AA/Baedeker
Paris

Baedeker's

AA

Paris

THE AUTOMOBILE ASSOCIATION

Imprint

Cover picture: Eiffel Tower

63 colour photographs
Map of Paris, plan of the Metro, 8 plans and diagrams

Conception and editorial work:
Redaktionsbüro Harenberg, Schwerte
English language: Alec Court

Text:
Manfred Kottmann

General direction:
Dr Peter Baumgarten, Baedeker, Stuttgart

English translation:
Babel Translations, Norwich

Cartography:
Ingenieurbüro für Kartographie Huber & Oberländer, Munich
Hallwag AG, Bern (Map of Paris)

Source of illustrations:
dpa (15), France (1), Historia-Photo (4), Messerschmidt (13), Prenzel (1), Retinski (1), Rogge (12), Rudoph (6), Sperber (10)

Following the tradition established by Karl Baedeker in 1844, sights of particular interest and hotels and restaurants of particular quality are distinguished by one or two asterisks.

To make it easier to locate the various sights listed in the A–Z section of the guide, their co-ordinates on the large map of Paris are shown in red at the head of each entry.

Only a selection of hotels and restaurants can be given; no reflection is implied, therefore, on establishments not included.

In a time of rapid change it is difficult to ensure that all the information given is entirely accurate and up to date and the possibility of error can never be entirely eliminated. Although the publishers can accept no responsibility for inaccuracies and omissions they are always grateful for corrections and suggestions for improvement.

2nd edition

Reprinted 1985

Licensed user:
Mairs Graphische Betriebe GmbH & Co., Ostfildern-Kemnat bei Stuttgart

Reproductions:
Golz Repro-Service GmbH, Ludwigsburg

Printed in Great Britain by Jarrold & Sons Ltd
Norwich

ISBN 0 86145 115 5

Contents

Page
The Principal Sights at a Glance . . . . inside front cover
Preface 7
Facts and Figures 9
General Information 9
Population and Religion 10
Communications 12
Culture 14
Industry and Commerce 17
Famous People 19
History of the City 21
The Arms of Paris 24
Paris A–Z 25
Practical Information 127
Useful Telephone Numbers at a Glance 175
Plan of the Metro 176
City Map . . . . at end of book

Preface

This Pocket Guide to Paris is one of the new generation of AA Baedeker guides.

These pocket-size guides, illustrated throughout in colour, are designed to meet the needs of the modern traveller. They are quick and easy to consult, with the principal sights described in alphabetical order and practical details about opening times, how to get there, etc., shown in the margin.

Each guide is divided into three parts. The first part gives a general account of the city, its history, prominent personalities and so on; in the second part the principal sights are described; and the third part contains a variety of practical information designed to help visitors to find their way about and make the most of their stay.

The new guides are abundantly illustrated and contain numbers of newly drawn plans. In a pocket at the back of the book is a large city map, and each entry in the main part of the guide gives the coordinates of the square on the map in which the particular monument, building, etc. is situated. Users of this guide, therefore, will have no difficulty in finding what they want to see.

Facts and Figures

General Information

Capital

Paris is the capital of France, the seat of the President of the Republic, of the Government and both Chambers of the French Parliament (National Assembly and Senate).

Region

Northern France (Région: Ile-de-France).

Geographical location

Latitude 48° 50′ N; longitude 2° 20′ E; altitude 27–127 m (90–415 ft) (highest point: Montmartre, 127 m – 415 ft).

International dialling codes

To Paris: from Great Britain: 010 33 1; from U.S.A.: 011 33 1; from Canada: 011 33 1.
From Paris: to Great Britain: 19 44; to U.S.A.: 19 1; to Canada: 19 1.

Population figures

Paris is one of the world's most densely populated cities (1975: 56,500 inhabitants per sq. mile – 21,820 per sq. kilometre), but its population has been diminishing over the past 50 years and between 1954 and 1975 it fell by 20% (550,000).
As of 1 January 1979 the City of Paris had a population of 2,102,900 while Greater Paris (Région Ile-de-Paris) with a population of over 10 million ranked fifth largest of the world's conurbations, after New York, Tokyo, Mexico City and Shanghai.

Arrondissements and quartiers

Paris is divided up into 20 "arrondissements" (precincts or wards) which are each further subdivided into four "quartiers" (quarters). When the poet Jean Cocteau called Paris a town made up of individual townships and villages he was alluding to the districts of the city which are also known as "quartiers" (or in many cases "faubourgs"). These traditional quartiers, whose popular names do not necessarily coincide with their official designation for administrative purposes, have in many cases retained their individuality and derive their names from villages that have subsequently been absorbed into the city (Montmartre, Chaillot), from churches (Saint-Germain de Prés), from buildings (Les Halles, Opéra) or from some special characteristic (Quartier Latin).
"Faubourg", literally "outside the town", means suburb, and as a rule these suburbs were named after the nearest village (hence Faubourg Montmartre was the suburb on the approach to the village of Montmartre). The suburbs outside today's city boundaries are called "banlieues".
A handy tip for finding your way around is that the arrondissements are arranged in a spiral that starts at the Louvre (1st arr.) then circles twice round the historic heart of Paris moving outwards from the Ile-de-la-Cité and ending (in the 20th arr.) at the Place de la Nation.

◀ *Eiffel Tower (view from the Palais de Chaillot)*

Administration

After the French Revolution France was divided up into 83 "Départements" (90 since 1918), each headed by a State-appointed "préfet" (prefect). There were times when Paris and its outlying districts were administered as a commune with a mayor (1789–94, 1848, 1870–1) but generally speaking it was a "département" with a prefect.
Under the administrative reform in 1964 the three départements of Greater Paris (Seine, Seine-et-Oise and Seine-et-Marne) were divided into eight to make up the "Région Parisienne":
Seine: Ville de Paris (75), Hauts-de-Seine (92), Seine-Saint-Denis (93) and Val-de-Marne (94);
Seine-et-Oise: Yvelines (78), Essonne (91) and Val-d'Oise (95);
Seine-et-Marne (77) remained as it was. (The reference numbers also occur in postal codes and vehicle number plates.)
In line with the move in French town and country planning in 1976 to keep more closely to the traditional provinces and regions the Région Parisienne was accorded the status of an administrative region with its historic title of Région Ile-de-France.
Under the administrative reform that took effect in 1977 the City of Paris became both a commune and a département.
Since that time Paris has been administered by a Mayor (Maire) and a City Council (Conseil Municipal) with 109 members, all of whom are directly elected by the people of Paris. The mayor in the Hôtel de Ville (Town Hall) is advised by local committees (Commissions d'Arrondissements) consisting of City officers and elected representatives from professional and occupational groupings and the population at large, which are based in the Mayor's Offices (Mairies Annexes) in each arrondissement.
The City Council is chaired by the Prefect of Paris and acts at the same time as the Council of the Départements (Conseil Général) and as such decides on the budget.
The Département of Paris is run by a Prefect and a Prefect of Police, both of whom are appointed by and answerable to the Government.
The Prefect of Paris is also the Prefect of the Ile-de-France region and presides in this capacity over the Regional Council (Conseil Régional) which decides on the budget plans for the region.

International organisations

Among the many international institutions which have their headquarters or are represented in Paris the three best known are: UNESCO (see Paris A–Z), here since 1946; the Secretariat of the Organisation for Economic Cooperation and Development (OECD); and the European Headquarters of INTERPOL, the organisation of national criminal police forces.

Population and Religion

Population

Paris had a population of 150,000 in the 14th c. By the time of Louis XIV, the "Sun King", the city had become a metropolis with half a million inhabitants. It was not until the 19th c., however, that Paris experienced the spurt in the growth of its

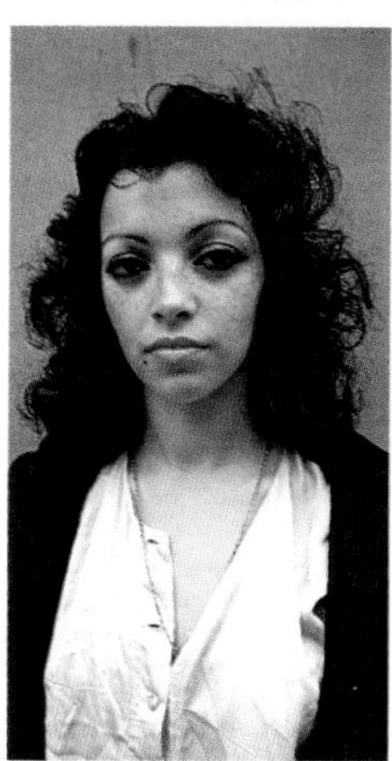

Faces of a metropolis

population that took it past the million mark (1846: 1,050,000; 1866: 1,800,000), and that was to be maintained until the end of the Second World War (2·8 million). Since that time its population figures have steadily declined. This is mainly because many old untenantable buildings in the heart of Paris have been pulled down, only to be replaced by accommodation which is more expensive and which houses fewer people.

Besides being a mecca for tourists, artists and students from all over the world, Paris also attracts workers from throughout France, from its overseas departments and from abroad. Every region of France is represented among the people of Paris:

many of its suburbs are firmly in the grip of migrants from the South, the Auvergne or Eastern France; they celebrate their regional festivals as they would if they were at home, and nearly all of them publish their own newspapers.
The foreign workers come chiefly from Algeria (51,000), followed by Portugal (44,500) and Spain (40,000). From the countries of the European Community, there are 28,700 in Paris including many from Great Britain.
Paris is also a haven for refugees from all over the world, many of them coming from South America and Indochina.
There are 289,700 foreigners living in Paris. (All these statistics are for 1978.)

Religion

Since the expulsion of the Protestants in the Religious Wars of the 16th and 17th c. the religion professed by the majority of the population is Roman Catholicism. Since 1905 there has existed an official division between Church and State.
Paris is the See of an Archbishop and accounts for 94 Roman Catholic parishes. It also has 15 Greek and Russian Orthodox churches and 7 synagogues (*c.* 220,000 practising Jews). There are two mosques catering for over 50,000 Muslims.

Communications

Port

Although the Port of Paris (Port Autonome) is declining in importance, as industry moves out of the city and freight has largely switched to road and rail, it is still France's major inland port, and, trans-shipping as it does almost 30 million tonnes a year, is numbered among the largest of Europe's inland ports. As the main trans-shipment areas now lie outside the city, the port installations on the Seine and the canals play nowadays only an ancillary role.
The pleasure boats, on the other hand, which cater entirely for the tourist trade, ply from moorings in the centre of the city.

Airports

The State Airports Company – "Aéroport de Paris" – administers Paris's three airports: Orly (in the S) and Le Bourget and Charles de Gaulle (in the N). Altogether they represent Europe's second largest airport complex after London, with, in 1979, *c.* 300,000 incoming and outgoing flights, 25 million passengers and 560,000 tonnes of freight. Orly continues to handle the most passenger traffic (14·2 million passengers), having weathered the steep fall in numbers that followed the opening of Charles de Gaulle (Roissy) Airport in 1974, while the latter has in the meantime become the largest handler of air freight.
In 1978 only 2% of the three airports' passenger traffic and 1% of freight traffic was being handled by Le Bourget.

Rail, Métro, RER

Although it lies on the western edge of the continent of Europe Paris is a hub of international communications. Thanks to the siting of its rail terminals and the building of its underground system, the Métro (Chemin de Fer Métropolitain), Paris has managed to avoid the fate of other major cities that have seen their historical centres carved up by railway tracks.
Two large companies are responsible for carrying the 8·6 million people that travel every day into, out of and through

Charles de Gaulle Airport at Roissy

Gare du Nord

Paris by public transport. In 1979 SNCF, the State Railway Company (Société Nationale des Chemins de Fer), carried 77·2 million long distance travellers and 450 million commuters. In 1979 RATP – which is part-owned by the State – recorded 1·5 billion passengers using the Métro and almost a billion bus passengers. The RER, or Regional Express Network (Réseau Express Régional), a relatively new transport subsidiary of the RATP, carried approximately 222·5 million passengers in 1979. It operates two lines, 59 stations and 92·2 km (58 miles) of track. The junction of the RER lines running from E to W and from N to S is the vast station of Châtelet (Les Halles). When completed the S–N line will end at the Gare du Nord.

A third RER line connecting suburbs in the W, including Versailles, with those in the S is operated by the SNCF.

The Métro network has steadily been extended, particularly in recent years. It has 15 lines, 353 stations and 183·5 km (115 miles) of track, 13·8 km (9 miles) of them above ground, the longest stretch (Balard–Créteuil) is 22·1 km (14 miles) and the shortest (Gambetta–Porte des Lilas) is 1·3 km (0·8 mile). The average distance between stations is 543 m (592 yds) and the trains run at 1½-minute intervals in the rush hour and at roughly 10-minute intervals at other times.

Motorways

Paris is the hub of the French motorway network, its system of "autoroutes". These are built and operated, as in Italy, by private companies and are subject to the payment of tolls. The Autoroute du Nord (A1) goes to Lille and the Channel Ports, with the A2 branching off at Péronne to Belgium (Charleroi–Liège–Brussels); the Autoroute de l'Est (A4) leads to Germany via Reims–Nancy–Strasbourg; the Autoroute du Sud (Autoroute du Soleil A6) leads down to the South of France via Lyons while Southwestern France is served by the Autoroute l'Aquitaine, via Orléans–Tours–Poitiers. Linking Paris with the West of France via Chartres is the Autoroute Océanie, currently ending at Rennes with extensions planned to Nantes and Brest, and the Autoroute de l'Ouest (Autoroute de Normandie A13) to Rouen and Caen.

The autoroutes all enter or leave Paris by the Boulevard Périphérique Extérieur, the outer ring-road encircling Paris and carrying between six and ten lanes of traffic.

The other long-distance highways, the "routes nationales", are well engineered, often more direct and free of charge.

Culture

General

Despite an upsurge in the seventies of public interest in France's provinces and regions, Paris remains the focal point of power, knowledge, learning, employment opportunities, culture and pleasure. The major universities, the most extensive and interesting museums and libraries (Bibliothèque Nationale with 7·7 million books), the greatest concentration of theatres and cinemas in one place, all the larger and many of the smaller publishers of books and newspapers, the national radio and television stations – everything that matters so far as France's public, intellectual and artistic life is concerned is to be found in Paris.

Paris, City of Art (Monet Exhibition in the Orangerie)

Art

From the time of the Impressionists until the beginning of the Second World War Paris was the art capital of the world and gave birth to or set the seal on the art movements of Impressionism, Symbolism, Fauvism, Cubism, Futurism and Surrealism.

In the forties New York took over from Paris as the internationally recognised centre of avant-garde art. However, its great museums and retrospective exhibitions of the collected work of important artists continue to attest to Paris's standing in the top flight of cities in the art world, as does the dealing in French and international art accounted for in present-day Paris at the three great exhibitions of the visual arts (Salons) that take place in the spring (Salon des Indépendants – paintings, Salon de Mai – sculpture) and autumn (Salon d'Automne – paintings).

The work of past and contemporary artists is on view all the year round in the "Galeries" – even for those not wishing to buy! – which are concentrated in and around the districts of Saint-Germain-des-Prés, the Faubourg Saint Honoré and Beaubourg.

Situated in the latter is the Pompidou Centre, the new centre for art and culture – known by most Parisians as the "Centre Beaubourg" after the name of the quarter – and it is undoubtedly the "Beaubourg" which is currently having the most vibrant impact and exerting the greatest pulling power on the Parisian art scene.

Colleges, Academies

In addition to the 13 universities (the Sorbonne itself was split up into four universities in 1968), in which in 1977 *c.* 300,000 students were enrolled, Paris also has its "Grandes Ecoles".

Entry to these colleges is by competitive examination only and their graduates are sure of subsequently obtaining top posts in industry or the Civil Service. Among the most important are the Ecole Polytechnique (engineers), Ecole des Hautes Etudes Commerciales (managers), Ecole Nationale d'Administration (civil service experts; many subsequent professional politicians), Ecole Normale Supérieure (teachers, lecturers).
The most outstanding of the many research institutions is the Centre National de la Recherche Scientifique (national centre for scientific research).
There is also the Institut de France which, although not a college as such, is an immensely respected authority in the intellectual and scientific field. Rich in tradition, the Institut has five scientific academies of which the best known is the Académie Française.

Theatre and Cinema

Of the 50 theatres in the French metropolis 8 are state-subsidised national theatres: Comédie Française, Théâtre National de l'Odéon, Théâtre National de Chaillot, Théâtre de l'Est Parisien, Opéra, Salle Favart (Opéra Comique), Théâtre Musical de Paris (formerly Châtelet) and Théâtre de la Ville.
Besides the many theatres offering a classical repertoire there are a number of experimental theatres, particularly in the suburbs. Paris also has forms of theatre which are unique in the "théâtre des boulevards" – internationally renowned variety theatres where witty repartee vies with raucous razzamatazz – and the "café-théâtres" used predominantly by very young acting companies for lively experimental theatre. There are also every conceivable hybrid forms of music hall, cabaret and "erotic" revue. These have at least one thing in common with the official theatre – standards of performance and price of admission vary enormously and mostly seem to bear absolutely no relation one to another.
With 250–300 films being screened every week, cinemagoers find themselves confronted in Paris with the greatest imaginable choice. Visitors with more time at their disposal can take advantage of the film seasons (hommages, rétrospectives) screened by some of the art cinemas and the two Cinémathèques (Palais de Chaillot, Centre Pompidou) and featuring the work of particular directors, stars, countries or periods in the history of the cinema. (Programmes change mid-week.)

Music and Dance

Paris has three classical opera houses (théâtres-lyriques): the Théâtre National d l'Opéra in the Palais Garnier, the Opéra Comique or Salle Favart (and occasionally Opéra Studio) and the Théâtre Musical de Paris in what was formerly Châtelet.
Innumerable great concert halls (Auditorium de Radio-France, Salle Gaveau, Palais des Congrès, Salle Pleyel, Théâtre des Champs Elysées and others) provide a wide range of classical music performed by internationally famous orchestras (Orchestre national de France, Orchestre de Paris, Nouvel Orchestre Philharmonique de Radio-France). The popular Sunday concerts given by the Orchestre des Concerts Lamoureaux, the Concerts Colonne and the Orchestre Pasdeloup are permanent features of the Parisian musical scene.
Lovers of classical ballet are recommended to visit the ballet performances staged at the Opéra and other theatres, depending on the season.

Théâtre Français, home of the Comédie Française

While many churches are venues for excellent concerts and recitals of church music, such as Notre-Dame on Sunday evenings, a different audience is catered for in the popular music halls, Olympia and Bobino, the Théâtre de la Ville and the Palais des Congrès, with their varied programmes of entertainment by the top names in French and international light music.

Spectacular combinations of music and dancers are the specialty of the "Revues" staged by the world-famous Moulin Rouge, Folies Bergère and the Lido, the last strongholds of the traditional French "can can".

Claiming to be more exclusive, esoteric, exotic and erotic are the "way-out dragshows" at the Alcazar and Paradis Latin and the stylish striptease at the Crazy Horse Saloon.

Industry and Commerce

Employment

The City of Paris provides employment for *c.* 2 million people in approximately 200,000 firms (1979) and thus accounts for almost a tenth of all the jobs in France. However, since the end of the war employment in Greater Paris has steadily shifted towards the surrounding Departments of the Ile-de-France Region – in 1954 Paris accounted for 55% of the Region's jobs and although the figure in 1975 was still as high as 40% Paris was losing jobs between 1972 and 1978 at the rate of 20,000 a year.

Employment figures have been falling as light industry moves out of Paris itself and is replaced by companies in the constantly expanding services sector. In 1975, for example, the services industry topped the employment league, providing 1·2 million jobs (63·2%), as compared with 392,700 (20·5%) and 213,600 (11·2%) in industry and commerce respectively, with the building trade in fourth place with 97,400 (5·1%).

Industries and Crafts

Industries traditionally located in Paris are those concerned with electronics, precision engineering, timber, textiles, pharmaceuticals, chemicals, aircraft and motor manufacturing – the Renault works at Boulogne-Billancourt are the largest in the Region.

The metal and engineering industries, timber, textiles and chemicals have been particularly affected by the drift away from the City, although most companies still retain their head offices in Paris. Their reasons for leaving include measures aimed at decentralisation, environmental protection costs and companies' inability to expand when necessary because land prices are too high.

Those left are mainly the small and medium-sized firms, often midway between a craft and an industry, which still largely determine the look of their "quartier": ready-to-wear trade (2nd arr.), newspapers and printing (2nd and 9th arr.), publishers (6th arr.), metalworking and precision engineering (10th, 11th and 12th arr.).

Craftsmen's products are traditionally to be found in the furniture workshops in the Faubourg Saint-Antoine (11th and 12th arr.) and the leatherworking district in the Marais (3rd arr. – see entry) while jewellery is fashioned in the Marais and the quarter between Opéra, Rue Royale and Place Vendôme (see entries). The highly lucrative "haute couture" trade is centred in the Faubourg Saint-Honoré (see entry).

Services

In France the services sector (financial and insurance institutions in the 8th and 9th arr., public administration in the 7th and 8th arr., transport, real estate and other service industries) also includes the wholesale and retail trade, which partly explains why it accounts for 80% of total employment.

Consumption

Since the market halls of "Les Halles" in the centre of Paris were demolished in 1969 the "stomach of Paris" is located outside the city in the southern suburb of Rungis where it occupies 450 hectares (1110 acres) and daily supplies the City and Greater Paris with thousands of tonnes of fresh fruit and vegetables, meat and other foodstuffs. Rungis also stores 25 million hectolitres (565 million gallons) of wine, 6 million (136 million gallons) of them for Paris.

The water supply of Paris consists of approximately equal parts of groundwater and river water (from the Seine and the Marne and of course chemically purified). The city uses about 1 million cub. m (200 million gallons) of water a day, approximately two-thirds of it drinking water (total length of piping: 3318 km, or 2075 miles).

At the end of the food chain, the network of sewers covers an overall length of 1550 km (970 miles), all of which can be visited.

750 refuse vehicles cart away 2740 tonnes of rubbish every day.

Paris's annual consumption of electricity totals approximately 7·5 billion kWh.

Famous People

Honoré de Balzac
(20.5.1799–18.8.1850)

Honoré de Balzac is regarded as being the founder of social realism in literature: eschewing the Romantic style of his period, he brilliantly described his characters and their settings in minute and realistic detail, and portrayed them caught up in the interplay of social forces and human passions.

His great work is "La Comédie Humaine", a series of 40 novels spanning French society from the Revolution to the Restoration. The most important novels in this series include "La Peau de Chagrin" (1831), "La Femme de Trente Ans" (1831–44), "Le Colonel Chabert" (1832), "Eugénie Grandet" (1833), "Le Médecin de Campagne" (1833), "Père Goriot" (1835), "Le Lys dans la Vallée" (1836), "César Birotteau" (1838), "Les Illusions Perdues" (1837–43), "Splendeurs et Misères des Courtisanes" (1839–47), "La Cousine Bette" (1846), "Le Cousin Pons" (1847). His other great work is the collection of short stories, "Contes Drolatiques" (1832–7).

In all Balzac was the author of 90 novels, 30 short stories and 5 (unsuccessful) plays. Driven by business failures, risky speculations and an extravagant life-style to produce this enormous literary output, he ruined his health and died, worn-out, when only 51. Shortly before his death he married his great friend of 13 years' standing, the Polish Countess Evelina Hanska-Rzewuska.

Jean Cocteau
(5.7.1889–11.10.1963)

Jean Cocteau was an artist of great versatility, able to express and combine a number of different talents. Not only was he a successful author ("Le Grand Ecart", "Les Enfants terribles"), film director ("La Belle et la Bête", "L'Eternel Retour"), scriptwriter ("Les Enfants du Paradis"), playwright ("Orphée"), painter, choreographer and librettist (for operas and ballets scored by Honegger, Stravinsky and Milhaud), he also embodied to a particular degree that quality of "esprit" – lightness, sharpness and brilliance of wit – for which others so admire the French.

In the vanguard of radical and literary movements, Cocteau played a decisive part in every manifestation of the avant-garde and was for decades one of the most fascinating celebrities on the French literary scene. His work encompasses futurism and dadaism but is more likely to be classified as a whole under the later heading of surrealism.

In 1955 Cocteau became a member of the Académie Française.

Victor Hugo
(26.2.1802–22.5.1885)

Victor Hugo, the son of an officer in the Napoleonic armies, was, with his plays, novels, writings and lyric and epic poetry, the leading figure among the French Romantics, whose programme he framed in the prologue to his play "Cromwell" (1827) and whose journal "La Muse Française" he founded and published. After the success of his poems ("Odes et Ballades", 1826) and his play "Hernani" (1830), his novel "Notre-Dame de Paris" (The Hunchback of Notre Dame) brought him fresh triumphs and its colourful and lively portrayal of life in medieval Paris inspired a sympathetic reappraisal of Gothic architecture (see Saint-Denis). In 1841 Hugo was made a member of the Académie Française.

Victor Hugo

After his daughter's suicide in 1843 Hugo temporarily lost his creative writing powers. He turned to politics (member of the Constituent and Legislative Assemblies, Presidential Candidate 1848) and although at first a sympathiser of Louis-Napoléon, he later became his bitter enemy when Louis seized power in 1851 and had himself proclaimed Emperor. Hugo was then forced into exile in the Channel Isles and became the idol of the radical Opposition.
After his return (1870) he completed "La Légende des Siècles" (1859–83), a masterly collection of epic poems.
In 1885 his remains were disinterred, in a State ceremony, from their resting place at the Arc de Triomphe and reinterred in the Panthéon.
Other works: "Les Orientales" (poems), "Les Feuilles d'Automne" (poems), "Marion Delorme" (play), "Lucrezia Borgia" (play), "Les Voix Intérieures" (poems), "Les Burgraves" (play), "Les Misérables" (novel), "William Shakespeare" (writings), "Les Travailleurs de la Mer" (Toilers of the Sea), "L'Homme qui rit" (novels).

Henry IV
(Henry of Navarre,
13.12.1553–14.5.1610)

Henry IV, still known today as "le Bon Roi Henri" (good King Henry), became King of Navarre in 1562 and was the leader of the Huguenots. Through his marriage with Margaret, the sister of Charles IX, he sought to reconcile the Catholics and the Protestants. This was prevented by the massacre of St Bartholomew when, on 24 August 1572, the flower of the Huguenot nobility, in Paris for the wedding, were murdered, together with thousands of fellow Protestants, on the orders of Catherine de Medici, the Queen Mother. Henry only saved his own life by renouncing his faith and he was held prisoner at the Court until he fled in 1576.
After the death of King Henry III (1589) Henry was the rightful successor to the throne but it was not until 1594, after long and bitter opposition and Henry's acceptance of Catholicism ("Paris is well worth a Mass"), that he was crowned the first king of the House of Bourbon.
Once king, Henry IV strove to restore French prosperity after the religious wars by promulgating the Edict of Nantes (1598), which secured religious freedom and equality of civil rights, reorganising the State's finances and opening up his country through the building of roads. As legend has it, his wish was that "in his kingdom every peasant should have a chicken in the pot on Sundays".
His reign saw the start of the colonisation of Canada and, with the restoration of central power to the monarchy, France was well and truly set on the road to absolutism.
When he was assassinated in 1610, Henry was mourned throughout France for his wise leadership and humane, tolerant and genial character.

Napoléon I
(15.8.1769–5.5.1821)

Napoléon Bonaparte, the son of a Corsican noble, won rapid promotion in the French Revolutionary Army to become a brigadier at the age of 24. As Commander-in-Chief in France and in the Italian and Egyptian campaigns he achieved a position of power that enabled him to overthrow the Directory (which after Robespierre's Reign of Terror was the supreme governing body of the State) and to seize power for himself as First Consul. Supported by plebiscite he made himself Consul for life in 1802 and finally, in 1804, France's first Emperor (Napoléon I).

The traditional enmity with England led him into wars with the Grand Alliance, the coalition led by England, and the conquest of Prussia and Austria. He seized Portugal and Spain in order to bring England to her knees through a continental blockade and finally he aimed at mastery of the whole of Europe by planning to conquer Russia which opposed the continental blockade.
The failure of the Russian campaign, defeat at the Battle of Leipzig (1813) and the occupation of Paris by the Allies forced Napoleon to abdicate (1814) and go into exile on the island of Elba. In 1815 he attempted to win back power in the famous 100 days but his troops were finally defeated at the Battle of Waterloo. He was banished to the British island of Saint Helena (South Atlantic) where he died in 1821. In 1840 his remains were brought back from Saint Helena to Paris to be interred, with great pomp and ceremony, under the Dôme des Invalides (see entry).
Unlike his nephew, Louis Napoléon (Napoléon III), Napoleon has lived on in the hearts of the French. His image as saviour of the Revolution was glorified by the Romantic movement (especially Victor Hugo) and monuments to him can still be seen today in every French town (in Paris he stands, in the garb of a Roman Emperor, on the column in the Place Vendôme (see entry).
In fact the "Code Civil" (the first civil legal code) which Napoleon drew up in 1804, codified the laws relating to property and society that were the fundamental achievements of the Revolution.

History of the City

From 300 B.C. onwards Celtic Gauls have settlements on the island in the Seine (today: Ile de la Cité). Their settlement "louk-teih" (place of the marsh) is conquered and destroyed by the Romans (first mention of "Lutetia Parisii" in Caesar's "De Bello Gallico" 53 B.C.). The Gallo-Roman town of Lutetia is founded and renamed Parisia after its inhabitants, the Parisii, by the Roman Caesar Julian Apostata in A.D. 360. 300 B.C.–A.D. 360

After defeating the Alemanni in the east and the last of the Romans in northern France, and conquering western France up to the Pyrénées, Clovis I, the king of the Franks, chooses Paris for the capital of his kingdom. A.D. 508

Hugh Capet becomes king of France. After being neglected under the rule of the Carolingians (Charlemagne's court was in Aachen), the Capetians make Paris the capital of the kingdom of France. 987

Under Louis VII work is begun on parts of the early Gothic choir of the cathedral of Notre-Dame. 1163

Philippe II (Philippe Auguste), considered the founder of France as a nation and great power, drives the English out of 1180–1223 their French territories. In his reign Paris becomes a large residential city (*c.* 100,000 inhabitants).

1200 Philippe II builds the fortress of the "Louvre" to protect Paris as the seat of his court.

1226–70 Saint Louis (Louis IX) strengthens his power base against the feudal nobles, establishes an effective administration and a supreme royal court of justice (Parlement) in Paris and allows the burghers of the capital to form their own (police) force instead of the royal guard.
After the death of the last "Staufer" Emperor (Frederick II, d. 1250) Louis IX becomes Europe's most powerful ruler and makes Paris the most important metropolis of the High Middle Ages.

1253 Robert de Sorbon, the cathedral canon, founds a college (later to become the Sorbonne) for poor theology students.

1358 Murder of Etienne Marcel, Provost of the Paris merchants, who had led the first civil uprising against the monarchy. The revolt collapses with his death.

1337–1453 During the Hundred Years War with England Paris is occupied twice by the English and is not finally recaptured until 1436.

1527 François I makes the City of Paris once more the seat of the royal court after its long absence from the city. He brings many Italian artists to France (including Andrea del Sarto, Leonardo da Vinci) and is responsible for building Paris's first Renaissance buildings (Town Hall).

1564 Catherine de Medici, widow of Henri II and the Regent of France, has plans drawn up for the Palace of the Tuileries.

1572 The religious wars reach their peak with the Massacre of St Bartholomew when on the night of 23 August 3000 Huguenots are murdered in Paris alone.

1635 Founding of the Académie Française by Cardinal Richelieu, chief minister of Louis XIII.

1682 Louis XIV moves the court to Versailles.

1789 The French Revolution begins with the storming of the Bastille on 14 July – the present national holiday.

1792 The first French Republic is proclaimed on 21 September. Four months later Louis XVI is guillotined in the Place de la Révolution (now the Place de la Concorde).

1800 Under Napoléon Bonaparte, first Consul of the Republic, France is divided up into 90 "Départements", each headed by a Prefect appointed by the Minister of the Interior. Paris comes under the Département de la Seine.

1804 Napoléon Bonaparte crowns himself Emperor Napoléon I in Notre-Dame.

The Allies occupy Paris, Napoleon is defeated. The monarchy is temporarily reinstated with Louis XVIII.	1814
Napoleon manages to regain power but the 100 days are soon ended with his defeat at Waterloo.	1815
First railway line in France – from Paris to Saint-Germain-en-Laye.	1837
The February Revolution finally abolishes the monarchy and the Second French Republic is proclaimed. Prince Charles Louis Napoléon Bonaparte (later Napoléon III) is elected President of the Republic by plebiscite on 10 December.	1848
A fresh plebiscite (97% in favour) grants Louis Napoléon the title of "Emperor of the French by the Grace of God and the Will of the Nation" (Emperor Napoléon III).	1852
Baron Haussmann, Prefect of Paris, begins the massive undertaking of re-planning Paris (boulevards, stations, parks, sewers).	1853
France loses the Franco-Prussian War. The Third French Republic is established in Paris (4 September 1870).	1870–1
The workers' uprising, the Paris Commune (March–May 1871), is bloodily suppressed (30,000 dead).	
Completion of the Eiffel Tower for the World Fair in Paris.	1889
Opening of the first métro line (Porte Maillot–Porte-de-Vincennes) for the World Fair.	1900
Occupation of Paris by the German Army. The City is liberated by the troops of the Allies on 26 August 1944.	1940–4
As Minister of Culture, the French writer and scholar André Malraux promulgates a law (the "Loi Malraux") for the conservation and rehabilitation of historical buildings whereby the monuments are given a face-lift and the Marais Quarter is rediscovered and reinstated.	1962
The number of France's Départements is increased to 95 by the administrative reorganisation of the Région Parisienne.	1964
Student protest in the Sorbonne and the Latin Quarter against the cultural and social policies of President de Gaulle. As workers join in the demonstrations and wild-cat strikes take place, the trade unions declare their solidarity and a General Strike brings the whole of France to a standstill.	1968
Greater Paris has its name changed from Région Parisienne to Région Ile-de-France.	1976
The City of Paris, previously administered by a government-appointed Prefect, gets its first elected Mayor (his 11 predecessors in office were appointed by the government of the day). The Centre National d'Art et de Culture Georges Pompidou is opened on 31 January.	1977

The Arms of Paris

The arms of Paris

"Fluctuat nec mergitur" is the motto under the ship in full sail that appears on the coat of arms of Paris.
The ship is the symbol of the City, or to be more precise, the old heart of Paris on the Ile-de-la-Cité, but it also symbolises in concrete form the merchant ships that plied on the Seine and to which Paris originally owed its prosperity.
The motto is therefore an apt one for the city – it rides the waves but does not go under.

Paris A–Z

Académie Française

See Institut de France

*Arc de Triomphe (triumphal arch; officially: Arc de Triomphe de l'Etoile) B2

The Arc de Triomphe de l'Etoile is dedicated to the glory of the victorious French armies of the Revolution and of the First Empire.

Napoleon ordered the building of this mighty edifice in 1806 but did not live to see its completion (in 1836, architect: Chalgrin). In 1920 the triumphal arch became the site of the tomb of the Unknown Soldier.

The arch is 50 m (164 ft) high and 45 m (148 ft) wide and its façades are covered with huge sculptures and friezes depicting the departure, the victories and the glorious return of the armies. (The inner surfaces bear the names of the generals and of other battles.)

From the viewing platform (lift) there is a remarkable panoramic view of the 12 avenues converging on the star-shaped square (see Place de l'Etoile, today officially Place Charles de Gaulle) and the straight line of the Champs-Elysées–Concorde–Louvre on one side and, on the other, the tower blocks of La Défense (NE), Montmartre with Sacré-Cœur (SE), the Eiffel Tower, the Dôme des Invalides and the Maine-Montparnasse tower.

Every evening at 6.30, when the stream of traffic around the Arc de Triomphe is beginning to abate slightly, a small delegation crosses the square. It consists of members of the Old Soldiers' Association who rekindle the flame at the tomb of the Unknown Soldier. (On 11 November, the anniversary of the Armistice of 1918, remembrance services are held here for the Fallen of both World Wars.)

A little museum below the platform houses an exhibition on the history of the building of the monument and mementoes of Napoleon and from the First World War.

Location
Place Charles de Gaulle (16th arr.)

Telephone
3 80 31 31

Métro
Charles de Gaulle (Etoile)

Buses
22, 30, 31, 52, 73, 92

Times of opening
10 a.m.–5 p.m., closed Tues.

Arc du Carrousel B3

(small triumphal arch; officially: Arc de Triomphe du Carrousel)

The Arc de Triomphe du Carrousel, the former gateway to the courtyard of the Tuileries Palace, is a copy of the triumphal arch of Septimius Severus (Rome).

It was erected (1806–8), to commemorate Napoleon's glorious victories, by the architects Percier and Fontaine. The quadriga (team of four horses) on the top is the work of the sculptor F.-J. Bosio (1828).

When the Tuileries Palace was destroyed the arch ceased to be the gateway to the Palace and today looks rather isolated.

Location
Place du Carrousel, between the two wings of the Louvre (1st arr.)

Métro
Louvre, Palais-Royal

Buses
27, 39, 48, 81, 95

Arènes de Lutèce (Roman amphitheatre) C4

The remains of the Roman amphitheatre give an idea of the huge size of the original structure: the elliptical arena (56×48 m – 184×157 ft) is almost the same size as the interior of the Colosseum in Rome. Gladiator and animal fights as well as theatrical performances were staged here.
It was built about A.D. 200 and although it had only 36 rows of seating, its 17,000 seats could hold almost the entire population of what was then the Roman town of Lutetia. The individual seats have the names of the "season ticket holders" scratched on them.

Location
Rue des Arènes,
Rue de Navarre
(5th arr.)

Métro
Monge

Buses
47, 67

Assemblée Nationale (National Assembly)

See Palais Bourbon

*Bagatelle (Bagatelle park and castle) B1

In the NW part of the Bois de Boulogne (see entry) lies a small château in an English garden, both bearing the name "Bagatelle".
These charming grounds date from the end of the 18th c. The young Count of Artois (later Charles X) bet his sister-in-law Marie Antoinette that he could have the little château built and the park landscaped in only three months. An international competition for rose-growers is held here each June. Besides the orangerie, with its evergreens, and a Japanese water-garden, the northernmost of the four lakes with its splendid display of water-lilies is of especial interest for visitors who can also visit the park on summer evenings when it is floodlit (between 9.30 and 11).

Location
Bois de Boulogne
(Sèvres–Neuilly road,
16th arr.)

Métro
Pont de Neuilly

Buses
43, 144, 244

Times of opening
Park: daily 8.30 a.m.–6 p.m.

Bastille (officially: Place de la Bastille) C5

Today there is a huge square on what was the site of the hated fortified prison of "La Bastille". Anyone hoping to find the remains of the Bastille is in for a disappointment; it was completely demolished within a few months of being stormed on 14 July 1789.
The Bastille (small bastion) was built between 1370 and 1382 in the reign of Charles V. The fortifications of the bastion of Saint-Antoine protected Charles V's newly built city wall at this point. The Bastille proved poor protection and was captured on several occasions. The people began to hate the fortress when Cardinal Richelieu, Louis XIII's minister, made it the State prison, where prisoners (including the Marquis de Sade) were held without trial merely by order of the king ("lettre de cachet").

Location
centre–E (3rd arr.)

Métro
Bastille

Buses
20, 29, 65, 69, 76, 86, 87, 91

◀ *Arc de Triomphe and Champs-Elysées by night*

The Bastille was often "full up", but on 14 July 1789, when the French Revolution began with the storming of the Bastille, the liberators could find only seven prisoners in the cells. These were petty criminals and a couple of madmen, but the mob gave them a triumphant reception.

François René, Vicomte de Chateaubriand describes the taking of the Bastille in his "Mémoires d'Outre-Tombe": "On 14 July the Bastille was stormed. As an observer I was a witness to this act against a couple of veterans and a faint-hearted governor: had the gates been locked the people would never have forced their way into the fortress. I saw how two or three cannon-shots were fired, not by the veterans but by the Gardes Françaises who had already occupied the towers. De Launay (the Governor) was fetched from his hiding place and after much manhandling was slaughtered on the steps of the town hall; Flesselles, leader of the merchants, had his skull shattered by a pistol-shot; this was a spectacle much enjoyed by the heartless onlookers. As in the Roman street-fights under Otto and Vitellius, people abandoned themselves to unbridled orgies in the midst of this slaughter. The victors of the Bastille, drunk with happiness and hailed as conquerors in the taverns, were driven round in carriages, prostitutes and Sans-culottes began to hold sway and keep them company.

"Passers-by raised their hats with the respect of fear to these heroes, some of whom died from exhaustion at the height of their triumph. The number of keys to the Bastille was constantly multiplying, such keys sent to pompous nincompoops in every corner of the world. . . . The experts proceeded to conduct the post-mortems on the Bastille. Temporary cafés were set up under canvas; the crowds came as to the fair . . . countless carriages drove past or stopped at the foot of the towers, whose stones were pulled down amidst great clouds of dust. . . . It was a rallying point for the most famous speakers, the best-known writers, the most celebrated painters, the most distinguished actors and actresses, the most popular dancers, the most aristocratic foreigners, the great lords of the court and envoys from all over Europe; the old France had come here to say farewell for ever, the new France had come here to make its début."

The July Column (with a statue of Liberty) stands today in the Place de la Bastille. It does not, however, commemorate 14 July, the French National holiday, but the Republicans killed during the July Revolution of 1830 whereby Charles X was deposed and the Citizen-King Louis-Philippe brought to power.

A model of the Bastille can be seen in the Musée Carnavalet (see entry). Similar miniature-Bastilles were sent to the provinces during the French Revolution to keep the Revolutionary spirit alive.

*Bois de Boulogne B1/2–C1

Location
On the western outskirts of the city

The 900 hectare (2224 acre) park is one of the most popular recreation areas in the immediate vicinity of Paris. It is right on the western edge of the city, bounded on the E by the

Boulevard Périphérique and on the W by the Seine. It is criss-crossed by footpaths, bridle-paths and roads.
The name of the park comes from a church (Notre-Dame-de-Boulogne-le-Petit) built by the inhabitants of a village on this spot in the 14th c. in honour of their place of pilgrimage, Boulogne-sur-Mer.
For a long time a royal hunting ground as well as a bandits' hideout, the forest had a wall built round it in the 16th c., during the reign of Henri II. Louis XIV ordered his minister Colbert to have a park laid out with paths converging in the form of a star, and opened it to the public. During the Regency (early 18th c.), and again from the middle of the 19th c. onwards, the park was a meeting place for the fashionable world. This was mainly due to the building of racecourses at Longchamp and Auteuil (*c.* 1850) and to the new landscaping of the park at around the same time by the Prefect, Baron Haussmann. (Napoleon III had given the park to the city.) Nowadays many people spend their leisure hours here going for walks, picknicking in the meadows, rowing or simply doing nothing. As evening falls there is a different public with different interests: night-time prostitution is well established (and so is voyeurism).
Anyone who is short of time for their visit to Paris should take a drive through the Bois de Boulogne by car.
The main things to see are:

1. Bagatelle (see entry – park and castle).
2. Grande Cascade (large waterfall) at the Carrefour de Longchamp.
3. Auteuil racecourse: this adjoins the western end of the upper lake. Its grandstand is on the slope of a small hill (Butte Mortemart) made when the two lakes were excavated. Only steeplechasing takes place here (see Practical Information, Sport).
4. Longchamp racecourse (1857): one of the best-known racetracks in the world (room for 10,000 racegoers, see Practical Information, Sport).
5. See Jardin d'Acclimatation (children's amusement park with Musée des Arts et Traditions Populaires (see entry) (Museum of Folklore).
6. Lac Inférieur (lower lake): this is over 1000 m (1100 yd) long and 1·5 m (5 ft) deep. Those not energetic enough to walk round the lake may like to take the ferry (from the W bank) to the two islands (café-restaurant) or hire a rowing boat (at the northern end).
7. Lac Supérieur (upper lake): it is also possible to walk round this 400 m (438 yd) long lake (also artificial).
8. Pré Catelan: these gardens, named after a troubadour (Armand Catelan) who was murdered here about 1300, contain two small châteaux and a majestic 200-year-old copper beech. The Jardin Shakespeare (guided tours: 11 a.m., 1.30, 3, 4.30 and 5.30 p.m.) contains all the plants mentioned in the plays of William Shakespeare.

Métro
Sablons, Porte Maillot, Porte Dauphiné, Porte d'Auteuil

Buses
32, 33, 43, 52, 63, PC

Bois de Vincennes

See Vincennes

Boulevards

The word "boulevard" (cognate with the English "bulwark") means a street built on the site of fortifications.
It is easy to see from a map of the city how Paris has grown outwards from the centre (Ile de la Cité) in a ring formation: the boulevards lie round this centre like the rings for every year of a tree.
The first ring (on the line of the 14th c. city wall) is formed by the Boulevards Beaumarchais, du Temple, the "Grands Boulevards" of Saint-Martin, Saint-Denis, Bonne-Nouvelle, Poissonnière, Montmartre, des Italiens, des Capucines, de la Madeleine and – linked by the Rue Royale, Place de la Concorde (see entries) and Pont de la Concorde – the Boulevard Saint-Germain on the left bank of the Seine.
The next ring consists, inter alia, of the Boulevards Rochechouart, de Clichy (N), de Courcelles (W), de Grenelle and du Montparnasse (S), Picpus and de Charonne (E).
The third ring is the so-called Boulevard Périphérique Intérieur (named exclusively after Generals and Marshals) and finally the fourth ring is the Boulevard Périphérique Extérieur (ring road) which today marks the bounday of the city.
The town-planning measures (1853–70) which Baron Haussmann (1809–91), Prefect of Paris, carried out under Napoleon III completely transformed the city and saw the construction of the boulevards, stations, the first indoor markets and department stores, new bridges (5) and parks.

Boulevard Rochechouart

Haussmann's town-planning (which called for the demolition of 30,000 houses and the resettlement of some 300,000 people) had several objectives. Besides improving the look of the city by making open spaces and wide streets, economic policy requirements were also of paramount importance. The new arterial roads facilitated fast transport and speeded up the circulation of goods and people between the different parts of the city in general and between the stations, markets and department stores in particular.

Grands Boulevards

The "great boulevards" (see above have always been a great attraction for those who enjoy taking a stroll or frequenting restaurants, theatres and, nowadays, cinemas. The concept of the "théâtre du boulevard" gives some idea of their special features – noise, sensation and spectacle which nowadays means amusement halls, sensational films and discothèques.
The "West End" of the "Grands Boulevards" in the area around the Opera House owes its worldly air to the presence of expensive boutiques and restaurants, but in the Faubourgs Montmartre, Saint-Denis and Saint-Martin, the "East End", one can soon sample the ordinary everday life of a big city.

Boulevard Saint-Michel C4

Location
Centre, on the Left Bank (5/6th arr.)

Métro
Saint-Michel

Suburban station
Luxembourg (RER)

Buses
21, 27, 38, 81, 84, 85

The Boulevard Saint-Michel, on the border between the 5th and 6th arrondissements, leads southwards away from the Seine. It crosses the Boulevard Saint-Germain and passes the Place de la Sorbonne (left) and the Jardin du Luxembourg (right – see entry) on its way to the Port Royal RER station, where it meets the Boulevard du Montparnasse and the Boulevard de Port-Royal.
The Saint-Michel métro station is a popular meeting place and, whether the rendezvous is the Place Saint-Michel in front of the fountain (Fontaine Saint-Michel) or one of the many cafés, this is a good starting point for walks along the Quais of the Seine, to the Cité, in the Quartier Latin, to Saint-Germain-des-Prés (see entries) or simply along the Boul' Mich' to the Jardin du Luxembourg.
Anyone looking for footwear (specialty: boots) or the latest fashion in jeans has plenty of choice in the shops on the Boul' Mich' or from the goods offered by the street traders: Indian scarves, leather ware, Far Eastern perfumes, jewellery.
During the school and university year (October–June) pupils and students from all over the world predominate on the streets. In the summer months, on the other hand, the Boul' Mich' is overwhelmingly peopled by tourists who are sometimes disappointed that all they find here are other tourists. It is a good idea to see what there is (to eat and drink) to the left and right in the narrow side streets of the Quartier Latin.

Bourse (des Valeurs) (Stock exchange; officially: Palais de la Bourse) B4

Location
Place de la Bourse (2nd arr.)

Like other buildings dating from the time of Napoleon (Arc de Triomphe, Madeleine), the Paris stock exchange (1808–27) is

Métro
Bourse

Buses
20, 29, 39, 48, 67, 69, 72

Visits
Mon.–Fri. 11 a.m.–1 p.m.

modelled on the buildings of antiquity. The architect A.-Th. Brongniart chose the form of a single-nave Graeco-Roman temple. It was not enlarged into its present cruciform style until 1902–3.
Trading in stocks and shares reaches a peak around midday. An undisturbed view of the hectic activities of the brokers and dealers can be obtained from the gallery (reached by a staircase in the left-hand vestibule). Most visitors are in the dark about what is going on, and so informative tours of introduction can be arranged (information in the gallery, tel. 2 33 99 83).

Bridges of Paris

See Ponts de Paris

Catacombes (Catacombs) C3

Location
Place Denfert-Rochereau (14th arr.)
Métro
Denfert-Rochereau
Times of opening
16 Oct.–30 June: 1st and 3rd Sat. in the month 2 p.m.;
1 July–15 Oct.:
every Sat. 2 p.m.

In Gallo-Roman times this was the site of underground stone quarries. Between 1785 and the mid 19th c. these old quarries were used to store skeletons from the many Parisian cemeteries which were removed to make way for new quarters of the city. The bones were arranged in the galleries according to the cemetery from which they had been removed, and stacked high against the walls of the twisting passages.
Remember to take a torch!

*Centre Pompidou/Beaubourg (Georges Pompidou national centre for art and culture; officially: Centre National d'Art et de Culture Georges Pompidou) B4

Location
Place Beaubourg (4th arr.)

Métro
Rambuteau, Les Halles, Hôtel de Ville

Between the Halles area (see Les Halles) and the Marais (see entry) lies the "Centre National d'Art et de Culture Georges Pompidou", to give it its official name, which since it was opened in 1977 has become a major attraction, with over six million visitors a year. In an area of 100,000 sq. m (over 1 million sq. ft) the public has a choice of temporary exhibitions,

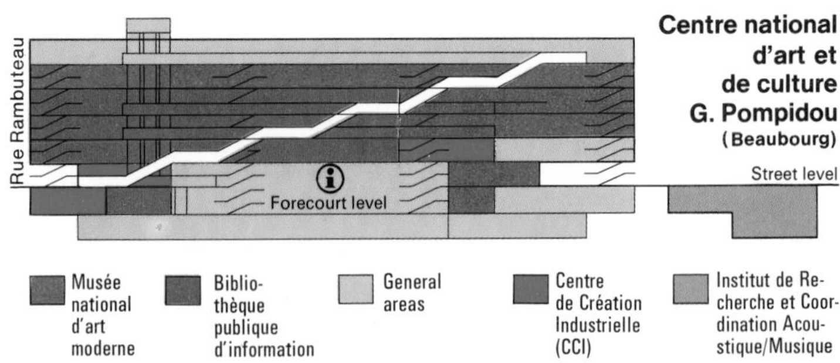

Centre Pompidou ("glass caterpillar" on the façade)

two libraries, the National Gallery of Modern Art (see Musée National d'Art Moderne), a cinémathèque, a theatre and a tour of the building itself.

Outside the building, on the forecourt, there is also the as yet unofficial street theatre provided by mimes, conjurers, musicians and soap-box orators.

The idea of taking Paris into the 21st c., heralded by the tower-blocks of Défense (see entry) on the outskirts of Paris, has been taken a stage further by the Centre Pompidou (as it is known for short), or Centre Beaubourg, in the heart of the city. The international architectural competition (almost 700 schemes were submitted from 50 countries) was won by the youthful team of Richard Rogers (39, England) and Renzo Piano (34, Italy). Under their direction a structure took shape over five years and at a cost of almost a thousand million francs, which immediately sparked off a lively controversy. Its opponents call it "that monstrosity, that refinery, that gigantic gadget, a useless toy". Its advocates see in the Centre Beaubourg (Beaubourg is the name of the district) an opportunity for Paris again to become what it was from the end of the 19th c. until the Second World War: the "art capital of the world".

Buses
38, 47, 75

Times of opening
Mon.–Fri. noon–10 p.m.; Sat. and Sun. 10 a.m.–10 p.m.; closed Tues.

Guided tours
Weekdays 3, 3.30, 4 p.m.; Sat. and Sun. 10.30 a.m.

Objective

The Centre Beaubourg is intended to stand for a new national cultural policy, not by amassing collections of documents and the usual objects to be found in museums, but by being creative, by producing works of art. This entails the regions of France being represented by exhibitions of their works and cultural events in the Centre Beaubourg, while exhibitions put together by the Beaubourg can be seen in provincial museums.

Architecture

The building, which is 166 m (547 ft) long, 60 m (197 ft) wide and 42 m (138 ft) high and is made of glass and steel, does in fact look a bit like a refinery: all the wiring and plumbing is channelled through coloured ducts on the E side of the exterior. Lifts and, in the "glass caterpillar", escalators are mounted on the main façade (W).
Leaving aside its outer aspect, the Beaubourg bears closer comparison with one of the time-honoured sights of Paris, the Cathedral of Notre-Dame (see entry). With its complicated building technique clearly visible, the "cathedral of culture", the Centre Beaubourg, is related to the Gothic architecture of Notre-Dame, particularly insofar as they share the same basic architectural principle: all load-bearing elements are contained in the outside walls. Thus the space on the ground floor and on the five upper floors (150×50 m – 492×164 ft) is not broken up by any form of support and can be arranged in any number of different ways, which is a great advantage for temporary exhibitions.

Useful information

The guided tours are in French and for individual visitors only. Groups may book guided tours in English in advance outside or during official visiting hours by writing to Centre Pompidou, F-75191-Paris Cédex 04, or by telephoning 2 77 12 33.
There is a charge for the temporary exhibitions on the 5th floor, the Musée National d'Art Moderne, the cinémathèque and for specific events (plays, concerts), but otherwise entrance is free. It is possible to buy tickets that are valid both for the museum and for the temporary exhibition.

Lay-out

Entrance: information desks on the right (general information) and left (that day's events). Guide booklets are available in English. Special exhibitions of large objects in the sunken central area ("forum"). Contemporary galleries (right). Sale of postcards, posters, catalogues, books (left). Bibliothèque d'actualité (left, behind the postcard and poster stall): newspapers, magazines, new books.
Bibliothèque publique d'information (open-access library): it is planned to have a million books here on shelves to which the public will have direct access. The books can only be read here, they cannot be borrowed. The same applies to slides, video and audio tapes: there are sets of slides and video tapes on various themes which can be viewed *in situ* and a "médiathèque" (language laboratory) with study programmes for up to 40 languages.
Musée National d'Art Moderne (National Gallery of Modern Art), entrance on the 5th floor: art of the 20th c. starting with the Fauves (Derain, de Vlaminck, Marquet, Dufy, Matisse) and Picasso's early 20th c. work through Cubism (Picasso, Braque, Gris), Expressionism (Nolde, Macke, Kandinsky), Constructivism (Klee, Mondrian) to Abstract Expressionism (de Staël, Hartung, Polikoff, Estère, Dubuffet), Pop-Art, Hard Edge and Minimal Art of the post-Second-World-War period, and a formidable collection of modern sculpture (Arp, Moore, Giacometti, Calder). The lay-out is chronological, starting on the 3rd floor and ending on the N side of the 5th floor.
Centre de Création Industrielle (CCI; Centre for Industrial design): arranges temporary exhibitions, discussion groups, provides information (mezzanine, left).

Cinémathèque: four screenings daily (from 3 p.m.) of films important in the history of the cinema.
Institut de Recherche et de Coordination Acoustique/Musique (IRCAM): an institute for research and development in contemporary music under the direction of Pierre Boulez, situated outside below ground level and open to the public only for concerts.
Large temporary exhibitions: 5th floor.
Café-restaurant (with a view over the roofs of Paris).
Administration.
Parking: the Centre's underground car park is linked with the "Forum des Halles" (see entry – entrance: Rue Rambuteau).
In the northern section of the forecourt there is a small two-part building containing a reconstruction of the studio of the Romanian sculptor Constantin Brancusi and many of his works. (Times of opening: Mon. and Wed.–Fri. 10 a.m.–6 p.m.; Sat. and Sun. noon–6 p.m.; closed Tues. Knock loudly!)

Palais de Chaillot B2

The two wings of the Palais de Chaillot were built in 1937 on a small elevation overlooking the Seine, on the site of an earlier palace (Palais du Trocadéro). The austere but imposing building was designed by the architects Jacques Carlu, Louis-Auguste Boileau and Léon Azème. The broad terrace (with gleaming bronze statues on both sides) between the two wings was the entrance to the 1937 World Fair, and there is a very good view from here of the Champ de Mars and the Eiffel Tower.
Under the terrace is the Théâtre de Chaillot with two stages. The palace also houses three museums: the Museum of Anthropology (see Musée de l'Homme), the Navy Museum (see Musée de la Marine) and the Museum of French Architecture (see Musée des Monuments Français). The E wing houses a cinémathèque (see entry) and the Musée du Cinéma (see Practical Information).

Location
Place du Trocadéro (16th arr.)

Métro
Trocadéro

Buses
22, 30, 82

Champ-de-Mars (field of Mars) C2

The Champ-de-Mars (field of Mars), originally a military training ground, today extends like a park between the Eiffel Tower (see Tour Eiffel) and the Ecole Militaire (see entry).
During the French Revolution this was the scene of the "Festival of the Federation" (14 July 1790) when Louis XVI and delegates from all the French provinces swore to uphold the new constitution which provided for a constitutional monarchy on the English model. It was here, too, that the mob demanded death for the royal family after their abortive flight.
In 1794 the painter Jacques-Louis David organised a "festival of the Supreme Being" (Etre suprême) which was to be worshipped as part of the new State religion decreed by Robespierre. This signalled for Robespierre the climax of his reign of terror. (Four months later he, too, was to lose his head beneath the guillotine.)

Location
W part of the city (7th arr.)

Métro
Ecole Militaire

Buses
42, 80, 82, 87, 92

World Fairs were held on the Champ-de-Mars in 1867, 1878, 1898, 1900 and 1937. Paris's first racetrack was also here for a time.

**Champs-Elysées (officially: Avenue des Champs-Elysées) B2/3

Location
Between Arc de Triomphe and Place de la Concorde (8th arr.)

Métro
George V., Franklin D. Roosevelt, Champs-Elysées-Clemenceau

Buses
28, 42, 49, 73, 80, 83

Famous throughout the world, this magnificent avenue, is 1·88 km ($1\frac{1}{6}$ miles) long and falls into two parts on either side of its main intersection, the Rond-Point. The upper part, towards the Arc de Triomphe (see entry), offers everything that the visitors from all over the world have come to associate with the Champs-Elysées – luxury shops and hotels, countless restaurants and pavement cafés, cinemas, theatres and the offices of the big banks and international airlines.

By contrast the lower section, towards the Place de la Concorde, is flanked by gardens surrounding museums, theatres and a few restaurants. Until the end of the 16th c. this area consisted of fields and marshland. The first approach road to it was the 17th c. "Cours de la Reine" running from the palace of the Tuileries but along the Seine. After the completion of the Tuileries Le Nôtre landscaped a broad shady avenue linking the palace with the hill where the Arc de Triomphe stands today. Early in the 18th c. this avenue was named the "Champs-Elysées" (Elysian Fields).

The entire Champs-Elysées forms only one section of the "voie triomphale" (the triumphal way) completed under Napoleon III and leading from the Arc de Triomphe de l'Etoile via the Place de la Concorde to the Arc de Triomphe du Carrousel.

The Marly horses, two masterly Baroque sculptures by Guillaume Coustou, were positioned between the Place de la Concorde and the Champs-Elysées in 1795.

Château de Chantilly (Chantilly castle)

Location
Chantilly, 40 km (25 miles) N of Paris on the N16

Rail
from Gare du Nord

Times of opening
1 April–30 Sept.:
1.30–5.30 p.m.; closed Tues., Fri. and on race days

The little town of Chantilly (12,000 inhabitants), famous for its horse-racing and the whipped cream named after it, lies on the N16 on the same latitude as Senlis. Its château and its park in particular are popular destinations for excursions from Paris.

In the 17th and 18th c. Chantilly was the seat of the Condé family, a branch of the royal house of Bourbon. The family bequeathed the castle to the Institut de France (see entry) in 1886. The "Grand" Château (built 1875–81) today houses the Musée Condé (see entry).

The "Petit" Château dates from the 16th c. Worth seeing: the sumptuously painted rooms, the chapel with magnificent high altar and the library (Galerie des livres) with valuable old manuscripts.

The park dates from 1663 and is the work of André Le Nôtre, the landscape gardener of Versailles. A small hunting lodge ("Maison de Sylvie", 17th c.), an indoor court for ball games (Jeu de Paume, 1757) and a hamlet or "hameau" (for acting out the pastoral fantasies popular at that time) are all charming

Pavement café on the Champs-Elysées ▶

LA
PERGOLA

Château de Chantilly

features of the fine park which, like Versailles, has a broad canal running across it.
To the W of the château are the Great Stables (Grandes Ecuries, 18th c.) and Chantilly racecourse (1834).

Châtelet C4

Location
Place du Châtelet (4th arr.)

Métro
Châtelet

Buses
21, 38, 47, 69, 74, 75, 85

The square and the enormous métro station are named after the "Grand Châtelet" which was a fortress, dating from the 12th c. and built to protect the Ile de la Cité (see entry), a prison and, until 1789, the law court of the chief administrator of Paris. (Prévôt des Marchands, head of the Paris merchants, see Hôtel de Ville.) Napoleon demolished the fortress in 1802 and the two theatres were built in the reign of Napoleon III. The "Châtelet" on the W side, which since 1980 has ranked as a National Theatre and is known as the Théâtre Musical de Paris, stages opera, light opera and ballet, while on the E side the "Théâtre de la Ville" (formerly the "Théâtre Sarah Bernhardt") mounts an ambitious programme of music recitals and modern classics.

Cité (Ile de la Cité) C4

Location
Centre (1st/3rd arr.)

Métro
Cité

The Ile de la Cité is the historical and geographical centre of Paris.
Here, on the island protected by the two arms of the Seine, were the first settlements in prehistoric times. Here stood the Gallo-Roman town of Lutetia. Here the inhabitants sought

refuge from the onslaughts of the Teutons, the Huns and the Normans. Not until the Middle Ages was the city able to spread permanently along both banks of the Seine.

Buses
21, 24, 27, 38, 81, 85, 96

From the 6th to the 14th c. the Cité was the seat of the kings, with the secular royal palace (see Palais de Justice) and its sacral counterpart, the "Cathedral of France": Notre-Dame de Paris. When the seat of the kings was moved elsewhere the face of the town changed, as broad squares and streets were no longer needed for the festivities of the royal court. There grew up a closely packed huddle of alleys and houses in the shadow of the towers of Notre-Dame. Baron Haussmann, the Prefect of the Seine in the 19th c. under Napoleon III, radically altered the face of the Cité again when he established a precedent for urban redevelopment by making room for the broad N–S streets, the Prefecture of Police, the commercial court, the extensions to the law courts, the rebuilding of the Hôtel-Dieu and an unobstructed view of Notre-Dame. This involved the destruction of the historical heart of the city and the resettlement of 25,000 people. Since then the term "Cité" in the sense of the ancient nucleus of a town is hardly applicable and the only inhabitants on the island live in a few narrow streets N of Notre-Dame.

The chief attractions of a visit to the Cité are (see entries): Notre-Dame, La Sainte-Chapelle, La Conciergerie, Le Palais de Justice (Law Courts); but there are also other squares and buildings worth visiting:

Square du Vert Galant: a small area of lawn on the north-western tip of the island, harking back to Henri IV and overlooked by his statue on horseback, this is a venue for vagrants and courting couples, for musicians and those who enjoy watching the sunsets over the Seine.

Place Dauphine: in 1607 Harlay, the wealthy chief justice, was given the site by Henri IV with instructions to construct a square fronted by houses sharing the same façade (only nos. 14 and 26 date from that time). The square, named after the heir to the throne (Dauphin), soon became a popular place for promenades.

Hospital "Hôtel-Dieu": the hospital, looking a bit like a barracks, was built between 1868 and 1878. A convent stood here as early as the 7th c. where nuns devoted themselves to the care of the poor and the sick; thus the Hôtel-Dieu is one of the oldest hospitals in Europe.

Mémorial de la Déportation: this monument on the south-eastern tip of the island commemorates those who suffered deportation to German concentration camps (1940–5).

Parvis de Notre-Dame (Cathedral square): in the south-eastern corner, in front of the Pont au Double, lies the little Square Charlemagne with a statue of Charlemagne (archaeological crypt – see Notre-Dame).

A stroll across the island is very pleasant, offering fine views, virtually unmatched elsewhere, of the Seine and its bridges and the city stretching along both sides of the river.

Collège de France — C4

The Collège de France (formerly: Collège des Trois Langues) is one of the most famous academic teaching and research

Location
Rue des Ecoles (5th arr.)

Métro
Odéon, Maubert-Mutualité, Saint-Michel

Buses
63, 86, 87

Visits
By prior application at the main gate

establishments in France. The 18th c. building was considerably enlarged in 1930.
François I established his reputation as "Father and Restorer of the Sciences" by founding in 1530 the "Collège des Trois Langues" (College of the Three Languages, also "Collège des Lecteurs royaux" = College of the Royal Lecturers). The king, an admirer of the Italian Renaissance, wanted to set up an independent scientific college where the three Classical languages, Hebrew, Greek and Latin, would be studied from the original texts (as in Italy). The lecturers were paid not by the students, as was usual elsewhere, but by the king and taught free of charge.
The freedom of these men of science from academic constraints and free access to the lectures for everyone have been preserved, but the Collège de France does not issue certificates or grant titles. Lectures given currently extend to all the humanities and natural sciences.
Well-known professors in the history of the College include the physicist André Ampère, the historian Jules Michelet, the poet Paul Valéry and the philosopher Henri Bergson. Today teachers at the Collège de France include the anthropologist Claude Lévi-Strauss and the philosopher Michel Foucault.

Comédie Française

See Théâtre Français

Concièrgerie C4

Location
1 Quai de l'Horloge (1st arr.)

Metro
Cité

Buses
21, 24, 27, 38, 81, 85, 96

Times of opening
1 April–30 Sept.: 10–11.25 a.m. and 1.30–5.25 p.m.; closed Tues.; 1 Oct.–31 March: 10–11.25 a.m. and 1.30–4 p.m.; closed Tues. and Fri.

The Conciergerie, part of the medieval royal palace (see Cité) and prison, is today a museum in which well-attended concerts take place. (Small sections of it are still used by the adjoining Palais de Justice (see entry) for prisoners on remand.)
About 1300 Philippe le Bel had the high-Gothic halls of the Conciergerie built and these are the only parts of the old palace still left today. The "concierge" in those days was the constable of the castle and hence the chief of the royal household (nowadays "concierge" means the caretaker of a block of flats). Presumably he also had some form of jurisdiction, as the building was soon turned into a palace prison and later a State prison. Many notorious prisoners awaited sentence here, including the assassins of Henri IV and the Duc de Berry, as well as Danton, Robespierre and Marie-Antoinette.
From the opposite bank of the Seine (Quai de la Mégisserie) there is a good view of the whole building (its neo-Gothic façade dates from the 19th c.) with its three round towers and its clock tower (Tour de l'Horloge) with the first public clock in Paris (*c.* 1370, destroyed in 1793, restored in the 19th c.). The entrance is to the right of this on the Quai de l'Horloge.
The following rooms are particularly interesting:
Kitchen (1353): banquets for two to three thousand royal guests could be prepared in this kitchen and it was directly supplied from the Seine (the quay did not exist at that time).

Place de la Concorde with obelisk ▶

The size of the open fireplaces was necessary for roasting whole oxen.
Salle des Gens d'Armes (Room of the Men-at-Arms, 1285–1314): this was used as a dining-room by the armed servants. The hall, with its ribbed vault, is divided into four aisles by three rows of pillars (dimensions: 70×30 m – 230×98 ft). It is the finest secular Gothic room still in existence in Paris.
Rue de Paris: named after the executioner ("Monsieur de Paris") to whom the condemned were handed over in this passage which is partitioned off from the Salle des Gens d'Armes.
Marie-Antoinette's cell in which the last queen of the "Old Régime" (Ancien Régime) was kept prisoner after an abortive escape attempt. Here, like thousands of other prisoners of the Revolution, she awaited execution.
Cell in which Danton and later Robespierre are said to have been held.
Women's courtyard (Cour des Femmes).
Chapelle des Girondins: the former chapel of the Conciergerie was used during the Revolution as a special prison for the supporters of the Girondist party (opponents of the dictatorship of the Jacobins). Exhibits: guillotine blade, prison rules, facsimile of Marie-Antoinette's last letter and other mementoes.
Salle des Gardes (14th c.): this was the room of the palace guards. The heavy vaults are supported by massive pillars with richly ornamented capitals.

**Place de la Concorde B3

Location
8th arrondissement

Métro
Concorde

Buses
24, 42, 52, 72, 73, 84, 94

The Place de la Concorde, at the intersection of the roads between the Louvre and the Arc de Triomphe and the Madeleine and the Palais Bourbon, is said to be one of the most beautiful squares in the world. It was chosen by the Senate as the site for an equestrian statue of Louis XV and laid out as the Place Louis XV by the architect Jacques Gabriel who had two magnificent buildings erected on the N side (1755–75), on either side of the Rue Royale: the present Ministry of Naval Affairs (until 1792 the royal furniture repository) on the right and what is today the Hôtel Crillon on the left (see illustration). During the French Revolution the statue of the king was destroyed, the name of the square changed to the Place de la Révolution and the guillotine set up here. Among the thousands executed in this square were Louis XVI, Marie-Antoinette, Madame du Barry, Charlotte Corday, Danton and in the end even Robespierre and his supporters.
In 1795, during the rule of the Directoire, the square was finally given its present name: Place de la Concorde.
In 1833 an obelisk 22 m (72 ft) high and weighing 220 tons, from Luxor, the Thebes of Ancient Egypt, was erected in the centre of the square. It dates from the reign of Ramses II (13th c. B.C.) and was a gift from the Egyptian Viceroy, Mehmed Ali. Between 1836 and 1854 Jacob Ignaz Hittorf completed the square by adding the fountains (N: allegories of Agriculture and Industry, see illustration; S: Seafaring and Fishing) and the eight statues of women symbolising (clockwise) France's

Place de la Concorde (with the Madeleine in the background)

eight largest cities: Marseilles, Bordeaux, Nantes, Brest, Rouen, Lille, Strasbourg, Lyons. (The small shelters in the plinths of the statues used to be occupied by "gardiens", city employees.)

*La Défense (Suburb – Défense quarter)

Location
Western outskirts

Métro
La Défense (RER)

In the W of the city, directly in line with the Champs-Elysées–Arc de Triomphe–Avenue de la Grand Armée, there has existed since the mid-sixties the business, exhibition and residential (!) quarter of La Défense. Its historical name (Defence) harks back to the war of 1870–1 when the French out up stubborn resistance to the Prussians on this spot. It does not quite seem to fit in with the aggressiveness of the skyscraper quarter which announces the French capital's breakthrough into the 21st c.

The "tours" (towers), as the French call the skyscrapers, are mainly occupied by large computer and oil multinationals. Thus La Défense is predominantly a quarter for business people but at the same time a residential quarter for people who like a "business-like" atmosphere, and here they have a large business centre, drugstore, restaurants, cinemas, a bank and boutiques.

An extravagant architectural feature is the large Centre National des Industries et Techniques, an exhibition building shaped like a mussel open to the sky. Its huge hall, which at

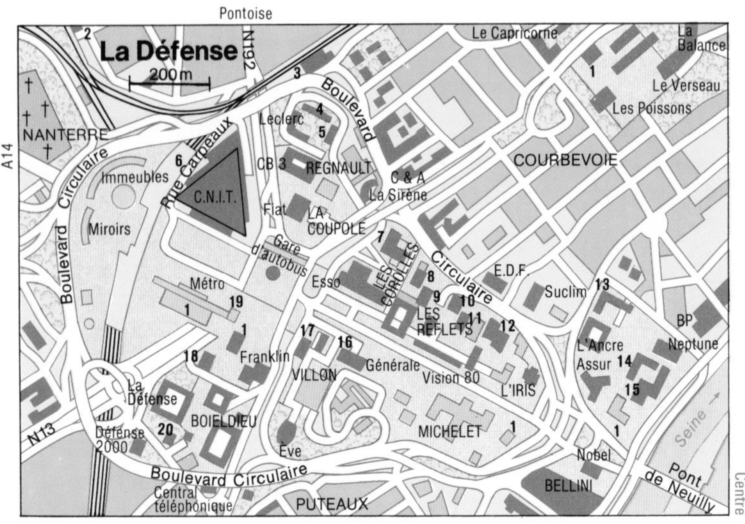

1 Hôtel
2 Centrale de Climatisation
3 Berkeley Building
4 Les Dauphins
5 Tour Gambetta
6 Gare S.N.C.F.
7 Septentrion
8 Europe
9 Aquitaine
10 E.D.F. - G.D.F.
11 Aurore
12 Manhattan
13 Damiers de Dauphiné
14 Damiers de Bretagne
15 Damiers d'Anjou
16 Crédit Lyonnais
17 Atlantique
18 Winterthur
19 Gare routière
20 Louis Pouey

90,000 sq. m (968,400 sq. ft) covers a greater area than the Place de la Concorde, is intended for fairs and exhibitions for which sufficiently large premises are not available in Paris itself.

*Dôme des Invalides (officially: Eglise du Dôme des Invalides) C3

Location
Place Vauban (7th arr.)

Métro
Latour-Maubourg, St-François-Xavier

Buses
28, 49, 69, 82, 92

Times of opening
1 Oct.–31 March: 10 a.m.–5 p.m.; 1 April–30 Sept.: 10 a.m.–6 p.m.

The Dôme des Invalides, the former "Royal Church" (see Hôtel des Invalides) of Louis XIV, is where Napoleon was entombed in 1840.

The work of the most important architect of the period, Jules Hardouin-Mansart, it is the outstanding ecclesiastical building of the French Classical period (1675–1706) and as such the counterpart of the secular masterpiece of the architecture of that period, the Palace of Versailles (see entry). With its impressive cupola (over 100 m (328 ft) in height) and façade of columns the Dôme des Invalides is an example of harmony in architecture.

The entrance is in the Place Vauban. In the open circular crypt (of the same diameter as the cupola: 11 m – 36 ft) Napoleon's red porphyry sarcophagus stands on a base of green granite. Twelve large goddesses of victory (by James Pradier) surrounding the crypt are a reminder of Napoleon's 12 major campaigns from 1797 to 1815.

Dôme des Invalides 

Tombs worth seeing in the side chapels:
Jérôme Bonaparte, king of Westphalia, one of Napoleon's brothers.
Marshal Turenne (killed near Sasbach in 1675).
La Tour d'Auvergne, military commander (killed near Oberhausen in Swabia in 1800), and Marshal Lyautey (1854–1934).
General Bertrand, Marshal of Napoleon's Household on Saint Helena (1773–1844).
Marshal Duroc (killed near Bautzen in 1813).
Marshal Foch (1851–1929).
Marshal Vauban, Louis XIV's master builder of fortifications (1633–1707).
Joseph Bonaparte, king of Spain, the Emperor's oldest brother (d. 1844).
Since 1969 there has been in a recess in Napoleon's crypt the tomb of his only legitimate son, Napoleon II. (He was king of Rome and duke of Reichstadt and died in Vienna in 1832 at the age of 21.)

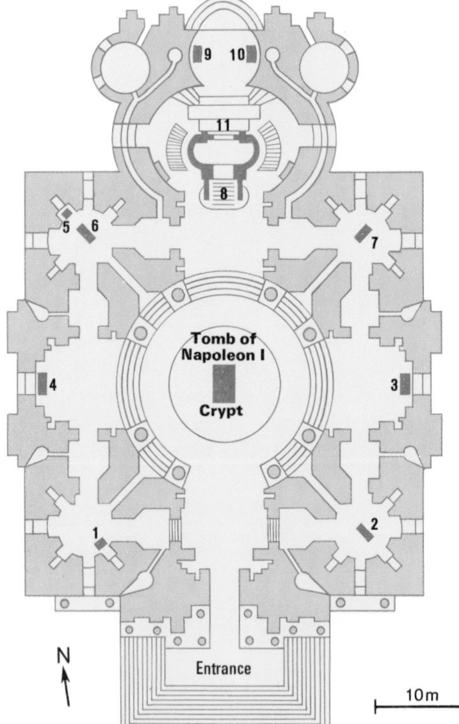

Eglise du Dôme des Invalides
(Tomb of Napoleon)

1 Tomb of Napoleon's brother Jérôme Bonaparte (d. 1860) in the Chapel of St Jérôme
2 Tomb of Napoleon's brother Joseph Bonaparte (d. 1844)
3 Tomb of Vauban (d. 1707), containing his heart
4 Tomb of Turenne (d. 1675)
5 Heart of La Tour d'Auvergne (d. 1800)
6 Tomb of Marshal Lyautey (d. 1934)
7 Tomb of Marshal Foch (d. 1929)
8 Altar with wreathed columns and baldachin
9 Tomb of General Bertrand (d. 1844)
10 Tomb of Marshal Duroc (d. 1813)
11 Entrance to the crypt: at the entrance two large bronze statues; inside surrounding Napoleon's tomb twelve colossal figures symbolising the Emperor's victories; at the back the tomb of Napoleon's son François Charles Joseph Bonaparte (d. 1832)

Ecole Militaire (former royal school for officers) C2/3

The Ecole Militaire, the former school for officers of the royal army, at the end of the Champ-de-Mars (see entry) opposite the Eiffel Tower (see Tour Eiffel), today houses the French military academy. It is the work of the architect Jacques-Ange Gabriel in accordance with whose plans it was built in two stages between 1759 and 1782. The clear-cut, simple, unadorned construction is a fine example of early Classicism.
In 1785 a little lieutenant left the officers' school. His superiors wrote on his certificate a meaningless phrase common at that time, "should go far". He did, and as Napoleon I became first Emperor of the French.
Behind the north façade of the main building (Place Joffre with the statue of Marshal Joffre) is the main courtyard (Cour d'honneur), its wings formed from two Doric colonnades.
The Saint-Louis chapel in the Louis XVI style is one of the masterworks of the architect Gabriel.

Location
Boulevard de la Tour-Maubourg (7th arr.)

Métro
Ecole Militaire, Champ-de-Mars

Buses
28, 49, 80, 82, 87, 92

Visits
Visits to the chapel on written application only: Général commandant d'armes de l'Ecole Militaire, 1 Place Joffre, 75007 Paris

Eiffel Tower

See Tour Eiffel

Etoile (officially: Place Charles de Gaulle; formerly: Place de l'Etoile) B2

The famous square, in the middle of which rises Napoleon's Arc de Triomphe (great triumphal arch – see entry), has, since 1970, borne the name of the former French President Charles de Gaulle. However, it is still popularly known as the Place de l'Etoile.
The points of the star (étoile) are formed by the 12 avenues which meet in a circular open space, the present aspect of which owes much to Baron Haussmann's town planning (see Boulevards).
France's general rule applies here too: traffic coming from the right has priority. From the platform of the Arc de Triomphe, besides enjoying a wonderful view of the city, one is also presented with the spectacle of the traffic in the square. The drivers entering the Etoile often seem under the impression that they are taking part in a race. Any foreigner who manages to get round in his own car without incident has already gone a long way to "conquering" Paris.

Location
16th arrondissement

Métro
Charles de Gaulle (Etoile)

Buses
22, 30, 31, 52, 73, 92

Faubourg Saint-Germain C3/4

The Faubourg Saint-Germain stretches from the quarter of Saint-Germain-des-Prés to the Hôtel des Invalides (see entries). The elegant aristocrats' quarter of the 18th c. today contains the residence of the Prime Minister (Hôtel de Matignon, 54 Rue de Varenne), and many former homes of the nobility are occupied by ministries and foreign diplomatic missions.

Location
7th arrondissement

Métro
Bac, Solférino, Varenne

Bus
69

Towards the end of the 18th c. the Marais quarter (see entry) went out of fashion and the aristocracy and the "nouveaux riches" moved here (and into the Faubourg Saint-Honoré – see entry). Some streets still give an impression of the town-planning of that time: Rue de Lille, Rue de Grenelle, Rue de Varenne. In the Rue de Grenelle stands the magnificent fountain "Fontaine des Quatre-Saisons" (1739–46), by Edmond Bouchardon, the most important sculptor of the reign of Louis XV.

Faubourg Saint-Honoré B3

Location
8th arrondissement

Métro
Saint-Philippe-du-Roulé

Buses
24, 38, 49, 52, 80, 83

Bordered by the Rue Royale, the boulevards Malesherbes and Haussmann and the Champs-Elysées lie a district and a street which bear the same name: Faubourg Saint-Honoré.
Haute Couture, the Presidential Palace and the Embassy quarter are all linked with the name of the street whose most interesting section lies between Rue La Boëtie and Rue Royale. Number 55–7 conceals the official residence of the French President, the Palais de l'Elysée (formerly the property of Madame de Pompadour, favourite mistress of Louis XIV). Almost opposite, in the Place Beauveau, is the Ministry of the Interior.
The window displays of the couturiers are a real centre of attraction: Daniel Hechter (No. 12), Lanvin (No. 22), Ted Lapidus (No. 23), Guy Laroche (No. 30), Yves Saint-Laurent (No. 38), Courrèges (No. 46), Castillo (No. 76), Louis Féraud (No. 88).
Well-known art galleries here are those of Hervé Odermatt (No. 85, contemporary) and Pacitti (No. 174, 19th and 20th c.).
The Faubourg Saint-Honoré, the Faubourg Saint-Germain (see entry) and the 16th arrondissement as a whole make up the prosperous, upper middle class West End of Paris.

Flea market

See Puces

**Château de Fontainebleau (Palace of Fontainebleau)

Location
Fontainebleau, 60 km (96 miles) SE (A6, N7)

Rail
From the Gare de Lyon

Times of opening
1 Oct.–31 March: 10 a.m.–12.30 p.m. and 2–5 p.m.; closed Tues.; 1 April–30 Sept.: 10 a.m.–12.30 p.m. and 2–6 p.m.; closed Tues.

The small town of Fontainebleau (20,000 inhabitants, the chief town of one of the cantons of the département of Seine-et-Marne) lies to the SE of Paris in the magnificent forest of the same name. Its great attraction is the Palace of Fontainebleau. Napoleon called it "the work of centuries and the home of kings", thereby epitomising the intimate relationship enjoyed by the French kings and emperors with their summer palace and hunting lodge.
The group of buildings making up the palace, with its beautiful park and lake, dates back to a 12th c. hunting lodge on the site of which François I ordered Gilles le Breton, Pierre Chambiges

Château de Fontainebleau (Cour des Adieux) 

Guided tours
For information ring 2 60 39 26

and Philibert Delorme to construct a Renaissance palace. This was extended several times by Henri II, Henry IV and Louis XV. It was here that Napoleon, who was especially fond of this palace, took leave of his army in 1814. This is recorded in the name "Cour des Adieux" given to the present entrance courtyard. It is also called "Cour du Cheval Blanc" (Courtyard of the White Horse) after a statue of the Roman Emperor Marcus Aurelius mounted on a white horse (since 1538 on the Capitol in Rome).

Exterior

The main façade of the palace as it is today is dominated by the double outside staircase in the shape of a horseshoe (1634) which, with its strong lines, announces the transition to the Baroque and overpowers the more delicate structure of the earlier (1615) central part. The outer parts of the façade date from the time of François I and are the work of the Bolognese master builder Primaticcio who worked at Fontainebleau from 1552 onwards.

The N wing of the Cour des Adieux is one of the oldest remaining parts of the palace. It was built about 1540 for François I's court officials; the S wing (18th c.) is the work of Louis XV's architect Jacques-Ange Gabriel and contains the apartments of the royal household.

The passage under the arcades to the right of the horseshoe staircase leads into the "Cour de la Fontaine", which on the right opens on to the large carp pond. On the left there is the François I Gallery (1st floor), behind which lies the Garden of Diana (Jardin de Diane).

Fontainebleau (carp pond, Cour de la Fontaine)

Interior

The most important rooms to see in the palace are the François I Gallery (Galerie François I), the ballroom and the chapel (Chapelle de Sainte-Trinité). The outside staircase leads directly into these rooms on the 1st floor.

The François I Gallery (1534–7) was used only as a corridor between the king's apartments and the chapel. Here merchants offered their fancy goods. Visitors are consequently astonished by the sumptuous furnishings in this room. It is unique in that artists (painters, sculptors and stucco workers) from Italy, the most outstanding of whom were Francesco Primaticcio (1507–70), Niccolò dell'Abbate and Rosso Fiorentino (1494–1541), created a synthesis of the arts in the Mannerist style (transition between Renaissance and Baroque). They founded the "Fontainebleau School" (as it was later known) whose showpiece this gallery is. They created a complex work of art, an ingenious unity of architecture, painting and stucco work with delicate coloration and a multitude of allegorical references. Incorporated into the 12 wall frescoes, the small paintings, the shapes of the frames and the stucco work are numerous symbolic references which can barely be deciphered today.

The ballroom (Henri II Gallery, 1552–6) was begun under François I (1547). The huge pilasters show that this room was to have had a vaulted ceiling (in the "medieval style"), but instead the "modern" flat ceiling was constructed which, nevertheless, spans an area of 30×10 m (98×33 ft). The numerous mythological scenes are by dell'Abbate (after sketches by Primaticcio). The scenes of Diana, the goddess of hunting, are also a tribute to Diane de Poitiers. She was François I's last favourite and after his death the favourite of his son, Henri II (who was almost thirty years younger than she was). Everywhere one looks in this room one finds the initials "D" and "H".

The Sainte-Trinité chapel is the height of both storeys (entrance on 1st floor). It was started by François I, continued by Philibert Delorme for Henri II, and was decorated under Henri IV (ceiling paintings by Frémiet).

Other rooms worth visiting on the 1st floor are the royal apartments. They consist of six rooms overlooking the Cour Ovale, including François I's suite which was altered by Louis XIV and contains the room where Louis XIII was born (Salon Louis-Treize), and 12 rooms overlooking the Jardin de Diane. These include:

The Queen's apartments (known as the Appartements de Marie-Antoinette).

The Throne Room (Salle du Trône).

The Council Chamber (Salle du Conseil).

Napoleon's rooms, in the Empire style. It was at the small round table in the Red Drawing-room (Salon Rouge) that Napoleon signed his Abdication in April 1814.

Worth visiting on the ground floor are:

Napoleon's private rooms (Petits Appartements de l'Empereur) next to the Jardin de Diane (formerly Louis XVI's apartments).

The former private rooms of Marie-Antoinette. Later they were used by Napoleon's wife Joséphine (Petits Appartements de l'Impératrice).

The Galerie de Diane, another wing of the palace, was constructed under Henri III and today houses a library and collection of paintings.

Fontaine des Innocents B4

Location
Square des Innocents next to the "Forum des Halles" (1st arr.)

Métro
Les Halles; Châtelet-Les-Halles (RER)

Buses
21, 69, 75

After the Halles district was altered the fountain "Fontaine des Innocents" (1549) was re-erected on its original site, the "Square des Innocents". Until 1786 this had been the location of the cemetery and the Church of the "Innocents" (Cimetière et Eglise des Innocents).
The architect of the fountain, which was converted into a temple in the 18th c., was Pierre Lescot ("Lescot-Façade" in the Cour Carrée of the Louvre – see entry). The reliefs on the older sides, the originals of which are today in the Louvre, are by the master of French Renaissance sculpture Jean Goujon. The fourth side of the fountain is decorated with the figures of nymphs (1788) by Augustin Pajou.

Grand Palais B3

Location
Avenue Churchill (8th arr.)

Métro
Champs-Elysées-Clemenceau

Buses
28, 42, 49, 72, 73, 83

Times of opening
Depending on the exhibition; usually daily (except Tues.) 10 a.m.–5 p.m.

Until the Centre Pompidou (see entry) was built the most important exhibitions in Paris were held in the Grand Palais, whether the collected works of individual artists (Monet, Matisse, Chagall, Miró, Picasso), periods (Impressionism, Symbolism) or countries. Today it shares this pre-eminence with the new arts centre. The Autumn Salon (Salon d'Automne), however, still takes place here all the year round.
Built for the 1900 World Fair, the inside is in the Art Nouveau style of the time (iron and steel construction), but the outside has predominantly been kept in the neo-Baroque style. The noteworthy glass dome inside is 43 m (141 ft) high.
Since 1965 the S wing has housed part of one of the Universities of Paris and since 1937 the W wing has contained the natural history museum, see Palais de la Découverte.

Les Halles (market quarter; officially: Quartier des Halles) B4

Location
Centre (1st arr.)

Métro
Les Halles

Suburban station
Châtelet-Les-Halles (RER)

Buses
21, 29, 67, 74, 75, 85

Since the demolition of the former market halls at the end of the sixties the market quarter, like the neighbouring Marais (see entry), has been in a state of upheaval.
For years there was the gaping hole of a gigantic building site ("Le Trou des Halles") where previously there had been the "Belly of Paris" (Zola wrote a novel of the same name about it, "Le Ventre de Paris"). Since then it has been filled with concrete and become one of the biggest underground traffic junctions in Paris (two RER lines intersect a métro line and the whole complex is connected with Châtelet station where four métro lines meet).
Above the métro and RER tunnels and underground car parks are (still underground) the commercial floors of the "Forum des Halles", opened in 1979, with cinemas, theatres, restaurants and cafés. It remains to be seen whether this "Forum" and the gardens laid out above it (at ground level) will fulfil the social function aimed at by the town-planners.

Forum des Halles

(The inhabitants never had any difficulty about being sociable before the market halls were demolished.)
The old streets surrounding the area are swarming with fashionable clothes shops, secondhand shops, cheap furniture shops and sex shops, which have sprung up in the Rue Saint-Denis as competition for the prostitutes who operate there.

Hôtel de Ville (Town Hall) C4

Since 1977 Paris, for a long time a "capital without a head", has had a mayor again. His official residence is the Hôtel de Ville (Town Hall), to which the mayor's offices (Mairies Annexes) of the 20 arrondissements are answerable. (For information on the special administrative structure of Paris and the surrounding area see General, Administration.)
The first town hall was built here in the 14th c. François I had it rebuilt in the Renaissance style. At the beginning of the 19th c. it was extended but an attempt was made to keep to the same style. In 1871 it was set on fire when the Commune was overthrown and then subsequently fully restored.
The present building dates from the same period as the Opéra (see entry) and can be compared with it in so far as the neo-Baroque style of the Opéra and the neo-Renaissance style of the Town Hall resulted in unduly ornate buildings which because of their overflowing decoration are impressive, but which on closer inspection appear to lack harmony and independence.

Location
Place de l'Hôtel de Ville
(4th arr.)

Métro
Hôtel de Ville

Buses
38, 47, 58, 67, 69, 70, 72, 74, 75, 76, 96

Guided tours
Information:
Bureau d'accueil,
tel. 2 78 13 00

Hôtel de Ville

In the Middle Ages the city's chief administrator was a provost (prévôt), the head of Paris's corporation of merchant shippers which belonged to the Hanseatic League. Though his appointment and dismissal were in the hands of the king, he still exercised considerable influence. In 1358 the provost Etienne Marcel led the first (unsuccessful) "citizens' revolt" against feudalism and the monarchy. In 1789 the last provost, who as a royal official represented the monarchy, was killed by the Revolutionary mob. After the Revolution Paris had a mayor for brief periods only (1789–94, 1848, 1870–1). The rest of the time it was "governed" by representatives of the State (Prefect and Prefect of Police).
The reception office of the Town Hall can supply information on guided tours of the civic chambers where the décor matches the exterior of the building. (The Parisians think the Town Hall has more rooms for gala occasions than for work.)

Ile Saint-Louis C4

Location
Centre (4th arr.)

Métro
Pont-Marie

Bus
67

In 1609, at the instigation of Cardinal Richelieu, two originally separate islands were joined together and then linked by two bridges to the right bank of the Seine. The contract for this work, and for developing the new unit as a whole, was awarded to Marie, Poulettier and Le Regrattier.
The 17th c. architecture still retains its (cold) aristocratic dignity. Besides the nobility, poets (Charles Baudelaire, Théophile Gautier), philosophers (Voltaire, Jean-Jacques

Rousseau) and statesmen (Georges Pompidou) have all lived here.
If you walk along the quays you can see the Hôtel de Ville on the right bank, the Quartier Latin with the Panthéon on the left bank, and the Cité (see entries) with Notre-Dame in the distance. Smart restaurants, many of them in vaulted cellars, are an enticing setting for dining in style.

Saint-Louis-en-l'Ile (church)

Location
Rue Saint-Louis-en-l'Ile

The church was begun in 1664 by Louis Le Vau and completed in 1726 by Jacques Doucet. Paintings by Charles Coypel (1694–1752): "The Disciples' Meal at Emmaus", Pierre Mignard (1612–95): "Rest on the Flight" and Francesco Vecellio (Titian's brother): "Entombment of Christ" (16th c,).

Hôtel de Lauzun

Location
17 Quai d'Anjou

The Hôtel (1657), by the architect Louis Le Vau, belongs to the city and is used for official receptions.
The Hôtel de Lauzun (famous frescoes and sculptures) may be visited only by prior arrangement (Directeur Adjoint, Les Beaux-Arts de la Ville de Paris, 14 Rue François-Miron, 75004 Paris). The poets Baudelaire and Th. Gautier lived here for a while in the 19th c.

Hôtel Lambert

Location
2 Rue Saint-Louis-en-l'Ile

This Hôtel, built in 1640 and also by Le Vau, is privately owned and cannot be visited. With its semicircular courtyard, open staircase, oval entrance hall, "Galerie d'Hercule" (depicting the legend of Hercules) and sumptuous original furnishings the Hôtel Lambert is an excellent example of the art and culture of its period.

Institut de France C4

(officially: Palais de l'Institut de France; formerly: Collège des Quatre-Nations)

Location
23 Quai de Conti (6th arr.)

Métro
Pont-Neuf

Buses
24, 27

Times of opening
Guided tour (in French) on application:
Secrétariat de l'Institut,
23 Quai de Conti,
75006 Paris

The Académie Française (founded in 1635 by Cardinal Richelieu to conserve the French language) is only one of France's five scientific academies which together form the Institut de France. Its members, "les 40 Immortels" (Immortals), decide on whether a word should be admitted to their authoritative dictionary of the French language, the "Dictionnaire de l'Académie", and thus "officially" rank as a "French word".
The other Academies carry out and promote research in the fields of classical history and archaeology (Inscriptions et Belles Lettres, 1663), natural sciences (Sciences, 1666), moral and social sciences and jurisprudence (Sciences morales et politiques, 1795) and art (Beaux-Arts, 1816). The Institut has its headquarters in the Palais de l'Institut de France on the Quai de Conti.

In 1661 Cardinal Mazarin founded a college to take 15 young nobles from each of the four provinces which had recently become part of France – Artois, Alsace, Piedmont and Roussillon. This Collège des Quatre-Nations was given its own building (1688) with a chapel (1674) and a library (1691), all designed by the architect Louis Le Vau (1612–70). The College was in existence from 1688 until 1790. In 1805 the five former royal academies, which since 1795 had been merged together to form the Institut de France, were moved, on Napoleon's orders, from the Louvre into the college building.

The Palais de l'Institut de France was designed, in town-planning terms, to offset on the left bank of the Seine the Cour Carrée of the Louvre (see entry) on the right bank. This accounts for its surprising size (for only 60 students) and imposing appearance with the typical features of "classical" French Baroque: prominent pavilions, with high-pitched roofs, that lend weight to the wings at the front of the building, alignment of the façade and the tambour at the base of the dome serried ranks of columns. A special feature is the semicircular arrangement of the façade with, in its centre, the dome of the former chapel behind the six-column portico. The chapel became the great council chamber and it is here that the individual academies and the Institut as a whole meet in plenary session. Here, too, elections are held on the death of a member and the ceremony of admittance takes place.

Despite what those who are critical (and envious) of this institution may say to the contrary, membership of one of the Academies is still in France the zenith of any career. Besides the internationally renowned figures who have been members, past and present, of the Académie Française (including Victor Hugo, Prosper Mérimée, Jean Cocteau, René Clair, Eugène Ionesco), many of France's great philosophers and writers have been refused admittance and a "reception under the dome": Blaise Pascal, Molière, Rousseau, Diderot, Balzac, Zola, Proust. In 1980, for the first time in the history of the Academy, women were admitted as members: Yvonne Choquet-Bruhat (Académie des Sciences) and Marguerite Yourcenar (Académie Française).

Inside the building, which can be visited by prior appointment only, the chief point of interest is the Great Council Chamber under the dome where one can see the memorial statue of Cardinal Mazarin by Antoine Coysevox based on Hardouin-Mansart's design.

Invalides (officially: Hôtel des Invalides) C3

Location
Between Place Vauban and Esplanade des Invalides

Métro
Latour-Maubourg, Varenne, Invalides

Buses
28, 49, 69, 82, 92

The Hôtel des Invalides still fulfils its original function as a home for disabled ex-servicemen. Although at one time it could accommodate 7000 pensioners, there are nowadays barely 200 living in what is the finest intact complex of 17th c. buildings in Paris. Most of the rooms are museums or are used by the military authorities. The Musée de l'Armée (Military Museum – see entry) and the adjoining Musée des Plans-Reliefs (Museum of relief maps) are of great interest to the visitor interested in military history, although the main attraction for most visitors is Napoleon's tomb in the Dôme des Invalides (see entry).

Prior to Louis XIV ("the Sun King") disabled ex-servicemen (if any) were given medical attention in hospitals and then in most cases forced to resort to begging. With the Hôtel des Invalides the "Sun King" founded the first home for men disabled while serving in his armies. It was built in 1671–6 under the direction of the architect Libéral Bruant with the church of Saint-Louis-des-Invalides in the centre. Today the nave of the church is festooned with flags and standards, the booty of the victorious French armies under Napoleon. (This church is the venue for outstanding organ recitals.)
Since the church's lack of adornment was not to the King's taste he commissioned Jules Hardouin-Mansart, one of the architects of Versailles, to build a second "Royal Church" (Eglise Royale, 1675–1706) which later became known as the Eglise du Dôme des Invalides (see entry) because of its characteristic dome.
In the main tourist season there are "Son et lumière" presentations in the courtyard (Cour d'Honneur) of the Hôtel des Invalides, chiefly featuring the history of Napoleon (in French: 3 April–12 Oct.: 10.30 p.m.; in English: 3 April–12 Oct.: 11.15 p.m.; 3 April–16 May and 10 Aug.–12 Oct.: 9.30 p.m.). There is a bronze statue of Napoleon as the "Little Corporal" under the central arcade of the S pavilion.
German tanks captured in the Second World War stand at the entrance to the gardens in front of the N front of the Hôtel des Invalides. The "Esplanade des Invalides" extending from here to the Seine was laid out (1704–20) by Robert de Cotte.

Times of opening
1 Oct.–31 March: 10 a.m.–5 p.m.;
1 April–30 Sept.: 10 a.m.–6 p.m.

Jardin d'Acclimatation (Children's amusement park) B1/B2

Children, including those of visitors to Paris, should get their money's worth, in terms of amusement, pleasure and edification, in this park where a Disneyland à la Paris has been set up on a former zoo site in the Bois de Boulogne (see entry). (Parents should accompany their children, if only to keep an eye on their spending!)
A children's zoo, donkey rides, miniature railway, mini road system, go-kart track, skate-board area, fair, children's museum and theatre are only some of the attractions on offer for ten hours every day.
For adults there is the Musée des Arts et Traditions Populaires (see entry), and obviously children are also welcome here.

Location
Bois de Boulogne (16th arr.)

Métro
Sablons, Porte Maillot (narrow-gauge railway to the park entrance)

Bus
73

Times of opening
9 a.m.–6.30 p.m. daily

Jardin des Plantes C4/C5

(National Natural History Museum; officially: Muséum National d'Histoire Naturelle)

The Jardin des Plantes offers the visitor a glimpse into the natural history research fields of botany (the school for botany has over 10,000 plant species), mineralogy, zoology, ecology and palaeontology (the study of extinct species of animals and plants). It is also a work-place for students at the nearby Paris-VII University (Jussieu).
Early in the 17th c. Louis XIII's doctors established a garden of medicinal herbs here which soon expanded into a great plant collection. A school for botany and pharmacy was set up and

Location
57 Rue Cuvier (5th arr.)

Métro
Jussieu, Gare d'Austerlitz

Buses
24, 57, 61, 63, 65, 67, 89, 91

Times of opening
Galleries: Mon., Wed.–Fri. 1.30–5 p.m.;
Sun. 10.30 a.m.–5 p.m.; closed Tues. and public holidays; Park: daily 9 a.m. until dusk

from 1650 onwards the garden was open to the public. Georges Louis Leclerc de Bouffon (1707–88), an aristocratic naturalist, extended the gardens and made them into a park, partly in the English and partly in the French (strictly geometrical) style. The 19th c. saw the erection of the iron and glass galleries for palaeontology, botany and mineralogy (greenhouses, bird cages and exhibition buildings) on the left of the main entrance. The acacia between the botany and mineralogy galleries is supposed to be the oldest tree in Paris (planted in 1636).
At the back (viewed from the Seine) there is a small maze.
The Parisians' first sight of the wild animals was during the French Revolution when they were moved from the royal court at Versailles to the English section of the Jardin des Plantes (beasts of prey, apes, elephants and birds). The park then became officially known as the "Musée d'Histoire Naturelle".

**Jeu de Paume (officially: Musée du Jeu de Paume) B3

Location
Jardins des Tuileries, Place de la Concorde (1st arr.)

Métro
Concorde

Buses
24, 42, 52, 72, 73, 84, 94

Times of opening
9.45 a.m.–5.15 p.m., closed Tues.

In the NE corner of the Tuileries gardens, on the left of the entrance in the Place de la Concorde (see entry), is the building where the ball game Jeu de Paume used to be played and which now houses the world-famous collection of Impressionist paintings from the Louvre. The building, erected in 1861 during the reign of Napoleon III, was turned into an exhibition hall in 1920 and received the Impressionist collection in 1947.
All the great masters of Impressionism, which between 1870 and 1900 began the modern art movement, are represented (Edouard Manet, Claude Monet, Camille Pissarro, Alfred Sisley, Auguste Renoir, Edgar Degas) as well as Post-Impressionism (Vincent van Gogh, Paul Gauguin, Paul Cézanne), Pointillism (Georges Seurat and Paul Signac) and the unclassifiable work of Henri de Toulouse-Lautrec.
At the exit to the terrace on the ground floor (this is a suitable place for a short rest) there are accounts in several languages of the history and nature of Impressionist painting.

**Louvre (officially: Palais du Louvre) B3/4–C4

Location
Palais du Louvre (1st arr.)

Métro
Louvre, Palais-Royal

Buses
21, 24, 27, 39, 48, 67, 69, 72, 74, 77, 81, 85, 95

Since 1793 half the former royal palace of the Louvre has been used as a museum (Musée du Louvre), which is one of the most famous in the world. Its collection of paintings ranges from the 13th to the 19th c.; the sculpture and other art treasures date back to the early history of the advanced civilisations; the valuable collections of period furniture and tableware are mainly 17th–19th c.
The Palace stands on the site of a fortress (*c.* 1200) built in the reign of Philippe Augustus which was partly demolished by the "Renaissance King", François I. In 1559–74 the architect Pierre Lescot and the sculptor Jean Goujon were responsible for the converging sections of the W and S wings of the old Louvre (the Cour Carrée). These oldest parts of the present Palace were extended in 1566 in a southerly direction by adding the Petite Galerie to Lescot's S wing. At almost the

Louvre (Arc de Triomphe du Carrousel)

same time (1564) the Tuileries Palace was built 500 m (550 yd) to the W of the old Louvre as a residence for the dowager queen Catherine de Medici (along the present Avenue du Général Lemonnier). During the reign of Henri IV this palace was joined to the Petite Galerie by the long S wing (Galerie du Bord de l'Eau) flanking the Seine. Louis XIII and Louis XIV had the Cour Carrée extended and completed.

The old Louvre and the Tuileries Palace were only occasionally occupied by the French kings and after Louis XIV left Paris for Versailles the buildings became so derelict that they were nearly demolished in 1750. Artists had set themselves up in the galleries, while the royal palace provided shelter for beggars and other forerunners of the "clochards" who would settle in for a couple of nights or even the whole winter: the stove pipes of the "tenants" poked out between the columns of the colonnade on the E façade.

Napoleon not only got rid of the "tenants" of the Louvre but also started to rearrange the area between the present N and S wings which at that time was tightly packed with buildings. He enlarged the square in front of the Tuileries Palace (today Jardin du Louvre and Place du Carrousel), had the Arc de Triomphe du Carrousel (see entry) set up there, and began building the N wing. But it was the architect of modern Paris, Baron Haussmann (see Boulevards) who, while completing the Cour Carrée and building the N wing (1852–70), had the remaining houses pulled down and the Jardin du Louvre and the Place and Square du Carrousel laid out in their present form. In the 19th c. all the buildings of the Louvre were also fully restored.

The Tuileries Palace was stormed three times by the people. In 1793, when Louis XVI was forced to return to the Tuileries after an unsuccessful flight, they mockingly placed the red ("Phrygian") cap of the Revolutionaries on his head. It was a less violent affair in 1848 when the "Citizen-King", Louis-Philippe, was overthrown but in 1871 the Tuileries Palace was set on fire during the Commune and never rebuilt.
Since then the palace complex has looked as it does now: abutting on to the W side of the Cour Carrée is the Square du Carrousel with the six pavilions of the inner wings on its N and S sides. This opens on to the Place du Carrousel and further W the "Parterres" of the Jardin du Carrousel with the Arc du Triomphe du Carrousel (see entry) and 18 statues by Aristide Maillol. The Jardin du Carrousel is bordered at the ends of the S and N wings on a level with the Pavillon de Flore (in the S) and the Pavillon de Marsan (in the N) by the Avenue du Général Lemonnier; the Tuileries Gardens begin on the other side of the Avenue.
The following sections of the exterior are most worth seeing:

Exterior

E front/colonnades: in 1665 Louis XIV sought to get the major architects of the time to produce an especially impressive design for the E front of the old Louvre by announcing a competition (entrants included the Frenchmen Jean Marot and Jacques Lemercier and the Italian Gian Lorenzo Bernini, the architect of St Peter's Square in Rome). The winning design was a joint effort by Claude Perrault, Louis Le Vau and Charles Lebrun. Their "colonnade", which today can be admired in its entirety thanks to the exposure of the base, as a result of the programme, since 1968, to refurbish Paris's monuments, represents a compromise between the styles of

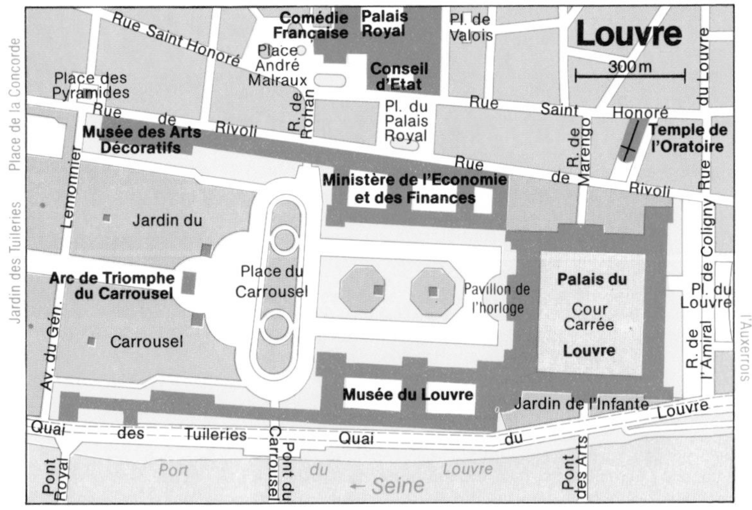

Musée du Louvre ("Mona Lisa" by Leonardo da Vinci) ▶

French Baroque and Classical Italian: the double columns and flat roof are Italian-Classical in style whereas the emphasis on the centre (triangular gable) and side sections is more typical of the French.

The exposure of the base has restored to the colonnade (18 Corinthian columns) its original spatial dimensions. The "classical severity" of this magnificent façade was to have been tempered by a row of statues on the roof balustrade but this did not materialise.

All work was stopped when the court moved to Versailles, leaving its completion to Napoleon. Consequently the figures in the central pediment (Minerva, 1811) and the reliefs below it (Goddess of Victory in a chariot drawn by four horses) date from the early 19th c. The medallions on the upper left and right contain the initials of Louis XIV.

Cour Carrée (Square Courtyard): the buildings enclosing this courtyard form the so-called Vieux Louvre (Old Louvre), the true Palace of the Louvre. This was approximately the site of Philippe Augustus' original fortress (its outline is marked out in the SW corner). Lescot's façade was begun under Henri II while work on the other wings began under Louis XIII and Louis XIV and was not finished until the time of Napoleon. (In summer there are open-air concerts and ballets here.)

Pavillon de l'Horloge: the Clock Pavilion, designed to harmonise with Lescot's façade, is the work of Jacques Lemercier (17th c.) who also added the N section of the W wing in imitation Renaissance style.

Lescot's façade (1559–74): the southern half of the W wing of the Cour Carrée is the oldest part of the Louvre Palace. This masterpiece of Renaissance architecture was created by the architect Pierre Lescot (1510–78) and the sculptor Jean Goujon (1510–68).

With its striking harmony the Lescot façade is an expression of the concern in Renaissance architecture to revive the symmetry of its Classical models in a distinct and "unassuming" but not necessarily unadorned form (unlike, for example, the monumental ordered Classicism of the late 18th c. – see Madeleine and Panthéon). It is clearly tripartite, both horizontally, in the alternation of the door and gable sections with those of the window, and vertically (if the narrow upper floor is considered part of the roof). Thus the ratio of door section to window section and of height of storey to (projecting) storey demarcation is in each case 1:3.

The round arches of the windows on the ground floor give the impression of an arcade; in the middle storey each pair of triangular-gabled windows flanks a round-gabled window (repetition of the triple theme!); the top storey is rightly famed for the marvellous relief decoration (Jean Goujon) on the round gables, which are linked by a richly ornamented balustrade. The gable reliefs are allegories: Nature (left: Ceres for Agriculture, Neptune for Shipping, Genius with cornucopia), War (centre: Mars God of War, Bellona Goddess of War, prisoners), Science (right: Archimedes for Astronomy, Euclid for Geometry, Spirit of science).

(The Lescot wing was built at the same time as the adjoining half of the S wing which contained the royal apartments, but this façade is of little artistic importance.)

Petite Galerie (1566): this short section is at right angles to the S side of the Cour Carrée and to the long wing of the Louvre

Musée du Louvre (Grande Galerie)

running along the Seine in a westerly direction. The ground floor is original. The upper floor contains the Galerie d'Apollon. Its frescoes by Charles Lebrun (1661) incorporate for the first time the allegorical relationship between Apollo and Louis XIV (cf. Versailles, Hall of Mirrors – see entry).

Pavillon Denon: the rooms in the N and S wings date from the time of Napoleon III. The main entrance to the Louvre museum is in the Pavillon Denon, in the Square du Louvre. Laid out by Baron Haussmann. The equestrian statue of General Lafayette (1900, P. W. Bartlett) was a gift from the U.S.A.

Guichet du Louvre in the Seine wing: triple-arched gateway with gigantic allegories of the Navy and the Merchant Fleet. The entire Galerie du Bord de l'Eau (Seine wing) was restored in the 19th c.

Place du Carrousel: "Carrousel" was the name given to the equestrian games and masked balls which evolved from the medieval tournaments and from which in turn we derive the term "carousel" for a fairground roundabout. The square owes its name to the "Carrousel" of 1662 which celebrated the birth of the Dauphin (crown prince) Louis XV.

To the W the Arc de Triomphe du Carrousel (see entry).

Pavillon de Flore: the Tuileries Palace which was burned down in 1871 stood between the Pavillon de Flore and the Pavillon de Marsan. The pavilion gets its name from the relief "Triumph of Flora" (1866) by Jean-Baptiste Carpeaux (on the Seine side).

Parterres du Louvre: the Parterres (formal lawns) contain 18 statues by the sculptor Aristide Maillol (1861–1944).

Pavillon de Marsan: houses the Musée des Arts Décoratifs (see Practical Information).
Pavillon de Rohan: the pavilion dates from the time of Louis XVIII. The N wing houses the Ministry of the Economy and Finance.

Musée du Louvre

Location
Palais du Louvre (1st arr.)

Métro
Louvre, Palais-Royal

Buses
21, 24, 27, 39, 48, 67, 69, 72, 74, 77, 81, 85, 95

Times of opening
9.45 a.m.–8 p.m., closed Tues. and public holidays

Guided tours
Mon., Wed.–Sat. (Information on guided tours in English can be obtained from the information desk or by telephone. Tel. 2 60 39 26)

It is not possible to reproduce a plan of the museum because it is currently being reorganised. A plan of the current arrangements can be obtained from the cash desk and it is advisable to obtain one of these in any case. (They are in fact given away free of charge during the week following publication.)
In this context it is possible to give only a general idea of the periods, schools of painting and artefacts on display.

1. Etruscan art (inc. "Sarcophagus of Cerveteri", 6th c. B.C.).
2. Oriental art (Mesopotamia, Persia, Phoenicia, Assyria).
3. Egyptian antiquities (Old, Middle and New Kingdoms).
4. Greek sculpture (inc. fragments from the Parthenon in Athens, "Venus de Milo", "Lady of Auxerre", "Winged Victory of Samothrace").
5. Classical bronze figures (inc. the "Athlete of Benevento" and the "Ephebe of Agde").
6. Roman sarcophagi, 2nd and 3rd c. B.C., frescoes and mosaics from Rome and Greece.
7. Greek ceramics.

"Venus de Milo"

Graeco-Roman department

8. Sculpture, 12th–19th c. (including the famous statue of Cupid by Edme Bouchardon; Michelangelo's "Slaves", Donatello's "St John the Baptist" and "Mary and Child").
9. Spanish painting, 14th–18th c. (inc. El Greco, Francisco Zurbarán, Estaban Murillo, José Ribera, Diego Velázquez, Francisco Goya).
10. Late-Gothic and Renaissance paintings from Germany and the Low Countries, 15th and 16th c. (inc. Dürer's "Self-portrait", works by Hans Holbein the Younger and Lucas Cranach).
11. Flemish and Dutch painting, 16th and 17th c. (inc. works by Peter Paul Rubens, Jan van Eyck, Hieronymus Bosch, Breughel the Elder, Rembrandt, Van Dyck, Frans Hals).
12. Italian painting, 13th–15th c. (inc. works by Giotto, Filippo Lippi, Botticelli, Mantegna).
13. Italian painting, 16th c. (Leonardo da Vinci's "Mona Lisa").
14. Italy, 17th c. masters ("Virgin Mary" by Caravaggio, Tiepolo, Caracci).
15. French 16th c. paintings (Jean Clouet, François Quernel).
16. French 17th c. painting (Lebrun, Poussin, La Tour, Le Nain).
17. French 18th and 19th c. painting.
18. Applied art and furniture.
19. Remainder of the French Crown Jewels.

The Louvre Museum can be visited free of charge on Sundays when, needless to say, it becomes particularly crowded.

*Jardin du Luxembourg — C3/4

Children and students (from the nearby Quartier Latin – see entry) are regular visitors to the Jardin du Luxembourg, which is the best-known park in Paris after the Tuileries. It dates from the 17th c. (coinciding with the Palais du Luxembourg – see entry) and owes its present appearance to the 19th c. architect J. F. Chalgrin (1739–1811).

Location
Main entrance:
Place Edmond Rostand (Boulevard St-Michel, 6th arr.)

Métro
Odéon

Suburban train station
Luxembourg (RER)

Times of opening
Daily 9 a.m. until dusk

The large octagonal pond with fountain is flanked by two terraces. This central part of the park is laid out in the French Classical style (straight lines, symmetry), while the outer sections are closer to the less formal English style of garden (winding paths, occasional stands of trees).

A number of statues of prominent men and women from the worlds of art and politics are dotted around the terraces and paths. The "Fontaine des Médicis", in its picturesque setting among the trees (opposite the E front of the Palace), is worth looking at. The basin of the fountain with its Renaissance statuary of the river gods of the Rhône and Seine dates from around 1620 and is a reminder of the former owner, Marie de Médicis, mother of Louis XIII.

The large pond is usually besieged by children who sail their boats here (these can also be hired at a stall); smaller children sit entranced in front of the "Grand Guignol" (Punch and Judy show) near the tennis courts in the SW part of the garden.

There are chairs and benches to rest on free of charge. (Until a few years ago elderly women still did the rounds collecting the city's charges for these.) At dusk the park-keeper's whistle indicates that the gates are about to be closed for the night.

Jardin and Palais du Luxembourg

Palais du Luxembourg C4

Location
15 Rue de Vaugirard
(6th arr.)

Métro
Odéon

Suburban station
Luxembourg (RER)

Buses
21, 27, 38, 84, 85, 89

Times of opening
Sun. 9.30–11.30 a.m.;
2–4.30 p.m.

The Palais du Luxembourg is the seat of the French Senate (Upper House) which together with the Assemblée Nationale (see Palais Bourbon) makes up the French Parliament. Only parts of it are open to the public, and then only on Sundays (apart from the exhibition rooms of the "Musée du Luxembourg" which are open daily, except Mondays, from 11 a.m. until 6 p.m.). Groups must apply in writing to the Secrétariat général de la questure du Sénat, 15 Rue de Vaugirard, 75006 Paris.

Marie de Médicis, the wife of Henri II, acquired the property in 1612 from Duke Francis of Luxembourg in order to have her dowager's residence built there – in the Florentine style of her homeland in accordance with her wishes. However, the architects of the palace, built between 1615 and 1631 according to the plans of Salomon de Brosse, closely followed the traditional French style: the principal and side wings, bounded by pavilions (domed structures with high-pitched roofs), form a courtyard (Cour d'Honneur); the living quarters in the "classical" sequence of garderobe, cabinet, antichambre, chambre (bedroom) each make up one unit. Two huge galleries were intended for series of paintings but Peter Paul Rubens' famous "Medici" series is now in the Louvre (see entry) and its counterpart for Henri IV was never painted. The remarkable paintings on the walls of the library are by Eugène Delacroix (1845–7).

Marie de Médicis never used the palace, as shortly after it was finished she had to flee the country – she had lost the game of political intrigue against her adversary Cardinal Richelieu. She died in exile in Cologne in 1642.
The palace changed hands several times before Napoleon decided it should be used for the Senate and had it altered by J. F. Chalgrin (garden wing).

*Madeleine (officially: Eglise Sainte-Marie-Madeleine) B3

The church of Saint Mary Magdalen, generally known as La Madeleine, is a pseudo-Grecian building (52 Corinthian columns) of considerable size (108 m (354 ft) long, 43 m (141 ft) wide, height of columns: 9 m – 20 ft). Although of minor significance from the art-historical point of view, it is always of interest to foreign visitors and affords a chance of glimpsing a spectacular wedding.
The story of the building of the Madeleine reflects the confused state of French history from the end of the Ancien Régime until the time of the Citizen-King: the foundation stone was laid in 1763 in the reign of Louis XV for a cruciform Baroque church with a dome. Under Louis XVI it was planned to remodel it on the Classical lines of the Panthéon (see entry), then under construction, with more emphasis on the dome. During the Revolutionary period building came to a complete standstill. Various plans for a completely different use (as a stock exchange, Parliament or bank) were advanced and rejected. In

Location
Place de la Madeleine
(8th arr.)

Métro
Madeleine

Buses
24, 42, 52, 84, 94

La Madeleine

1806 Napoleon decided on a Hall of Fame for the army in the style of the Parthenon in Athens but shortly before his abdication he reverted to the idea of a church. Louis XVIII, protagonist of the Restoration, wanted a church of expiation to atone for the Revolution. It was not until the reign of Louis-Philippe, the Citizen-King, that the church dedicated to Saint Mary Magdalen was completed as a "Greek temple" (1842).
The gable frieze on the façade (1833, Philippe-Henri Lemaire) is of the Last Judgment. The reliefs on the bronze door relate to the Ten Commandments.
Light enters the interior (vestibule, nave, semicircular choir) through three huge domes. The spandrels are decorated with reliefs of the 12 Apostles and the main altar with a group of figures in marble (1837), Ascension of Mary Magdalen). Above the altar is a vast fresco showing Constantine the Great, Frederick Barbarossa, Joan of Arc, Saint Louis, Michelangelo, Raphael, Dante, Cardinal Richelieu, Napoleon and other historical figures. Famous Cavaillé-Coll organ (recitals).

*Malmaison (château; officially: Musée National du Château de Malmaison)

Location
Rueil-Malmaison
(suburb 16 km (10 miles) W on the N13)

Suburban station
Défense (RER)

Bus
158A (from Défense)

Times of opening
1 Oct.–31 March: 10 a.m.–noon and 1.30–4.30 p.m.;
1 April–30 Sept.: 10 a.m.–noon and 1.30–5.30 p.m.;
closed Tues. and holidays.

This château, situated in the western suburb of Rueil-Malmaison, contains many mementoes of the Emperor Napoleon I and the Empress Joséphine. It has been a French national museum since 1906.The château of Malmaison was built in 1620 in the early Baroque style and bought in 1799 by Joséphine de Beauharnais, the wife of Napoléon Bonaparte. After their divorce the Empress lived here withdrawn and alone. She died here in 1814, ten months before Napoleon – after the failure of the "100 days" – took his leave of family and country here to go into final exile on the island of Saint Helena.
The interior furnishings date back to the time of the Empire. Most of the objects were originally in the château but some come from the palaces of Saint-Cloud and Fontainebleau and from the Tuileries Palace.
The ground floor houses the billiard room, Golden Drawing Room (Sèvres porcelain), Music Room (complete 1812 décor), Dining-room (the gilded dinner service was a coronation gift from the city of Paris in 1804), council chamber, study (military décor) and library (in its original state).
The rooms on the first floor: Emperor's drawing-room and bedroom, Marengo drawing-room (after the wall painting of the victory of Marengo), Empress's rooms, exhibition rooms.

Maisons-Laffitte (château; officially: Château de Maisons)

Location
Maisons-Laffitte (western suburb)

Telephone
Tourist information office:
9 62 68 96, ext. 361

This impressive château was built between 1642 and 1650 by François Mansart for the president of the Royal Court of Justice (Parliament), René de Longueil. It is the most important example of the early period of Classical French château-architecture in the 17th c. The whole of the interior dates from

Marais, Hôtel Sully ▶

Rail
from Gare Saint-Lazare

Bus
262 from Pont de Neuilly métro

that time. Especially worthy of note are the many double pilasters with their fine detail.
This is where Mansart first used the high gable windows that later entered the French language as "mansardes".

Quartier du Marais (Marais quarter; officially: Le Marais) B/C4/5

Location
4th arrondissement

Métro
Saint-Paul, Rambuteau

Buses
29, 75, 96

The Marais quarter covers more or less the same area as the 4th arrondissement. In the last 20 years costly restoration work has saved a chapter in the history of the city of Paris from ruin and demolition.
In the 16th and 17th c. what had been a swamp (*marais*= marsh, swamp, bog) was turned into an elegant residential area.
The Marais is the "birthplace" of the "hôtel", the magnificent Paris town houses of the French landed gentry. A "hôtel" is always laid out with a courtyard (Cour d'Honneur) opening on to the street, main section with lateral wings, terrace and gardens at the back.
At the end of the 17th c. the Marais, whose showpiece in town-planning terms is the Place des Vosges (see entry), lost its attraction for the nobility and rich bourgeoisie who moved out to Versailles or the Faubourg Saint-Germain. Craftsmen and small tradesmen moved into the district. The Revolution left terrible scars, the hôtels fell into decay or were demolished by the people to make way for new housing and subsequent attempts at restoration in the 19th c. were fruitless. Not until 1962 did the French Ministry of Culture under André Malraux tackle the pressing task of conserving the heart of the city of Paris, valuable both in town-planning and in historical terms, thereby rediscovering the almost forgotten hôtels of the Marais.
The restoration and development of the quarter may have brought the speculators on to the scene, but the Marais has managed to retain its charm which can be experienced by sampling its lively combination of medieval settings and modern everyday living or by visiting the "Festival du Marais" (see Practical Information, Calendar of Events).
The hôtels most worth seeing are:
Hôtel de Sens (1475–1507); 1 Rue du Figuier, tel. 2 78 17 34; métro: Pont-Marie, Saint-Paul.
Hôtel d'Aumont (built 1630–50 by Louis Le Vau, altered by François Mansart 1656); 7 Rue de Jouy; métro: Saint-Paul.
Hôtel de Beauvais (1658–60, Antoine Lepautre); 68 Rue François-Miron, tel. 8 87 74 31; métro: Saint-Paul.
Hôtel Amelot de Bisseuil (Hôtel des Ambassadeurs de Hollande; 1657–60); 47 Rue Vieille-du-Temple; métro: Rambuteau.
Hôtel de Rohan-Soubise/Archives Nationales (1705–9, Pierre Alexis Delamaire); 60 Rue des Francs-Bourgeois, tel. 2 77 17 34; métro: Rambuteau.
The French National Archives housed here are among the largest in the world. The Rococo rooms, especially the "Salon ovale" (1735–8), are well worth seeing.
Hôtel Guénégaud (1648–51, François Mansart); 60 Rue des Archives, tel. 2 72 86 43; métro: Rambuteau.

Musée de la Chasse (see Practical Information, Museums).
Hôtel Lamoignon (1594–8, Jean-Baptiste Androuet du Cerceau); 24 Rue Pavée, tel. 2 72 10 18; métro: Saint-Paul.
This contains the Library of the City of Paris (Bibliothèque Historique de la Ville de Paris); open: daily except Sundays and holidays, 9.30 a.m.–6 p.m. (with reading-room).
Hôtel de Béttune-Sully (1625, Jean Androuet du Cerceau); 62 Rue Saint-Antoine, tel. 8 87 24 14; métro: Saint-Paul.
Hôtel Carnavalet – see Musée Carnavalet.

Monnaie (mint; officially: Hôtel des Monnaies) C4

The former royal, now State, Mint is one of Paris's few monuments (1771–7) in the early Louis XVI style.
It was begun towards the end of Louis XV's reign (plans by Jacques Denis Antoine), and the notable feature of its architecture is that it lacks the ornamentation usually found to a large degree in Rococo and Baroque. On the portal of the 117 m (384 ft) long façade there are allegories of Trade and Agriculture.
Besides the ordinary one-franc coins special gold and silver coins are also minted here. Visits to the workshops can be arranged.
Guided tours (in French): Monday and Wednesday 2.15 and 3.30 p.m.; groups by special arrangement (tel. 3 29 12 48 ext. 511).

Location
Quai de Conti (6th arr.)

Métro
Pont-Neuf

Buses
24, 27

Visits
daily (except Sun. and holidays)
11 a.m.–5 p.m.

*Montmartre (hill of Montmartre; officially: La Butte Montmartre) A/B3/4

There are two common explanations for the name Montmartre. One is that it is derived from "Mont de Mercure" (mount of Mercury) after one of the Roman temples dedicated to Mercury which is supposed to have stood here. The other is connected with the legend of Saint Denis (or Dionysius), the first bishop of Paris, who is supposed to have been beheaded here along with his companions Rusticus and Eleutherius (see Saint-Denis), hence "Mont des Martyrs" (Mount of the Martyrs).
Today Montmartre stands for three things: "La Butte Montmartre" is the hill of Montmartre (130 m (426 ft) above sea level) with the Sacré-Cœur and the Place du Tertre (see entries); Montmartre also means the residential quarter of Montmartre, and, finally, also stands for the entertainment quarter of Montmartre (see entries) on the Boulevard de Clichy.
The "Butte Montmartre" is not only a place where legends were created but also where history was made. From the 12th c. the hill was the site of a powerful Benedictine convent run by abbesses (see Saint-Pierre-Montmartre) which was razed to the ground during the French Revolution (1794) (hence the name "Abbesses' for the métro station). At that time the hill was temporarily named "Mont-Marat" after the Revolutionary leader Jean-Paul Marat.
In 1871 Montmartre was the scene of the bloody beginning and even bloodier end of the Paris Commune, whose defenders made their last stand here (and on the Buttes Chaumont)

Location
the northern part of the city (18th arr.)

Métro
Place Clichy, Blanche, Pigalle, Anvers, Abbesses

Buses
30, 54, 80, 85

against the troops of Thiers' bourgeois-reactionary government. Today Montmartre still proudly calls itself "commune libre" (free commune).
The former vine-growing village, which was only incorporated into the city in 1860, owed its international fame to the artists' colony that settled on the hill before the turn of the century and attracted from everywhere singers, writers and above all painters: Manet, Van Gogh, Toulouse-Lautrec, Utrillo, Apollinaire, Max Jacob, Picasso and many others. After the First World War the artistic and intellectual centre of Paris shifted to the quarter of Montparnasse (see entry).
But it is not only the memories that linger on. Although art and commerce may have become one and the same thing in the Place du Tertre and people may argue about the "wedding-cake" style of the "Sacré-Cœur", if one takes the time to explore the narrow alleys and steep steps of la Butte Montmartre, with their views of Paris, many of them quite unexpected, one gets the feeling of what Paris has to offer – her "infinite variety". When one is "down below" in the centre and thinks back to Montmartre, one understands better why it is said that there is more of Montmartre in Paris than there is of Paris in Montmartre.
As Montmartre is the highest "mountain" in Paris it has its only funicular railway which travels daily from 6.45 a.m. to 0.45 a.m. between the Place Saint-Pierre and the Sacré-Cœur.

*Montmartre (entertainment quarter) B3/4

Location
Boulevard de Clichy (between Place de Clichy and Place Pigalle; 18th arr.)

Métro
Place Clichy, Blanche, Pigalle

Buses
30, 54, 74, 80, 95

On the SW fringe of the Butte Montmartre lies one of the night-time centres of attraction of Paris with a lot to offer in a very small area: the Boulevard de Clichy between Place Pigalle and Place de Clichy. Here and in the adjoining side streets running into Place Pigalle, Place Blanche and Place de Clichy there is everything that commercialised sex can offer: sex shops, cinemas showing pornographic films, striptease shows, cabarets, bars and prostitution.
Night-life begins with the illumination of the neon signs at dusk: at the entrances to the "establishments" the touts take up their positions as do the women and girls on the corners and in the doorways around the Place Pigalle.
Those who still have enough money left and feel like eating are well catered for in the Place Clichy and several restaurants also stay open after midnight (with full menu).

Montparnasse C3

Location
On the border between 6th and 14th arr.

Métro
Vavin, Montparnasse-Bienvenue

Buses
48, 58, 82, 89, 91, 94, 95, 96

The quarter of Montparnasse is today almost better known for its 52-storey "tower" than for its former artists' colonies, the last remnants of which still linger on in the southern part of the 14th arrondissement.
While Montmartre and Saint-Germain-des-Prés (see entry) may have served as the rendezvous for artists and intellectuals before the First World War and in the decade that followed the Second World War, it was Montparnasse that fulfilled this function in the twenties and thirties. Simone de Beauvoir and

Montmartre, Place Pigalle

Jean-Paul Sartre, Ernest Hemingway, Henry Miller and James Joyce met in the cafés, bars and restaurants at the junction of Boulevard du Montparnasse and Boulevard Raspail (Dôme, Coupole, Select, Rotonde). The painters Henri Matisse, Wassily Kandinsky, Amedeo Modigliani and Marc Chagall worked in this quarter. The café-restaurant "Closerie des Lilas" (171 Boulevard du Montparnasse, RER station Port-Royal) was the domain of the poets Paul Fort and Guillaume Apollinaire, and Jean-Paul Sartre was a regular customer.
Today Montparnasse is dominated by a tower block ("Tour Montparnasse") from the restaurant and open terrace of which there is a view of Paris from 200 m (656 ft) up which can only be compared with the view from the Eiffel Tower. The "tower" rises up near the entrance to the railway station of Montparnasse, built in the seventies, from which trains leave for the W of France, especially Brittany (there are many Breton Crêperies around the station).

*Mosquée (mosque) C4

The Islamic house of prayer was built between 1922 and 1926. The building also houses the Islamic Institute for Religious Studies. Its minaret is 33 m (108 ft) high. The prayer room may be visited every day except Friday. Remember that the religious custom is to remove one's shoes before entering the prayer room.

Location
39 Rue Geoffroy-Saint-Hilaire (5th arr.)

Métro
Censier

A Turkish bath, a small Arab restaurant and a bazaar also form part of the complex of buildings.
The mosque is open daily, except on Friday.

*Musée de l'Armée/Musée des Plans-Reliefs B2

(military museum with museum of relief maps)

Location
See Hôtel des Invalides (7th arr.)

Métro
Latour-Maubourg

Buses
28, 49, 69, 82, 92

Times of opening
1 Oct.–31 March: 10 a.m.–5 p.m.; 1 April–30 Sept.; 10 a.m.–6 p.m.; closed 1 Jan., 1 May, 1 Nov., 25 Dec.

The various wings around the courtyard of the Hôtel des Invalides (see entry) house the military museum, which was founded as an artillery museum in 1794 and has since assembled a substantial collection of equipment and uniforms, weaponry, figures and curiosities from all ages and all countries (36,000 objects, 32,000 drawings and engravings). In addition to mementoes of Napoleon there are also memorabilia honouring famous generals or describing the plans of French campaigns. Some exhibits from the Late-Gothic and Renaissance periods are important from the art-historical point of view.
The entrances to the museum are in the middle of each side wing of the courtyard.
The E wing contains the associated museum of relief maps (Musée des Plans-Reliefs) which has a collection of models as well as engravings and plans illustrating the history of French fortifications for towns, harbours, fortresses and castles. This collection was begun by Marshal Vauban, Louis XIV's master of fortifications.

Musée d'Art Moderne de la Ville de Paris B2

(municipal museum of modern art)

Location
11 Avenue du Président-Wilson (16th arr.)

Métro
Iéna

Buses
32, 63, 82, 92

Times of opening
10 a.m.–5.45 p.m.; Wed. 10 a.m.–8.30 p.m.; closed Mon.

The collection in the W wing of the Palais d'Art Moderne (see Palais de Tokyo), built for the 1937 World Fair, represents the intermediate stage between the art treasures of the Jeu de Paume (Impressionists) and those of the Centre Pompidou (see entries) which are modern, mainly since Cubism. The Musée d'Art Moderne de la Ville de Paris has a collection of important post-Impressionists: Paul Cézanne, Georges Rouault, Raoul Dufy, André Dunoyer de Segonzac, Maurice Utrillo. Also represented are: Pablo Picasso, Georges Braque, Fernand Léger, Robert Delaunay; the "Fauves": André Derain, Albert Marquet, Maurice de Vlaminck, Suzanne Valadon and Amedeo Modigliani. The sculpture includes work by Jacques Lipchitz, Chavigné and Ossip Zadkine.
There are also temporary exhibitions of modern art on the 1st floor of the museum.

*Musée Carnavalet/Hôtel Carnavalet C5

(officially: Musée Historique de la Ville de Paris)

Location
23 Rue de Sévigné (3rd arr.)

Carnavalet is a mocking distortion of the name of the former owner, the widow of the Breton Sire de Kernevenoy. The hôtel was built in the 16th c. (probably by Pierre Lescot, the architect

of the Renaissance façade of the Louvre). The entrance with sculptures of lions (by Jean Goujon) and the section opposite date from that period. The other sections of the courtyard, in which stands a remarkable statue of Louis XIV by Antoine Coysevox (1698), were altered in the 17th c. by François Mansart. Madame de Sévigny lived in the Hôtel Carnavalet between 1677 and 1696. Her letters to her daughter (over 1500 of them) describing life in Paris and at the court in Versailles are an exceptionally valuable account of the period of Louis XIV. Around the turn of the century the hôtel was enlarged to its present size for the purposes of the museum.
Since 1880 it has housed the museum of the history of the city of Paris. Although visitors can be shown only part of its enormous collection of paintings, drawings, prints and sculptures, lovingly arranged displays afford a vivid impression of the history of the city of Paris from the 15th to the 19th c. Lately there have also been temporary exhibitions here.

Métro
Saint-Paul

Buses
29, 66, 96

Times of opening
10 a.m.–5.40 p.m.; closed Mon.

**Musée de Cluny/Hôtel de Cluny C4

The former Hôtel de Cluny, today the Museum of Medieval Art and Culture, stands on part of the site of the former Roman baths (see Thermes) the ruins of which can be seen on the corner of the Boulevard Saint-Michel and the Boulevard Saint-Germain.
At the beginning of the 14th c. the Benedictine abbey of Cluny (in Burgundy) acquired the site to build accommodation in Paris for its abbots. The Hôtel de Cluny was built by Abbot Jacques d'Amboise between 1485 and 1500 and today it and the Hôtel de Sens (see Marais) are Paris's only large private residences dating from the late medieval period. After changing hands frequently, even in the Middle Ages, it fell into decay after the French Revolution but was acquired by the State in 1842 and has been a museum since 1844.
The Musée de Cluny houses an important collection of medieval art (showpieces: valuable tapestries) based on the private collection of the antiquarian Alexandre du Sommerard. Especially noteworthy are:
Cour d'Honneur (courtyard): this reveals the charm of this Late-Gothic/early-Renaissance complex as a whole. The fine well, on the left, is 15th c.
Statues of the Apostles from Notre-Dame and Sainte-Chapelle (rooms IX and X).
High-Gothic and Late-Gothic sculpture (room VIII).
Gold and enamelled artefacts, 7th–13th c. (room XIII).
Stained glass (rooms XV and XVI).
French, Italian and Spanish faïence (room XVIII).
Treasure items such as the gold altar frontal from Basle cathedral (11th c.) (room XIV), which was presented by the Emperor Henry II.
Tapestries, the finest example being the famous series of the "Lady with the Unicorn" (15th c.) from the Loire valley (rooms XI, II).
The Late-Gothic chapel, formerly the abbot's oratory. The priceless Auxerre tapestries (15th c.) depict 23 scenes from the "Legend of Saint Stephen" (Saint Etienne) (room XX).

Location
24 Rue du Sommerard (5th arr.)

Métro
Saint-Michel, Odéon

Buses
21, 27, 38, 86, 87

Times of opening
9.45 a.m.–12.30 p.m. and 2–5.15 p.m.; closed Tues.

Musée Condé

Location
Chantilly, 40 km (25 miles) N (autoroute de Lille; N16)

Rail
from Gare du Nord

Times of opening
Closed 1 Oct–31 March: open 1 April–30 Sept.: 1.30–5.30 p.m. (except Tues., Fri. and race days)

The Musée Condé, housed in the Château of Chantilly (see entry), stems from a donation by the Condé family to the Institut de France.
The art gallery contains paintings by Italian, Flemish, French and English masters (Raphael, Caracci, Van Dyck, Watteau, Delacroix, Ingres, Reynolds).
The splendid library, with 12,500 rare books and 1500 manuscripts, contains one of the world's finest illuminated manuscripts, the book of hours (prayer book) of the Duc de Berry ("Très riches Heures du Duc de Berry") with 15th c. hand painting.
In the Jewel Room (Cabinet des Gemmes) one can admire the "Grand Condé", the rose diamond belonging to the former owners of the château.

*Musée Guimet B2

Location
6 Place d'Iéna (16th arr.)

Métro
Iéna

Buses
32, 63, 82

Times of opening
9.45 a.m.–12.30 p.m. and 1.30–5.15 p.m.; closed Tues. and public holidays

The Musée Guimet houses the most important collection of Indian, Indonesian, Japanese, Nepalese and Tibetan art in France.
The foundations for the collection of Far-Eastern treasures to be seen here were laid by the Lyon industrialist and explorer Emile Guimet at the end of the last century when he made a donation of his collection to the city of Paris. The collection has since been continuously expanded in close cooperation with the affiliated Research Institute for East-Asian Culture.
Especially noteworthy are the art treasures on display from the following countries:
India: Buddhist and Brahmin works of art, including "Shiva's cosmic dance" (ground floor).
Cambodia: Khmer art (ground floor).
Indonesia: bronzes from Java (ground floor).
Tibet: ritual weapons, jewellery, articles connected with Lamaism. Pièce de résistance: dancing Dakini in gilded bronze (ground floor).
China: lacquered furniture, jade and porcelain (1st floor), paintings (2nd floor), frescoes (rotunda).
Japan: theatrical masks, jewellery, paintings (2nd floor).

*Musée de l'Homme (Museum of Anthropology) B2

Location
Place du Trocadéro (16th arr.)

Métro
Trocadéro

Buses
22, 30, 82

One-third of the area (altogether 10,000 sq. m – 108,000 sq. ft) of the Museum of Anthropology in the Palais de Chaillot (see entry) is taken up with the prehistoric and anthropological collections of the museum proper. The other part is reserved for temporary exhibitions and the library (180,000 volumes) on the top floor. On the 1st floor: prehistoric finds relating to the development of Man; including Menton man, a cast of the Hottentot Venus and the famous "Venus of Lespugue" carved from a mammoth tusk.

The anthropological section on the 1st floor is devoted to Africa (inc. Ethiopian medieval frescoes, West African sculpture).
On the 2nd floor: anthropological collections from the Arctic regions, Asia and America (esp. the art of the Mayas and Aztecs).

Times of opening
10 a.m.–6 p.m; closed Tues.

Musée du Jeu de Paume

See Jeu de Paume

Musée de la Marine (Navy Museum) B2

The collections of the Navy Museum in the Palais de Chaillot (see entry) recount the history of the French navy and merchant marine (from the galley to the steamer). Its 13 rooms of pictures and models of ships and port installations, nautical equipment, old charts and figureheads give one an excellent idea of its theme.
Especially interesting: Columbus' "Santa Maria" (room 1), the "Louis XV", one of the young king's toys (room 2), the "Valmy", a ship made of ebony, ivory and silver (room 5), one of the first steamers (room 5) and "La Gloire", the world's first iron-clad (room 6).

Location
Place du Trocadéro
(16th arr.)

Métro
Trocadéro

Buses
22, 30, 82

Times of opening
10 a.m.–6 p.m.; closed Tues. and public holidays

*Musée des Monuments Français (Museum of French Monuments) B2

The E wing of the Palais de Chaillot (see entry) houses a museum with full-size reproductions and models of important French works of art.
The museum was set up in 1880 at the suggestion of the architect Viollet-le-Duc. It gives a vivid idea of the history of styles (sculpture, painting, architecture) in chronological order covering 12 centuries of the development of art in France from early Romanesque to Classicism.
The wall paintings are on the right of the entrance hall (on all three floors) and the sculpture department (in the E wing of the palace) is on the left.
Wall paintings
Ground floor: early Romanesque works (*c.* 800–1000) inc. crypt painting from Auxerre, "Life of Saint Stephen" (*c.* 850).
1st floor: Romanesque art (*c.* 1000–1200), inc. the impressive representation of biblical history (from Genesis to Revelations) from the abbey church of Saint-Savin-sur-Gartempe in Vienne (southern France).
2nd floor: Early and High Gothic (*c.* 1200–1400).
3rd floor: Late-Gothic art (*c.* 1400–1550).
Sculptures
In chronological order:
Early Romanesque: sarcophagi (6–7th c.), first tomb with three-dimensional portrait (11th c., room 1).
Romanesque: 11th c. tympana (sculptures and reliefs), and church doorways (rooms 2–6).

Location
Place du Trocadéro
(16th arr.)

Métro
Trocadéro

Buses
22, 30, 82

Times of opening
9.45 a.m.–12.30 p.m. and 2–5.15 p.m.; closed Tues.

Crusader architecture in Palestine: (12–13th c., room 7).
Early Gothic: reproductions of reliefs and statues from the cathedrals of Chartres, Reims, Paris and Strasbourg (12th–13th c., room 8).
High Gothic: burial chapel of the Dukes of Burgundy (14th c., rooms 14 and 15).
High and Late Gothic: (14–15th c., rooms 16–18).
Late Gothic and early Renaissance: (15th–16th c., rooms 19–21).
Renaissance (16–17th c.): works by Jean Goujon (1510–68), Ligier Richier (1500–66), Germain Pilon (1536–90, rooms 22–4).
French Classical (Baroque, 17th–18th c.): works by François Girardon (1628–1715), Antoine Coysevox (1640–1720), the Nicolas brothers (1658–1733) and Guillaume Coustou (1677–1746, room 25).
Rococo (18th c.): represented by Maurice-Etienne Falconet (1716–91), Edme Bouchardon (1698–1762), Jean Antoine Houdon (1741–1828) and Jean Baptiste Pigalle (1714–85). Busts of Voltaire, Mirabeau, Rousseau (rooms 26 and 27).
Early 19th c. Classicism, inc. the "Marseillaise" of the Arc de Triomphe (room 28).

Musée National d'Art Moderne

See Centre Pompidou

Musée de l'Orangerie

See Practical Information, Museums

*Musée Rodin C3

Location
77 Rue de Varenne (7th arr.)

Métro
Varenne

Buses
69, 82, 92

Times of opening
10 a.m.–6 p.m.; closed Tues.

The sculptor Auguste Rodin lived in the former Hôtel Biron (constructed 1728–31) until his death in 1917. Having been given some of his works and his personal collections, the State was able that same year to open the museum and its lovely gardens to the public.
Full-size copies of his monumental world-famous statues: "Le Penseur" (The Thinker), "Les Bourgeois de Calais" (The Burghers of Calais), "Ugolino", "L'homme qui marche" (The Walker) – are all displayed in the garden; smaller works and studies of models are inside the museum, including "Le Baiser" (The Kiss), the bust of Clemenceau, "Eve", "L'Age d'Airain" (The Age of Brass), "Saint-Jean-Baptiste" (John the Baptist), studies of "Balzac" and "Victor Hugo".
Rodin's private collection (furniture, paintings and sculptures) complement the exhibition of his works.
For a long time two other internationally famed artists lived in what was then the Hôtel de Biron without getting to know each other: a young man, who had lodgings in one of the wings, by the name of Jean Cocteau, and a German who worked as Rodin's secretary by the name of Rainer Maria Rilke.

Musée Rodin, Park

**Notre-Dame (officially: Cathédrale Notre-Dame de Paris) C4

The Cathedral of Notre-Dame de Paris was begun in 1163. Louis IX (Saint Louis) and Canon Maurice de Sully wanted to build a church on the Ile de la Cité (see entry) similar in style and beauty to that built by the Abbot of Saint-Denis (see entry), where the first Gothic church had been begun in 1135. In the 150 years it took to build, all the various stages of Gothic architecture (partly borrowed from the other great cathedrals of Chartres, Reims and Amiens) were used in the design of the Cathedral of Notre-Dame. (For the history of the Gothic style, see Saint-Denis.) The Choir was constructed in 1163–82 and the Nave in 1180–1200 in the Early-Gothic style. The transition to High Gothic is shown on the W Front (=main façade; 1200–20). The Nave was later reworked in the High-Gothic style (1230–50). The transepts are pure High Gothic (1250–60). Finally the Choir was also reworked in High Gothic (1265–1320).

Location
Ile de la Cité (4th arr.)

Métro
Cité

Buses
24, 27

Here, as later in Saint-Denis, the great 19th c. restorer Viollet-le-Duc made a marvellous job, from 1841 to 1864, of restoring the almost dilapidated cathedral.

Parvis de Notre-Dame (cathedral square)

It is possible to get an unobstructed view of the W Front (main façade), even when there are hordes of tourists, from the broad Parvis (square) of Notre-Dame, which itself conceals interesting treasures of the past under its paving. Since 1980 the 117 m (384 ft) long "crypte archéologique" (archaeologi-

Visits to the archaeological crypt
10 a.m.–5.30 p.m. daily

cal crypt) under the Parvis has been open to the public. The remains of 16th and 18th c. houses (see Cité), of the Merovingian church of Saint-Etienne and of Gallo-Roman buildings were discovered when an underground car park was being built. The entrance to this historical dig, which is clearly laid out with explanatory notes and is unique in size, is by the staircase leading to the underground car park.
The bronze plaque in the centre of the Parvis denotes the "administrative geographical centre" of Paris from which all distances are measured.

Exterior

The W Front: the monumental overall view of the main façade of Notre Dame reveals on closer inspection the sequence of the stages of construction and hence the development into the High-Gothic style. The doorway (*c.* 1200), the windows (*c.* 1220), the tracery balustrade above the rose window and the unfinished towers (1225–50) illustrate the progressive refinement of the Gothic language of form. The three vertical divisions are to be regarded as corresponding to the three aisles of the Nave. The five horizontal divisions (doors, kings' gallery, windows, tracery gallery, towers) also correspond to the interior: the portal corresponds to the arcades, the kings' gallery to the balcony and the window area to the windows inside the cathedral.
The Kings' Gallery: the identities of the figures of the kings seem to be as yet unresolved. For a long time they were considered to represent the kings of Judah but there is also reason to think that they are statues of the French kings from Childebert I (511–588) to Philippe Augustus (1180–1223). The fact that they had their heads chopped off during the French Revolution has not helped to solve the problem.
Sides: The richness of High-Gothic form is illustrated on both sides.
On the N front (1250–60) Jean de Chelles completed the transept in 1250 with the Portail du Cloître which led to the former cloister (cloître). The door of the S transept, Porte de Saint-Etienne (St Stephen's door) was the work of Pierre de Montreuil. The pointed false gable of the portal, rising up almost to the rose window, and the upper half of the end wall of the transept broken up into glass and rosette arches, together with the bold sweep of the flying buttresses, give this front the typical appearance and vibrant forcefulness of the High-Gothic cathedral.

Times of opening
1 Nov–28 Feb.: 10 a.m.–4.45 p.m.; 10 March–31 Oct.: 10 a.m.–5.45 p.m.

Tower: The view over the city centre from 70 m (230 ft) up is one of the finest in Paris: unlike the views from the Eiffel Tower, Sacré-Cœur (see entries) or the "tower" of Montparnasse, here the historical heart of the city seems to be within tangible reach (Hôtel de Ville, Louvre, Sorbonne, Panthéon, Ile Saint-Louis).

Portals

Portail du Cloître (cloister doorway, 1250): tympanum: childhood of Jesus (below), Deacon Theophilus' pact with the Devil, Redemption through Mary (centre), the Bishop shows the people the pact (top). Pier: original statue of Mary (13th c.). The rose window (1270) shows Mary encircled by figures from the Old Testament.
Porte Rouge (red door, by Pierre de Montreuil): tympanum: Mary, Louis IX and his wife Marguerite de Provence.

Portail Saint-Etienne (St Stephen's door): tympanum: sermon, capture of St Stephen (bottom), stoning and entombment (centre), ascension (top). Centre pillar: St Stephen.
Portail de Sainte-Anne (St Anne's door, 1210–20): tympanum: story of Mary's parents, Anne and Joachim, before the Temple, in the desert, the Annunciation of Mary's birth, at the wedding (bottom); Mary in the Temple, Mary's Annunciation, the birth of Jesus, Herod and the Three Kings (centre); Mary and Jesus, left and right next to the angels the founders of the cathedral, Maurice de Sully and Louis IX, kneeling (top). The sculptures in the top and centre sections are the oldest in the cathedral and were made between 1165 and 1175 for another doorway but then installed here. Intrados: the heavenly choir. Pier: St Marcellus (Bishop of Paris, 19th c. copy). Splays: kings, queens and saints.
The four figures in the recesses between the flying buttresses represent (from left to right): St Stephen, the "Church triumphant", the "vanquished Synagogue", St Denis (see Saint-Denis).
Portail du Jugement Dernier (Door of the Last Judgment, 1220–30): tympanum: Resurrection (bottom); the Archangel Michael sending the Good to Heaven and the Wicked to Hell (centre); Christ the Supreme Judge. This tympanum was destroyed in the 18th c. and restored by Viollet-le-Duc but the figure of Christ the Supreme Judge is the original Gothic. Intrados: Choir of the Blessed being received by Abraham (left), Hell with Demons (right). Pier: Christ (19th c.). Jambs: the wise (left) and foolish (right) virgins. Splays: the 12 Apostles (19th c.). Medallions: Virtues (top row) and Vices

Notre-Dame, S front

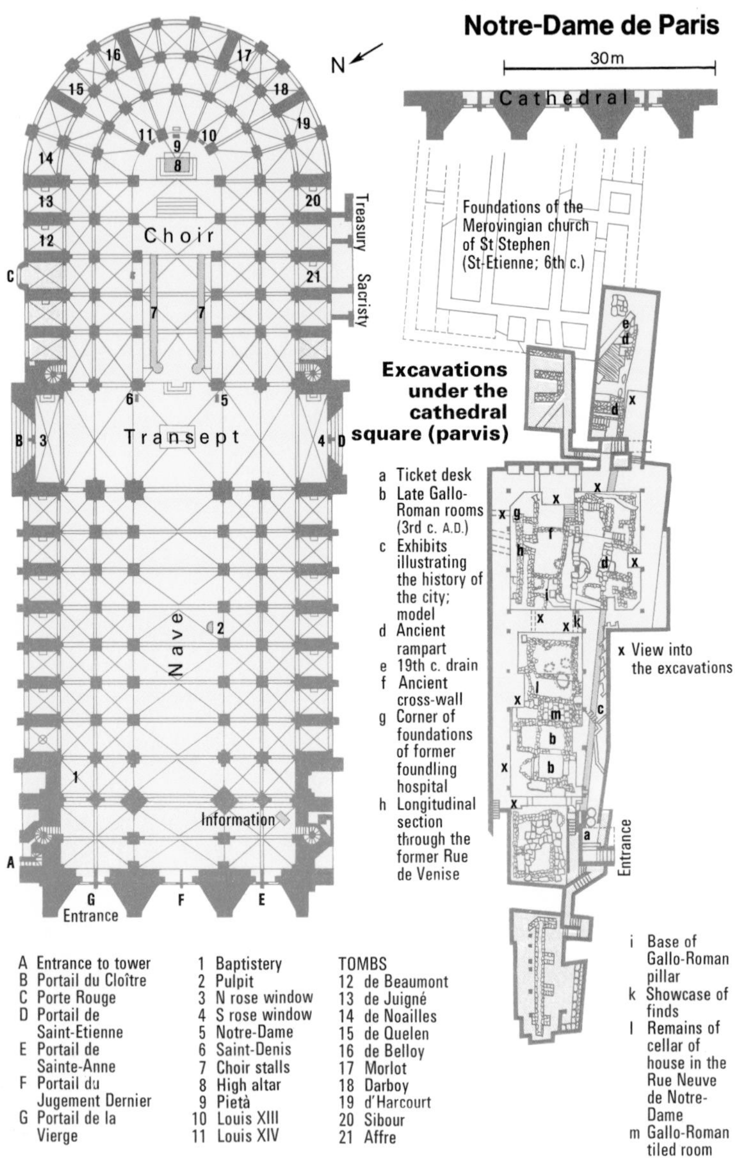

Excavations under the cathedral square (parvis) see right

(bottom row); the figures on the right-hand side are original. Portail de la Vierge (Door of the Virgin, 1210–20): tympanum: bottom section: Ark of the Covenant with Old Testament kings and prophets; middle section: entombment of Mary, surrounded by Christ and the Apostles; top section: Mary's Assumption. Intrados: angels with censers and candlesticks, patriarchs, prophets and Christ's forefathers. Pier: 19th c. statue of Mary by Viollet-le-Duc, with symbols of the months on both sides. Jambs: signs of the Zodiac. Splays: St Denis (see Saint-Denis), kings (left); John the Baptist, St Stephen, St Genevieve, figure of a pope (right).

Interior

A special feature of the architecture of the interior is the reworking of the Early-Gothic side walls of the nave which already had galleries built into them. Those were retained and not replaced with a triforium, the narrow arcade usually found with High-Gothic side aisles and transepts. The windows modelled on Chartres (double windows with pointed arches and round windows above) were incorporated above the galleries. In the first span of the nave Viollet-le-Duc, while carrying out his work of restoration, began to convert the High-Gothic (tripartite) arrangement back to the Early-Gothic (four-part) arrangement. Fortunately he gave up this plan, so that we can acknowledge the greater elegance in comparison of the High-Gothic solution.
The cathedral is 130 m (426 ft) long, 48 m (157 ft) wide, and 35 m (115 ft) high and can hold 9000 people (1500 of them in the galleries).

Notre-Dame, rose window in S transept

Free and therefore well-attended organ recitals take place in Notre-Dame every Sunday evening at 5.45. High Mass is celebrated every day at 10 a.m. (There is an information desk at the entrance.)
Besides the many important tombs and statues, the pulpit and altar, the following are of particular interest:
The interior as a whole, with its 75 round pillars, effectively picked out by indirect lighting.
The large rose window in the N transept with 80 illustrations from the Old Testament (*c.* 1270).
The large rose window in the S transept (1257).
Statue of Mary "Notre-Dame de Paris" (*c.* 1330), the best-known miraculous image of the Patron Saint of the cathedral (in front of the pillar to the right of the entrance to the choir).
23 stone reliefs of the life of Christ (1319–51) by Jehan Ravy and his nephew Jehan de Bouteiller, painted and partly gilded (choir screen).
Tomb of the Count d'Harcourt (d. 1718) by Pigalle (second apsidal chapel on the left of the entrance to the sacristy).
Cavaillé-Coll organ, recently restored, with 8500 pipes; its 110 stops make it the largest in France.

Times of opening
10 a.m.–5 p.m.; closed Sun.

Trésor (treasury): in addition to the Holy Relics, for which Louis IX originally built the Sainte-Chapelle (see entry), the displays here include precious ecclesiastical treasures (monstrances, crucifixes, chalices) and Napoleon's coronation robe.

Obelisk of Luxor

Place de la Concorde (see entry)

*Opéra (officially: Académie Nationale de Musique et de Danse) B3

Location
Place de l'Opéra (9th arr.)

Métro
Opéra

Buses
20, 21, 22, 27, 29, 42, 52, 53, 66, 68, 81, 95

Visits
11 a.m.–4.30 p.m. daily (auditorium only 1–2 p.m.)

The construction of the Paris Opera House saw the creation of a "style Napoléon III" and resulted in a splendid neo-Baroque building.
Charles Garnier (1825–98), hitherto unknown, won the competition for its design, and the biggest opera house in the world (over 11,000 sq. m (118,000 sq. ft) of floor space but "only" 2200 seats) was built according to his plans between 1862 and 1875.
The façade is horizontally divided into three. The seven arches on the ground floor are flanked by allegorical figures (from the left): Poetry (by Jouffroy), Music (Guillaume), Idyll (Aizelin), Recital (Chapu), Song (Dubois), Drama (Faguière), Dance (Carpeaux, the most important sculpture; the original is in the Louvre), Lyric Drama (Perraud). Over the statues there are medallions with portraits of Cimarosa, Haydn, Pergolesi and Bach.
The loggia (with 16 large and 14 small Corinthian columns) is decorated with the busts of Halévy, Meyerbeer, Rossini, Auber, Spontini, Beethoven and Mozart.
On the attic storey there are four gilded groups glorifying Poetry and Fame.

Opéra

On the Rue Scribe side is the Pavillon d'Honneur which used to give the President direct access to his box from the approach road. Today this houses a small library and a museum of opera props (Monday–Friday 10 a.m.–5 p.m.).
The interior of the building can be visited only at certain times but the magnificent grand staircase (Escalier d'Honneur) in multi-coloured marble can be admired at any time. The large foyer is decorated with an allegorical ceiling painting and wall paintings by Paul Baudry (1828–86). In the auditorium, which is decorated entirely in red and gold, the painting in the cupola is by Marc Chagall (1964).

*Palais-Bourbon (National Assembly; officially: Assemblée Nationale) B3

The former Palais-Bourbon is directly in line with the Madeleine and the obelisk in the Place de la Concorde (see entries). It is the seat of the French National Assembly (Assemblée Nationale), the lower house of the French Parliament (the upper house is the Senate, see Palais du Luxembourg). Until 1946 this legislative body (which corresponds to the British House of Commons) was called the Chambre des Députés (Chamber of Deputies).
The Palais was built in 1722–8 for the Duchess Louise-Françoise de Bourbon, legitimised daughter of Louis XIV and Madame de Montespan. It was seized during the Revolution, later converted into the parliamentary building, and since 1827 has been the meeting place of the French Parliament.

Location
Quai d'Orsay (7th arr.)

Métro
Chambre des Députés

Buses
24, 63, 83, 84, 94

Visits
On written application only to: Questure de l'Assemblée Nationale, 126 Rue de l'Université, 75007 Paris. Application may also be made to sit in on a session.

The imposing design of the side facing the Seine with its portico dating from the time of Napoleon (1806) is reminiscent of the façade of the Madeleine (see entry) which also drew on the Classical model (columns and triangular gables). One gets a good view of this example of 18th and 19th c. urban architecture (Madeleine, see Rue Royale, see Place de la Concorde, Palais-Bourbon) from the Pont de la Concorde (see entry).
The monumental statues in front of the portico represent ministers of the kings of France (from left): Sully (Henri IV), l'Hospital (François I and Henri II), d'Agnesseau (Louis XV) and Colbert (Louis XIV). The allegories on the tympanum (Liberty, France, Order) were done by the sculptor Cortot between 1839 and 1841. Left and right of the open staircase: Minerva (Wisdom) and Themis (Justice).
The Place du Palais-Bourbon at the rear of the building provides a very good idea of what a square in the elegant quarter of the Faubourg Saint-Germain (see entry) was like in the 18th c. The façade of the Palais-Bourbon facing on to this square has been retained from the 18th c. and contains the entrance used by the Deputies.
The French Ministry for Foreign Affairs (Ministère des Affairs Etrangères) adjoins the W of the Palais.
The former Hôtel de Salm at No. 64 Rue de Lille is the Palais of the French Legion of Honour.

*Palais de la Découverte B3

Location
Avenue Franklin-D.-Roosevelt (8th arr.)

Métro
Champs-Elysées-Clemenceau

Buses
24, 42, 84, 94

Times of opening
10 a.m.–6 p.m.; closed Mon.

The Palais de la Découverte (Palace of Discovery) is housed in the W wing of the Grand Palais (see entry). It is an exceptionally interesting museum which seeks to impart to the visitor the history of the natural sciences and their practical results.
There are guided tours (in French only; on Wednesdays the museum is overrun with classes of schoolchildren!), experiments which visitors can do themselves, a planetarium (2, 3.15, 4.30 p.m.; on Sundays 12.45 and 5.45 p.m.) and film shows.

*Palais de Justice (Law Courts) C4

Location
Boulevard du Palais (1st arr.)

Métro
Cité

Buses
21, 24, 27, 38, 81, 85, 96

Visits
Mon.–Fri. 9 a.m.–noon and 1–6 p.m.

On the site of the present Law Courts, on the Ile de la Cité (see entry), the Celtic Gauls, followed by the Romans and later the Frankish Merovingians, built fortified squares, fortresses and royal castles. This was the birthplace of French royal power. Under Louis IX (Saint Louis, 1226–70) the royal palace here, with its newly constructed chapel (see Sainte-Chapelle), reached the peak of its magnificence, but soon after the French kings moved to the Louvre (see entry). (In 1358 the palace was stormed by the rebellious merchants led by Etienne Marcel, see Hôtel de Ville.)
From the 16th c. onwards the palace was the seat of the "parlement" (law court) whose approval was required before

Palais de Justice, main gate ▶

royal decrees acquired the force of law. This purely formal privilege was removed, after the "parlement" had made a half-hearted stand against the power of the king (war of the "Fronde", 1648–52), by Louis XIV when he was a young ruler on the way to becoming an absolute monarch.
The French Revolution in its turn removed both the king and the "parlement" (all its members were sent to the scaffold). The new (citizens') courts moved into the building which is now known as the Palais de Justice.
The palace has been damaged and destroyed by fire several times. The present building dates from the turn of the century; the S wing was not added until 1911–14.

Especially worth seeing are:
The entrance with the fine wrought-iron gate from the time of Louis XVI (see picture, p. 87) and the forecourt, the Cour de Mai (where the maypole used to be set up). Steps leading up into the interior.
Galérie Marchande (Merchants' Hall): at the time of Louis IX this was the passage joining the royal palace to the Sainte-Chapelle. Until the Revolution merchants offered their wares for sale here amid a throng of advocates, judges and attorneys.
Galérie Duc (named after the architect and great restorer of many important monuments, Eugène Emmanuel Viollet-le-Duc – 1814–79): view of the Sainte-Chapelle and, at the other end, of the Cour des Femmes of the Conciergerie (see entry).
Vestibule de Harlay with statues of Charlemagne, Philippe Augustus, Louis IX and Napoleon (rulers who have been especially concerned with law-making).
Première Chambre Civile (1st Civil Chamber): formerly the bedroom of Louis IX; later the meeting place of the "parlement"; in 1793 "Salle de la Liberté" where the Revolutionary tribunal condemned over 2500 people to death.
Salle des Pas Perdus (Hall of the lost steps, a poetic reference to the lost causes of those waiting to be tried here): this room is situated above the Salle des Gens d'Armes of the Conciergerie (see entry). This was the pièce de résistance of the royal palace, the famous Palace Hall. The present neo-Classical décor dates from the time of the restoration work carried out after the great fire of 1871.
Musée de la Police (1 bis Rue des Carmes), which portrays the history of the criminal police of Paris.

Palais-Royal B4

Location
Place du Palais-Royal
(1st arr.)

Métro
Palais-Royal

Buses
21, 27, 39, 48, 67, 69, 72, 74, 81, 85, 95

The Palais-Royal is today the official seat of the Council of State (Conseil d'Etat) and the Directorate of Fine Arts (Secrétariat de la Culture et de la Communication).
Between 1634 and 1639 Cardinal Richelieu (1585–1642) had the Palais built for himself near the Louvre and later left it to the king in his will. After the death of Louis XIII his widow Anne of Austria moved into the Palais which was thenceforward known as the Palais-Royal (Royal Palace). Her son, Louis XIV, moved back into the Louvre in 1652. (Later, after a period spent in the Château de Vincennes, he moved his court to Versailles.) The king then granted the palace to his aunt, Henrietta Maria, widow of England's King Charles I and it subsequently came

Palais-Royal

into the hands of the House of Orléans. Louis-Philippe of Orléans, called Philippe-Egalité (because although a nobleman he sided with the Revolutionaries – which did not save him from the guillotine), had the palace altered to its present form (late 18th c.) and laid out the small park with colonnades, shops and apartments.
It was under these colonnades that on 13 July 1789 the advocate and journalist Camille Desmoulins led a revolutionary assembly which next day stormed the Bastille. Before and during the Revolution and during the First Empire the Palace was a social meeting place with restaurants, cafés, gambling halls and brothels. (The gaming halls and the brothels were closed in 1830.)

Palais de Tokyo B2

The Palais de Tokyo, the E wing of the Palais de l'Art Moderne, was the home of the Musée National d'Art Moderne until the Centre Pompidou (see entries) was opened. Besides a permanent museum (Musée d'Art et d'Essai) housing educational exhibitions with art objects from the Louvre, there are now plans for temporary exhibitions illustrating trends in avant-garde art. Non-European modern art is also displayed in the Palais de Tokyo.
The whole Palais d'Art Moderne, today split into the Musée d'Art Moderne de la Ville de Paris (see entry) and the Palais de Tokyo, was constructed for the 1937 World Fair. The architects

Location
13 Avenue du Président-Wilson (16th arr.)

Métro
Iéna

Buses
32, 63, 82, 92

Times of opening
9.45 a.m.–5.15 p.m.; closed Tues.

(Aubert, Dastugne, Dondel and Viard) created a functional building in the Bauhaus tradition which is also apparent in the nearby Palais de Chaillot (see entry). Traces of the Classical style are evident in both buildings. The allegories of "Strength" and "Victory" (1861–1929) in the peristyle and the allegory of "France" (1927) in the pool are the work of Antoine Bourdelle.

*Panthéon C4

Location
Place du Panthéon (5th arr.)

Suburban station
Luxembourg (RER)

Buses
84, 89

Times of opening
1 Oct.–31 March; 10 a.m.–5 p.m. (daily except Tues.);
1 April–30 Sept.; 10 a.m.–6 p.m. (daily except Tues.)

The Panthéon, originally built as a church, is the national monument and burial place of France's "famous men".

In 1756 Louis XV commissioned the architect Jacques-Germain Soufflot (1713–80) to start building what was planned to be a magnificent church on the site of the dilapidated abbey church of Saint Genevieve (the patron saint of Paris, see church of Saint-Etienne). The church was finished in 1790, ten years after Soufflot's death, with the completion of the cupola, and during the Revolution, in 1791, the National Assembly voted for it to be turned into a "Panthéon français" (in classical Greece a "pantheon" was a temple dedicated to all a country's gods). 42 windows of the former church were walled up; this gave the building the cold outer aspect and the gloomy inner aspect of a mausoleum which characterise it today.

The architecture of the Panthéon is a clear indication of the break with the ornate Rococo style (Louis XV style, see Marais, Hôtel de Soubise) which in turn had been a reaction against the distinct "classic" French Baroque style under Louis XIV. The Panthéon is the first monumental building in Paris in the Classicist style which attempted to revive the simplicity and monumentality of the architecture of Classical times. It set the standard for the period before and after Napoleon (see Arc de Triomphe, see Madeleine, see Bourse).

In his design Soufflot wanted to distinguish himself from Sir Christopher Wren (Saint Paul's Cathedral) on whom he modelled himself. This is why the portico projects right out in front of the façade, preventing the observer looking at it from the front from seeing the cupola. This was supposed to make the cupola appear to be hovering above the lower part of the building.

The triangular pediment on 18 Corinthian columns bears the inscription "To great men, their grateful country" and a relief by David d'Angers of the history of the French Nation: left, among others, Mirabeau, Voltaire and Rousseau; right, Napoleon and his generals.

The interior was designed by Soufflot to give the idea of transmitted light and clarity, an effect that was to be attained by having a great many windows and using slender columns, even when it came to supporting the cupola. However, faults in construction meant that massive pillars had to be used and most of the windows were sacrificed when the church became a mausoleum.

The cupola was decorated with a fresco "Ascension of Saint Genevieve" (1811) on the orders of Napoleon, in whose time

Panthéon 

restaurants

the Panthéon was a church for a while. Several frescoes on the side walls (Puvis de Chavannes) depict the life of the Saint. (Others show Charlemagne, Louis IX and Joan of Arc.)
In the crypt are the final resting places of famous men (60 altogether) including Voltaire and Rousseau, whose graves were plundered in 1814 by fanatical royalists, and Soufflot, Victor Hugo and Emile Zola.

*Petit Palais B3

Location
Avenue W.-Churchill (8th arr.)

Métro
Champs-Elysées-Clemenceau

Buses
28, 42, 49, 72, 73, 83

Times of opening
10 a.m.–5.40 p.m.; closed Mon.

Apart from interesting temporary exhibitions (mostly relating to the history of civilisation) the Petit Palais has since 1902 housed the valuable art collections of the city of Paris (Musée des Beaux-Arts de la Ville de Paris): paintings, furniture, books and tableware.
The collections are partly based on endowments such as those of the Dutuit brothers (ancient, medieval and Renaissance works of art together with paintings, icons, drawings, books and ceramics) and the Tuck collection (18th c. furniture and sculpture). The city has mainly bought 19th c. art, including paintings by Géricault, Ingres and Delacroix.
Its architecture is similar to that of the Grand Palais (see entry) which was also built for the 1900 World Fair. It has a magnificent main entrance, crowned by a cupola, and a wealth of sculptural decoration.

Place du Tertre B4

Location
Montmartre (18th arr.)

Métro
Abbesses

Buses
80, 85

The former village square on the Butte, Montmartre (see entry) is, together with Sacré-Cœur (see entry), one of the most popular tourist attractions on the "highest mountain" in Paris. Painters, portrait artists and caricaturists display their wares and offer their services.
The 18th c. houses (No. 3, built in 1790, was formerly the mayor's office) still form a picturesque backdrop for the tourist traffic that dominates the square. Certainly the paintings on display have less to do with art than with the souvenir trade.
Near the square is the little Musée de Montmartre (see Practical Information, Museums).

*Place Vendôme B3

Location
Centre W (1st arr.)

Métro
Madeleine, Tuileries, Concorde

Buses
29, 72

This unique square on the N side of the Tuileries Gardens (see entry) dates from the late 17th and early 18th c. when Jules Hardouin-Mansart, one of the outstanding architects of the 17th c. – the "Grand Siècle" – drew up the plans for the square as it is today. The façades and houses around the square – originally to be called "Place Louis-le-Grand" – were built between 1686 and 1720 and were intended to house the Royal Academies (see Institut de France), the Mint (see Monnaie), the Royal Library and the Palace for Ambassadors Extraordinary. The city, granted the land when the king ran into financial difficulties, sold users' rights to aristocrats and

wealthy citizens who, behind the façades, constructed an adjoining garden and palaces modelled on those of the nobility (see Marais).
During the Revolution, in 1792, the equestrian statue of Louis XIV was pulled down and replaced, in Napoleon's reign, by a column "in honour of the army". This 44 m (144 ft) high column, an imitation of Trajan's Column in Rome, was topped by a statue of Napoleon in the garb of a Roman Emperor which was destroyed during the Paris Commune (1871) but later replaced by a copy of the original.
Encircling the Column is a spiral bronze relief depicting the glorious deeds of the French army. An internal staircase leads to the top but is not open to the public.
One of the finest examples of harmony in urban architecture in Europe, the charm of the Place Vendôme is that it has retained, unspoilt, the consistency of the overall design, successfully blending royal opulence with civic simplicity.
Famous jewellers – Boucheron, Van Cleef et Arpels, Cartier – are to be found on the Place Vendôme and in the Rue de la Paix leading from the N side of the square to the Opéra. Ernest Hemingway, Scott Fitzgerald and Gertrude Stein frequented the "Bar Américain" of the Ritz Hotel (No. 15).

Place Vendôme

*Place des Vosges C5

Location
Centre E (4th arr.)

Métro
Saint-Paul, Bastille

Buses
29, 69, 76, 96

In the eastern part of the Marais (see entry), the spacious and uniformly planned Place des Vosges is the oldest public square in Paris and served as a model for the design of others (Place Dauphine, Place Vendôme, Place de la Concorde).
The completion of the square – or "Place Royale" as it was then called – in 1612 confirmed the Marais as the heart of the aristocratic part of the city. At the instigation of Henry IV an unknown architect laid out a magnificent setting, its symmetry reflecting the architectural concepts of the Renaissance, for tournaments, royal receptions, weddings and – despite a ban by Cardinal Richelieu – for duelling when this was a fashionable activity.
Incorporated into the façades of this "royal square" are the royal residences, and their arches, with the "Pavillon de la Reine" on the N side and the "Pavillon du Roi", bearing Henry IV's initials, on the S side. The remaining houses were privately owned.
In 1800 the square was renamed Place des Vosges in honour of the first Département to pay its taxes to the French Republic. Today the square, with its trees and fountains, is a children's playground and a place for the people of the Marais, old and young, to meet and relax in.
In the south-eastern corner stands the house that Victor Hugo lived in from 1833 to 1848 (see Information, Museums, Maison Victor Hugo).

Ponts de Paris (bridges of Paris)

The actual city of Paris itself has 33 bridges across the Seine. It takes 13 of them alone to connect the two Seine islands, Ile de la Cité, Ile Saint-Louis (see entries), with one another and the rest of the centre. These are among the oldest of Paris's bridges, most of the others upstream and downstream from the centre having been built in the 19th c. The cast-iron Pont des Arts suffered flood damage some years ago and is due to be replaced by a new bridge.

The bridges of medieval Paris served as promenades and meeting places for people to gossip and do business. Merchants built shops on them, with their living quarters above, but as modern times dawned these vanished to make room for roads and their traffic.

Pont au Change

C4

Métro
Châtelet

Buses
21, 24, 27, 38, 81, 85, 96

During the reign of Louis XIII the two 14th c. wooden bridges between Châtelet and Conciergerie (see entries) were replaced by the Pont au Change, and the occupants of the old bridges (merchants, hawkers, dealers and moneychangers, i.e. "changeurs") moved to the new bridge. During the Revolution those condemned to death passed over the Pont au Change on their way to be guillotined in the Place de la Concorde (see entry).

In 1859–60 the bridge was aligned with the present Boulevard du Palais.

Pont de la Concorde

B3

Métro
Chambre-des-Députés

Buses
24, 73, 83, 84

On a level with the Palais Bourbon (National Assembly), the Pont de la Concorde connects the square of the same name with the right bank of the Seine. Stone from the demolished Bastille was used in the building of the bridge (1787–91).

▼ *Pont Neuf, the oldest bridge in Paris*

The view on the left bank from the bridge is of the Place de la Concorde, the Obelisk and the Madeleine beyond (see entries). Looking upstream you can see the Tuileries Gardens and the Louvre, with the Ile de la Cité and the towers of Notre-Dame rising above the Seine in the distance (see entries). On the right bank there is a very good view of the Eiffel Tower (see Tour Eiffel) and the Hôtel (see entry), and Dôme, des Invalides. An excellent spot to get your bearings – and take photographs!

Pont Marie

C4

Métro
Pont Marie

Bus
67

The five-arched bridge linking the Ile Saint-Louis (see entry) with the right bank of the Seine was built between 1614 and 1635 at the behest of Louis XIII by its architect, Christophe Marie, whose name it bears.
121 people were killed when part of the bridge broke away during a major flood disaster in 1658, and all its occupants were evacuated when, in 1740, Paris was again hit by flooding. A year later it was made illegal to build new houses on the Seine bridges and the old ones were gradually demolished. The Pont Marie's "hump" was straightened out in the 19th c.

Pont Neuf

C4

Métro
Pont Neuf

Buses
21, 24, 27, 58, 67, 70, 75, 85

A popular catch question on the history of Paris is "Which bridge is the oldest?" The answer is "the New Bridge" – the Pont Neuf – which, though restored in the 19th c., was begun in 1578 and completed in 1607. It is one of the most beautiful

and also, at 330 m (1080 ft), the longest of the old Seine bridges and spans both channels of the river at the western end of the Cité (see entry). (The "Square du Vert-Galant" was added subsequently.)
It was built like a modern road bridge, without houses and with pavements, and until the Revolution, when it began to decline in importance, was a popular attraction for strollers with its pedlars and entertainers and makeshift stalls.

Pont Royal — C3/B3

Métro
Bac

Bus
681

After several failures to build a bridge that could withstand floods downstream from the Cité (level with the Tuileries – see entry), public money was used up and when the bridge was finally built in 1685–9 (as designed by Jules Hardouin-Mansart) it was paid for by Louis XIV from his own privy purse – hence its name, literally "bridge of the king". Its "hump" was flattened in 1850 to make way for a road.

Puces (fleamarket; officially: "Marché aux Puces") — A4

Location
Northern outskirts

Métro
Porte de Clignancourt

Buses
50, 254, PC

Times of opening
Sat., Sun., Mon. 6 a.m.–5 p.m.

This great kingdom of "bric à brac" lies between the Porte de Clignancourt and the Porte de Saint-Ouen (outside the Boulevard Périphérique) on the northern outskirts of Paris. Walking towards the fleamarket from the Métro at the Porte de Clignancourt the visitor's heart may well sink at first on seeing the stalls selling cheap plastic wares that line the pavement, but the fleamarket proper does not begin until you pass under the motorway.
Here, too, the goods on offer are rather mixed: brand new jeans jostle with worthless junk and genuine (?) antiques: pictures, furniture, books, china – when buying anything here you need to know what you are about! The visitor who goes simply to browse can happily immerse himself in this welter of junk, skilful reproductions and valuable antiques.
It's worth knowing which parts of the market specialise in particular items, viz. Malik – spectacles, records; Jules-Vallès – country furniture; Paul Bert – china; Cambo – household articles, pictures; Biron – valuable antiques; Vernaison – period furniture, trinkets.

Quais (quays) — B/C3–C4/5

Location
Centre (bank of the Seine between Pont Sully and Pont Royal)

Métro
Cité, Saint-Michel

It used to be possible to walk along the "Quais de la Seine" on two levels but the lower level along the right bank and part of the left is now completely given over to traffic. However, a walk along the upper level (next to the surging traffic) offers ample compensation in a beautiful panorama, with the Iles de la Cité and Saint-Louis, of the heart of Paris and the displays of the "bouquinistes" (bouquin=book, novel) whose wooden box-type stalls selling new and secondhand books, postcards, posters, prints and the like, often also specialise in postcards,

detective novels, exhibition posters, etc., affording many a pleasant surprise for the collector.
The finest walks along the quays are undoubtedly on the Ile Saint-Louis and Ile de la Cité (see entries).

Quartier Latin C4

The Quartier Latin (or Latin Quarter) is bordered by the Seine on the N, the Boulevard de Port-Royal on the S and the Boulevards Saint-Marcel and de l'Hôpital on the E, while demarcation on the W from the quarter of Saint-Germain (see entry) is less well defined (roughly on a level with the Odéon métro station). In addition to the University of the Sorbonne (see entry) (Université de Paris IV), the Latin Quarter houses most of the "Grandes Ecoles" (exclusive colleges that do not belong to the University system, e.g. Ecole Polytechnique, Ecole Normale Supérieure) as well as Censier University (Paris III) and Jussieu Universities (Paris VI and VII). A number of grammar schools, with a wealth of tradition – Lycée Henri IV (next to the Panthéon – see entry), Lycée Louis-le-Grand (behind the Sorbonne) and Lycée Saint-Louis (Boulevard Saint Michel) – together with the Collège de France (see entry) complete this panorama of scholarship.

Location
Centre (5th arr.)

Métro
Saint-Michel, Cardinal Lemoine, Monge

Buses
63, 84, 86, 89

Towards the end of the Middle Ages lack of space forced the Schools of Latin and Theology to move from the Cité around Notre Dame to the left bank of the Seine, thus establishing the "Latin" Quarter as it was popularly known, because Latin was the official language in everyday use there.
Nowadays the student quarter is also a great tourist attraction. The lower part of the quarter is packed with cinemas, discos and restaurants (mostly Arab, some Greek and Indochinese). The 80-seater Théâtre de la Huchette (23 Rue de la Huchette) has staged the same programme (to full houses!) every night for over 20 years – Eugène Ionesco's two famous one-act plays "La Cantatrice Chauve" (The Bald Primadonna) and "La Leçon" (The Lesson).
Chinese and Vietnamese restaurants are to be found around the Montagne Sainte-Geneviève (between the Rue des Ecoles and the Panthéon).
In the Rue Mouffetard it is Greek cooking that takes pride of place in the many eating places. Several students' bistros have old cellars where, after a meal upstairs, one can hear poetry, music and drama.

Rambouillet (officially: Château de Rambouillet)

Although the summer residence of the President of the Republic, the Château is open to visitors.
In 1706 the Château, which had been built on the site of an old manor-house, was bought by the Count of Toulouse, a legitimised son of Louis XIV. Sections dating back to the Gothic, Renaissance and Baroque eras testify to the fact that it has undergone constant extension and renovation. When Louis XVI acquired Rambouillet in 1783 it was, like his predecessors and those that came after him, to use it mainly as a

Location
Rambouillet, 56 km (35 miles) SW (N10 and N306)

Rail
from Gare Montparnasse

Times of opening
1 Oct–31 March 10 a.m.–noon and 2–5.30 p.m.; closed Tues. 1 April–30 Sept. 9.30 a.m.–noon and 2–6 p.m.; closed Tues.

hunting lodge. He had a "Laiterie" (dairy) built there for Marie-Antoinette in the form of a Greek temple and set up a sheep farm where today about 800 sheep are reared.
Napoleon I made the Château his residence and since 1959 it has been the summer residence of the President and is also occasionally used for cabinet meetings.
The elegant interior is sumptuously decorated and furnished (Delft tiles, period furniture).

*Rue de Rivoli — B3/4–C4/5

Location
Between Place de la Concorde and Place de la Bastille (1st and 4th arr.)

Métro
Concorde, Palais-Royal, Châtelet

Buses
21, 67, 69, 74, 75, 81, 85

The Rue de Rivoli on the right bank (rive droite) of the Seine runs between the Place de la Concorde and the Place de la Bastille. The oldest and most interesting section is between the Place de la Concorde (see entry) and the Place du Louvre (Métro station: Louvre), running the whole length of the Tuileries and the N wing of the Louvre.
This section was designed in Napoleon's time and he named the street after Rivoli, near Verona, which was the scene of his victory over Austria in the Italian campaign (1797). It took a long time to plan (1802–11) and to build, and it was not until 1833, 12 years after Napoleon's death, that work on the street – a blend of the traditional (uniform façades, round-arched arcades) and the contemporary (multi-storeyed buildings, metal roof structures) – was finished, only to be resumed in 1853 when Baron Haussmann, the architect who transformed Paris into a modern city, extended the Rue de Rivoli (together with the Rue Saint-Antoine) as far as the Place de la Bastille.
At the time of the French Revolution, when what is now the street was a maze of houses and alleyways, between the Place de Pyramides and the Rue Castiglione there stood the Royal Riding School, whose main building in 1789 was made the chamber of the Revolutionary Parliament and it was here that the Republic was proclaimed in 1792, a fact recalled by a commemorative plaque opposite No. 230.
In 1862 Ivan Turgenev, the Russian writer, wrote his celebrated novel "Fathers and Sons" at No. 210, and the French author and diplomat René de Chateaubriand lived at No. 194 from 1812 to 1814.
A stroll through the arcades of the Napoleonic section, with their jewellers, art galleries, antique shops and tearooms, is today as inviting a prospect for the window-shopper as ever it was.
Three of Paris's largest department stores (Samaritaine, Belle Jardinière, Bazar de l'Hôtel de Ville – BHV) are situated between the Louvre and Hôtel de Ville.

Rue Royale — B3

Location
N of the Place de la Concorde (8th arr.)

Métro
Concorde, Madeleine

The Rue Royale linking the Place de la Concorde with the Madeleine (see entry) is one of the most elegant streets in Paris.

Sacré-Cœur ▶

Buses
24, 42, 52, 84, 94

Its luxury establishments such as Villeroy et Boch, Christofle (tableware), Fauchon (delicatessen) and Cerutti (clothing) are not quite as expensive as those in the nearby Faubourg Saint-Honoré (see entry) but are nevertheless in the top price bracket. Maxim's, the restaurant at No. 3, whose Art Nouveau décor dates from the Belle Epoque, is famous throughout the world.
The Rue Royale dates from the 18th c. and some houses from that period are listed monuments.

Sacré-Cœur (Basilique du Sacré-Cœur de Montmartre) B4

Location
25 Rue du Chevalier de la Barre (18th arr.)

Métro
Anvers, Abbesses

Buses
30, 54, 80, 85

Times of opening
1 Oct.–31 March: 9 a.m.–5.30 p.m.
1 April–30 Sept.: 9 a.m.–6.30 p.m.

The "Basilica of the Sacred Heart" (Sacré-Cœur) is one of the landmarks of Paris and its gleaming domes seem to shine out from the hill of Montmartre far over the city.
After France's defeat by the Prussians and the suppression of the Paris Commune (1871), the Catholics of France vowed to build a church on the hill of Montmartre as a symbol of contrition and hope. The National Assembly of 1873 declared the project to be "of public utility" and building work began under the supervision of Paul Abadie in 1876. This proved extremely difficult and protracted because of the porous sandstone base and the Basilica was not consecrated until 1919.
Its architectural style, which to some resembles a wedding cake, is reminiscent of Byzantine-Romanesque. Although the exterior is not particularly interesting, architecturally speaking, its oppressively ornate interior is impressive if only on grounds of the scale of its dimensions – 100 m (330 ft) long and 50 m (165 ft) wide. The huge mosaic of the vault of the choir depicts Christ and the Sacred Heart, with the Archangel Michael and the Maid of Orleans to the left and Louis XVI and family to the right.
For a magnificent panoramic view over Paris it is well worth going up to the top of the dome (entrance on the left of the main doorway). You also have one of the finest views of the city from the broad flight of steps, thronged on summer evenings with youthful musicians, in front of the church (Notre-Dame, with the Centre Pompidou just in front of it, almost straight ahead; the Opéra, and behind it the Dôme des Invalides, slightly to the right).

**Saint-Denis (officially: Basilique de Saint-Denis)

Location
Saint-Denis
4·5 km (3 miles) N (A1)

Métro
Saint-Denis-Basilique

Bus
156 (from Porte de la Chapelle)

The building of the façade and the choir of the Basilica of Saint-Denis, the necropolis of the kings and queens of France, marked the beginning of Gothic architecture.
The northern and central European Gothic style of architecture, painting and sculpture was born in France, in the French province of Ile-de-France centred on Paris. It comes between Romanesque and Renaissance and covers the period from the 12th c. to the onset of the 16th. The concept stems from the Italian art historian, Giorgio Vasari (1511–74), who, from the standpoint of the Italian Renaissance, considered it to be a

barbarian (northern) art form and associated it with the Goths! Eventually objectively reassessed because of the 19th c. Romantic movement's enthusiasm for history, Gothic has come to be regarded as medieval architecture at its zenith.
Since early Christian times Saint-Denis has been an important place of pilgrimage. Legend has it that St Dionysius (or St Denis), missionary, martyr and first bishop of Paris, walked from Montmartre after he had been beheaded, carrying his head in his hands, to the place where he wished to be buried. A church was built on this site as early as the 5th c. and an abbey was added in the 7th c. The work on transforming the basilica from Romanesque to Gothic was begun in the 12th c. under Abbot Suger (1081–1151) with the Early-Gothic façade and porch (1137–40) and choir (1140–3). The middle section of the church was not demolished until a century later when Pierre de Montreuil (d. 1267), the architect of Louis IX (see Sainte Chapelle), built the High-Gothic outer choir, transept and nave.
Over the centuries the basilica fell into decay but in the early 19th c. restoration began on an amateur basis and was finally completed between 1858 and 1879, in accordance with the historical records, by Viollet-le-Duc who left the church as we see it today.

Exterior

The early Gothic W façade brings together for the first time the characteristic features of Gothic architecture: simple, clear-cut structure (the narrative additions date from the 19th c.), symmetrical arrangement of the towers (the N tower was demolished in 1837 after being struck by lightning), the transition from round to pointed arches, the insertion of a rose window (a feature found on a larger scale in the later High-Gothic cathedrals) and three portals (symbolic of the Holy Trinity) serving as focal points for the art of the ecclesiastical Gothic sculptor.

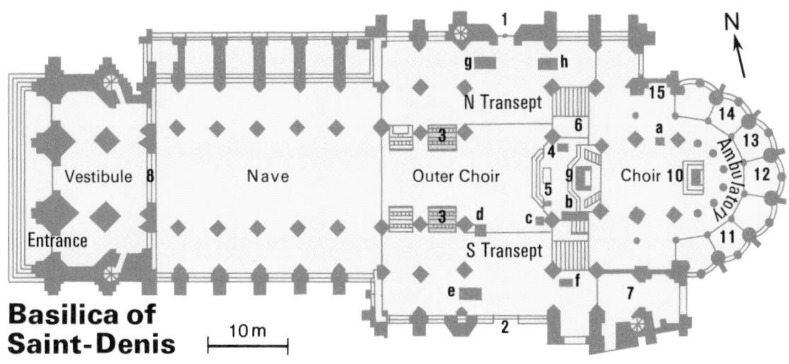

Basilica of Saint-Denis

1 Porte des Valois
2 S Portal (13th c.)
3 Choir stalls (by Gaillon)
4 Bishop's throne
5 Mary with Infant Jesus
6 Entrance to crypt
7 Treasury
8 Cavaillé-Coll organ

ALTARS
9 High Altar
10 St Denis
11 Crucifixion
12 Childhood of Jesus
13 St Pérégrin
14 St Eustache
15 Evangelists (mosaics)

TOMBS
a Clovis
b Dagobert I/Nantilde
c Pépin le Bref (Pippin)
d Charles Martel
e François I/Claude de France
f Charles V
g Louis XII/Anne de Bretagne
h Henri II/Catherine de Médicis

None of the original portal sculpture remains apart from the robed figures (central doorway: the wise and foolish virgins; right: the months; left: the signs of the Zodiac). The spandrel of the central doorway (restored) represents the Last Judgment; that on the right (recarved) the Last Communion of St Denis and that on the left (also recarved) the torture of the Saint and his companions Rusticus and Eleutherius.
With its crenellations and massive buttresses the exterior of the basilica has retained something of the "fortified" air that characterised Romanesque churches built as "God's fortresses".

Interior

The interior of the church is 108 m (355 ft) long and almost 30 m (100 ft) high and makes an impressive effect with its soaring pillars and 37 windows, each 10 m (33 ft) high. It is divided into the vestibule, nave, outer choir, intersection, transepts and choir. Here one finds the final and possibly most important element of the Gothic style, perfected in High Gothic, namely, the "architecture of light", by which is meant light not only in its literal sense but as an integral part of the structure and spatial disposition of the building: the way the light falls (depending on the angle of incidence and how much light) breathes life into the spatial dimensions. Walls as load-bearing elements can be dispensed with and replaced with a great sweep of windows. The load-bearing function is performed by the ribbed vaulting which distributes the loading on to the underpinning arrangements of buttresses and pillars (the external buttresses provide stability). The use of the pointed Gothic arch makes for higher vaulting and greater spatial freedom.
Besides bringing together Early and High Gothic, the basilica also enjoys the special feature of having windows in the triforium which runs between the arcades and high windows of the aisles and transepts.

Times of opening
1 Oct.–31 March: 10 a.m.–noon, 1–4 p.m.;
1 April–30 Sept.: 10 a.m.–noon, 1.30–6 p.m.;
closed: 1 Jan., 1 May, 1 Nov., 25 Dec.

Royal tombs: almost all of France's kings and queens, their children and certain great servants of the crown were buried in the basilica of Saint-Denis. Their tombs were plundered during the Revolution but since 1817 their mortal remains have again reposed in the church.
There are two communal tombs in the crypt, one for the royal house of Bourbon (including Louis XVI) and the other for about 800 members of the Merovingian, Capetian, Orléans and Valois royal families. The most notable of the many tombs are those of Louis XII (d. 1515) and his wife Anne de Bretagne (d. 1514), erected between 1517 and 1531 (in the N transept); Henri II (d. 1559) and his wife Catherine de Médicis (d. 1589), completed in 1573 (in the N transept); and Dagobert I (13th c.) with a statue of Queen Nantilde (on the right of the High Altar).

*Saint-Etienne-du-Mont (church) C4

Location
Place Sainte-Geneviève
(5th arr.)

The present church dates from 1492 and was built for the servants of the Benedictine Abbey which used to be on this site. It is dedicated to St Stephen (Etienne) but St Genevieve, the patron saint of Paris and its supposed saviour from

destruction by the Huns in the 5th c., is also venerated here. The quarter in which the church is situated (Montagne Sainte-Geneviève) is named after her.
The period and style of the building range from Late Gothic to early Renaissance. The choir and transept were completed in 1540 and the nave in 1610. Despite the Gothic ground plan and the Flamboyant vaulting above the intersection with a 5½ m (18 ft) pendant keystone ("Angus Dei"), the most prominent feature was already the plain round pillars of the Renaissance. The richly decorated façade (1610–18) is pure Renaissance, the work of Claude Guérin. The small tower on the right probably survives from an earlier 13th c. building.
The triforium around the central nave constitutes a special architectural feature for a Renaissance church of this kind, since it is usually only to be found in Gothic churches.
The church is famous for its rood screen (1530–41, marble centrepiece) with spiral staircases on both sides, the only one left in Paris.
To the right of this, at the entrance to the Chapel of the Virgin, are the memorials of the philosopher Blaise Pascal (1623–62) and the playwright Jean-Baptiste Racine (1639–99) who are buried in the church. The second side chapel on the left contains a sarcophagus supposed to hold a stone from the grave of St Genevieve.
Stained glass in the N transept ("Revelations", 1614) and the S aisle ("Parable of the feast", 1586) dates from the church's construction.

Métro
Cardinal Lemoine, Maubert-Mutualité

Suburban station
Luxembourg (RER)

Buses
84, 89

Saint-Eustache (church) B4

The church of Saint-Eustache, dedicated to the early Christian martyr Eustachius, is generally considered the finest Renaissance church building in Paris. It is the parish church of the quarter of Les Halles (see entry).
Its foundation stone was laid in 1532 under François I but it was not completed until 1640. Modelled on Notre-Dame, it is Gothic in its ground plan, five-span nave, triforium (gallery under the windows) and fan vaulting. Its unique blending of Gothic and Renaissance forms is seen most clearly in the columns which, though built on the Gothic model, are Renaissance in outward appearance, and the church as a whole is as impressive as befitted the size and importance of its parish. It measures 100 m (330 ft) in length, 44 m (145 ft) in width and 34 m (110 ft) to the ceiling.
The choir windows date from 1631 (Philippe de Champaigne) and show St Eustache surrounded by the Apostles and Fathers of the Church. The Martyrdom of St Eustache is depicted on the left spandrel of the portal (Simon Vouet, *c.* 1635). A noteworthy tomb is that of Colbert, Minister of Finance to Louis XIV, sculpted by Coysevox, designed by Lebrun and situated in the side aisle of the choir on the left of the apse.
Saint-Eustache is famous for its concerts (at 11 a.m. on public holidays), and works by Berlioz ("Te Deum", 1855) and Liszt (Mass, 1866) were heard here for the first time. Large Ducroquet/Gonzalès organ.

Location
Rue Rambuteau (1st arr.)

Métro
Les Halles

Suburban station
Châtelet-Les Halles

Buses
29, 67, 74, 75, 85

*Saint-Germain-des-Prés (church) C3

Location
Place Saint-Germain-des Prés (6th arr.)

Métro
Saint-Germain-des-Prés

Buses
39, 48, 63, 70, 86, 87, 95, 96

The church of Saint-Germain-des-Prés was part of the Benedictine Abbey established here in the 8th c. and destroyed during the French Revolution. It has borne the name of St Germain, Bishop of Paris, since his canonisation in 754.
The church which already stood here on the meadows (prés) of the Seine in the 6th c. was the burial place of the Merovingian kings Childerich I, Chlothar II and Childerich II (tombs plundered during the Revolution). Destroyed several times by the Normans, the church was rebuilt between 990 and 1021. Parts of it are late Romanesque (nave) and Early Gothic (choir completed in 1163).
The tombs of John Casimir, king of Poland (d. 1672) and a statue of St Francis-Xavier by Nicolas Coustou can be found in the right transept. In the second side chapel on the right of the choir are the headstones of the philosopher Descartes (d. 1650) and the two scholar monks Mabillon (d. 1707) and Montfaucon (d. 1719).

Saint-Germain-des-Prés (quarter) C3/4

Location
6th arr.

Métro
Saint-Germain-des-Prés. Odéon

Buses
39, 48, 63, 95, 96

The quarter of Saint-Germain-des-Prés, celebrated for the Existentialist circle around Jean-Paul Sartre and for the writers and artists of the forties and fifties, adjoins the western section of the Quartier Latin (see entry). Its borders are broadly the Seine (N), the Rue des Saints-Pères (W), the Rue de Vaugirard (S) and the Odéon métro station (E).
The artistic and intellectual atmosphere lingers on in the numerous art galleries, the Paris Academy of Art (Rue Bonaparte) and a number of cafés (Aux Deux Magots, Café de Flore) and restaurants. Saint-Germain-des-Prés is also famous for its sophisticated jazz bars.
As in the neighbouring Quartier Latin, the cinemas of Saint-Germain screen excellent programmes throughout the year (almost all foreign films are shown in the original version, i.e. sub-titled, not dubbed).

*Saint-Germain-en-Laye (château and park)

Location
Saint-Germain-en-Laye (suburb 20 km (12 miles) W of Paris)

Times of opening
9.45 a.m.–noon and 1.30–5.15 p.m.;
closed Tues.

Saint-Germain-en-Laye, birthplace of the French composer Claude Debussy, has one of the Ile-de-France's many royal palaces.
In the 12th c. Louis VI built a castle on the ridge above the Seine which François I had demolished retaining only the keep and the Sainte-Chapelle (the predecessor of its namesake in Paris). The château that he built in its place was the home of Mary Stuart between the ages of 6 and 16 and James II of England ended his days here after being deposed. Louis XIV was born in the château in 1643. The Renaissance château fell into decay in the 18th c. but was restored, together with the chapel, by Napoleon III in 1862–7.

Since 1867 the rooms of the former royal palace have housed the "Musée des Antiquités Nationales (Musée de la Préhistoire)", an outstanding and ever-growing collection of archaeological finds from all over France. (The times of opening are the same for the museum as for the château.)
The chapel, probably the work of Pierre de Montreuil who built the Sainte-Chapelle on the Ile de la Cité (see entries), was begun in 1245 and is one of the great works of early High Gothic in the Ile-de-France.
Saint-Germain is also famous for the château's terraces which afford superb views of Paris and the Seine.

*Saint-Germain-l'Auxerrois (church) C4

The former royal parish church of Saint-Germain-l'Auxerrois is situated on the square at the E entrance to the Louvre (Place du Louvre) opposite the town hall (Mairie Annexe) of the 1st arrondissement). It is dedicated to St Germanus, bishop of Auxerre.
The present church is a mixture of styles (Romanesque belfry, Gothic chancel, Late-Gothic porch and nave and a Renaissance side porch). The front porch (1435–9) is an outstanding example of Late Gothic and the very fine royal pew (1684) in the nave is well worth seeing.
Many artists who served the French kings are buried in the church: the architects Le Vau and Robert de Cotte, the painters François Boucher and Jean-Marc Nattier, the sculptor Coysevox and the brothers Nicolas and Guillaume Coustou.

Location
Place du Louvre (1st arr.)

Métro
Louvre

Buses
21, 67, 69, 72, 74, 76, 81, 85

*Saint-Julien-le-Pauvre (church) C4

This little church on the Quai-Saint-Michel behind the Square Réne-Viviani is today the church of the Greek Orthodox community.
It was built in the High-Gothic style between the middle of the 12th and 13th c. The elections of the Chancellors (Recteurs) of the Sorbonne (see entry) were held here in the 15th and 16th c. and its bell summoned the students to lectures. Today its interior is dominated by an iconostasis (a screen of icons) dating from 1901.

Location
Quai-Saint-Michel (5th arr.)

Métro
Saint-Michel

Bus
24

*Saint-Pierre-de-Montmartre (church) B4

Four black marble pillars (two in the choir and two against the inner wall of the façade) date from the Merovingian church erected here in the 7th c. on the site of a Roman temple. The present church is Early Gothic (choir, apse, transept) and was consecrated in 1147.
The Church of Saint-Pierre is all that remains of the large 12th c. Benedictine Abbey of Montmartre the last Abbess of which was guillotined in 1794.

Location
Rue du Mont-Cenis
(18th arr.)

Métro
Anvers, Abbesses

Bus
80

*Saint-Séverin (church) C4

Location
1 Rue des Prêtres-Saint-Séverin (5th arr.)

Métro
Saint-Michel

Buses
21, 24, 27, 38, 67, 81, 85, 96

The Church of Saint-Séverin (named after the hermit who lived on this spot in the 6th c.) is in the lower part of the Quartier Latin and is one of the finest examples of "style flamboyant", the Late-Gothic form of Flamboyant art.
This was at one time the site of an oratory (destroyed by the Normans), a chapel and then a church. The present building was begun in the first half of the 13th c. Parts of it were probably destroyed by fire in the 15th c. and it was completed in the Late-Gothic style about 1520.
The first three sections of the nave are in the simple style of the 13th c. but from the 4th span onwards one finds richly decorated pillars and imaginatively worked keystones. The choir has a double ambulatory of great beauty and with its wonderfully intricate fan vaulting is a masterpiece of Late-Gothic art. The 14th c. stained-glass windows depicting the Apostles in the first three sections come from the choir of Saint-Germain-des-Prés (see entry), whereas the other windows in the nave are 15th c. and contrast sharply with the modern windows (1966, Jean Bazaine) in the chancel. The side door on the right leads into a small garden covering the old cemetery and surrounded by ossuaries.

*Saint-Sulpice (church) C3/4

Location
Place Saint-Sulpice (6th arr.)

Métro
Saint-Sulpice

Buses
63, 70, 84, 86, 87, 96

The Abbey of Saint-Germain-des-Prés commissioned the plans for this new parish church in 1634 but building was not finished until the façade was completed in 1766. Six architects were involved in the work.
The Place Saint-Sulpice in front of the church was originally intended by the Florentine architect Jean-Nicolas Servandoni (1695–1766) to be a half-circle fronted by uniformly designed houses but this project was abandoned. The square in its present form dates from 1808 while the fountain (1844) with the four bishops (Bossuet, Fénelon, Massillon, Fléchier) is by Louis Visconti.
The façade, modelled on Sir Christopher Wren's St Paul's Cathedral, is the work of Servandoni and with its two tiers of columns (Ionic above, Doric below) is a rare example of simple, unadorned Classicism.
The N tower (73 m – 240 ft) was built (1777) by Jean François Chalgrin, while the S tower is incomplete (68 m – 220 ft).
The nave was begun by Christophe Gamard in 1646 and continued by Louis Le Vau from 1655 onwards. The barrel-vaulted interior is impressively spacious and is evenly lit by high side windows.
Items of special interest:
Two stoups near the entrance, the gift of the Venetian Republic to François I, bequeathed to the church by Louis XV
Frescoes by Eugène Delacroix (in the first side chapel on the right): St Michael and the dragon, Heliodorus driven out of the temple, Jacob and the angel (completed in 1861).
Statues near the choir pillars by Bouchardon of Christ, Mary and eight Apostles (from 1734).

In the chapel of the Virgin: four paintings by Carle van Loo (1705–65), a fresco in the cupola by François Lemoyne (1688–1737) and a marble statue of the "Queen of Heaven" by Jean-Baptiste Pigalle (1714–85).
In the right and the left transepts: a copper plate and a marble obelisk that together form a sundial (1744). Victor Hugo and Adèle Foucher were married in the church in 1822. – Enormous Cliquot organ, rebuilt and enlarged by Cavaillé-Coll in 1860 (recitals).

Saint-Vincent-de-Paul (church) B4

This church – completed in 1844 and the most important church to be built in the reign of Louis-Philippe (1830–48) – was designed by Jacob Ignaz Hittorf (1792–1867) who hailed from Cologne. Hittorf combined the Christian architectural form of a five-sectioned basilica with elements of Roman (triumphal arch) and Greek (Ionic and Corinthian columns). Outstanding features of the magnificent interior are the fresco "Procession of the Saints" (1849–53) by Hippolyte Flandrin and the altar sculpture by François Rude (1784–1855).

Location
Place La Fayette (10th arr.)

Métro
Poissonnière

Buses
32, 42, 43, 49

**Sainte-Chapelle (church C4

A palace chapel on two levels, the Sainte-Chapelle (Holy Chapel) is the brightest of all the Gothic jewels of Paris. Mass is celebrated only on special occasions but concerts are given here frequently.
This magnificent High-Gothic masterpiece – probably the work of Pierre de Montreuil – was built in under 33 months by St Louis (Louis IX) to house the holy Christian relics obtained from the Emperor of Constantinople (at a cost 2½ times as much as the actual building).

Location
4 Boulevard du Palais (1st arr.)

Métro
Cité

Buses
21, 24, 27, 38, 81, 85, 96

Sainte-Chapelle

CHAPELLE HAUTE
UPPER CHAPEL

SEQUENCE OF SCENES IN STAINED-GLASS WINDOWS (Total area c. 618 sq. m (6672 sq. ft) – partially restored)

1 Creation, Adam and Eve, Noah, Jacob
2 Flight from Egypt, Joseph
3 Pentateuch, Leviticus, Laws of Moses
4 Deuteronomy, Joshua, Ruth and Boas
5 Judges: Gideon, Samson
6 Isaiah, Root of Jesse
7 John the Evangelist, Life of Mary, Childhood of Jesus
8 Christ's Passion
9 John the Baptist, Daniel
10 Prophecies of Ezekiel
11 Jeremiah, Tobias
12 Judith, Job
13 Esther
14 Kings: Samuel, David, Solomon
15 Legend of the Holy Cross, Discovery of Christ's Cross, Acquisition of the Relics by Louis IX and their Deposition, Consecration of the Sainte-Chapelle

Times of opening
1 Oct.–31 March: 10–11.45 a.m. and 1.30–4 p.m.; 1 April–30 Sept.: 10–11 a.m. and 1.30–5 p.m.

Guided tours
daily except Tues.

At that time what was then the palace chapel stood in the great courtyard of the royal palace on the site of the present Palais de Justice (see entry). (The entrance to the Sainte-Chapelle is on the left inside the great ironwork railing at the main entrance to the Palais de Justice.) In the 18th c. a wing of the Palais de Justice was linked to the side of the chapel. Until its restoration (1841–67) the chapel served for a 30-year period as the legal archives.

Today the Sainte-Chapelle stands in an inner courtyard on the left of the Palais de Justice's main entrance. It is 33 m (110 ft) long, 17 m (55 ft) wide and 42 m (140 ft) to the gable. All that can be seen from the outside is the tip of the spire (la flèche) rising to a height of 75 m (246 ft).

The lower chapel (chapelle basse) was originally for the servants. Its vault, which is only 6·6 m (22 ft) high, is not load-bearing but is supported by 14 pillars at intervals along the walls.

The upper chapel is the actual Sainte-Chapelle. It was dedicated to the Holy Relics and reserved for the king, his family and high officials. (The relics – fragments of the Holy Cross and the Crown of Thorns, and a nail from the Cross – are today kept in the Treasury of Notre-Dame – see entry.)

On entering the upper chapel one is immediately struck by the breathtaking beauty of the light filtering through the stained-glass windows that act as its walls, seemingly transcending earthly gravity. Apart from a low blind arcade around its base, decorated with scenes of martyrdom, the chapel has no walls as such and no supporting pillars or columns other than the 14 22 m (70 ft) high pillars that provide the framework for the great 4×15 m (13×50 ft) windows and buttress the superb vaulting.

The chapel is famous for its stained glass depicting 1134 scenes from the Bible and flooding the interior with all the colours of the rainbow. About two-thirds is the original 13th c. glass and the rest has been restored to its original state.

The Late-Gothic rose window, with scenes from Revelations, dates from the reign of Charles VIII (1493–8).

Each pillar in the nave has the statue of an Apostle at its foot but only half of these are originals (3, 4, 6, 11, 12, 13). In the 3rd bay (on the left) there are two recesses that were reserved for the royal family, and St Louis was able to hear mass without being seen from his oratory in the 12th bay (on the right).

There is a small dais under a wooden baldachin in the apse where the reliquary for which the chapel was built used to stand; it is reached by two wooden staircases (the one on the left is original). The French kings were the only keyholders to the reliquary, the contents of which were displayed to the royal household on Good Friday.

Sorbonne C4

Location
Rue des Ecoles, Place de la Sorbonne (5th arr.)

Métro
Odéon, Saint-Michel

The influential cathedral canons (chanoines) of medieval Paris are often described as hungry for power and possessions but Robert de Sorbon, canon and father confessor to St Louis (IX),

Sainte-Chapelle ▶

Buses
21, 27, 38, 63, 81, 85, 86, 87

Times of opening
Mon.–Fri., 8 a.m.– 8 p.m.

seems to have been an exception. With the king's help he established a college (la Sorbonne) in 1257 where poor theology students could live and study at his expense. The college soon became a leading school of theology and later a university, only to decline in importance towards the end of the Middle Ages. Cardinal Richelieu, when Rector of the University, stopped the buildings deteriorating and had them partly rebuilt by Jacques Lemercier (1624–42). Napoleon made the Sorbonne a State university and considerably extended it.

The present building, with 22 large lecture theatres, 38 smaller rooms, 37 academics' studies, 240 laboratories, a library, observatory and numerous offices, dates from between 1885 and 1901 (architect: Nenot).

The Sorbonne was one of the centres of the student unrest of May 1968 which spread to become a general strike throughout France. Subsequent reform of the university system split the Sorbonne into four universities. These still have their headquarters and some departments here but most faculties have been distributed throughout the city and its suburbs. (Greater Paris now has a total of 13 universities.)

The main façade on the Rue des Ecoles bears allegorical representations of the sciences. Arrangements can be made in the office on the right of the main entrance to visit the largest of the lecture theatres, the Grand Amphithéâtre, which seats 2700 and contains Puvis de Chavannes' famous classical mural "the Sacred Grove".

The church in the courtyard of the Sorbonne (Eglise de la Sorbonne) was built between 1635 and 1642. The tomb of Cardinal Richelieu (1694) which stands in the S transept was designed by Charles Lebrun (1619–90) and executed by François Girardon (1628–1715). (Entrance to the church in the courtyard; if closed, apply to the concierge at 1 Rue de la Sorbonne under the arch.)

Théâtre Français

B4

Location
Place du Théatre Français (1st arr.)

Métro
Palais-Royal

Buses
21, 27, 39, 48, 67, 69, 72, 74, 81, 85, 95

Times of opening
Advance bookings (a week ahead); 11–6 p.m.

The Théâtre Français is the home of France's national theatre company, the Comédie-Française.

Founded by Louis XIV in 1680, the Comédie-Française was originally the troupe headed by Molière until his death in 1673. In 1812 Napoleon enacted a decree giving the company its official status, with a Director appointed (as today) by the government.

The original building into which the Comédie-Française moved in 1792 burnt down in 1799 and was rebuilt in 1807. The present façade dates from 1867 and the interior from the turn of the century (restored and extended after a second fire in 1900).

In the foyer visitors can see the chair in which Molière died on stage during a performance of "Le Malade Imaginaire", and the famous bust of Voltaire by Jean-Antoine Houdon (1781). The Comédie-Française only performs the classics: plays by Corneille, Racine, Molière, Marivaux and Beaumarchais, as well as "modern" classics by Claudel, Giraudoux and Anouilh.

Thermes (Roman baths) C4

The remains of these Roman baths are on land next to the Musée de Cluny (see entry). It is not known exactly when they were built but their destruction is put at about A.D. 380. It is not possible to enter the ruins (on the corner of Boulevard Saint-Michel and Boulevard Saint-Germain) but they can be seen from the outside.
The Frigidarium is the only room still intact and this was due to the building of the Hôtel de Cluny (entrance).
The ruins are of the following:
Caldarium (hot bath): farthest W of the three main rooms, visible from Rue du Sommerard.
Tepidarium (warm bath): visible from Boulevard Saint-Michel.
Two Gymnasiums: visible from Boulevard Saint-Germain.
Swimming pool, 10 m (33 ft) long.
Frigidarium (cold bath) with the "Autel des Nautes": the best preserved of the baths, 21 m (65 ft) long, 11 m (40 ft) wide and 14·5 m (47½ ft) high. The capitals of the pillars supporting the cross vaulting on the N side look like ships' prows, hence the supposition that the baths were financed by the "Nautes", the rich corporation of Paris boatmen. The "Autel des Nautes" (altar of the Nautes) is from the excavations of the temple of Jupiter located beneath the choir of Notre Dame. Bearing a dedication by the "Nautes", its sculpture of Gallic and Roman deities is the oldest found in Paris to date (1st c. B.C.).

Location
24 Rue du Sommerard (5th arr.)

Métro
Saint-Michel, Odéon

Buses
21, 27, 38, 86, 87

Times of opening
9.45 a.m.–12.30 p.m. and 2–5.15 p.m.; closed Tues.

Tour Saint-Jacques (St James' tower) C4

On the N corner of the Place du Châtelet stands the Tour Saint-Jacques, the Late-Gothic steeple of what was the parish church of the butchers' guild, Saint-Jacques-la-Boucherie, built 1508–22 by Jean de Félin under François I.
In the Middle Ages the church was the assembly point for pilgrims setting out for Santiago de Compostela (NW Spain), the reputed tomb of St James the Apostle and the most important pilgrim shrine of medieval Christendom.
Pilgrims proceeding from the N by the Rue Saint-Martin passed along the Rue Saint-Jacques on their way S. On top of the 52 m (170 ft) high tower stands a statue of St James (in French, Saint Jacques; in Spanish, Santiago).
The pilgrims' symbol was the scallop shell or "coquille Saint-Jacques", which has subsequently also become famous as a culinary delicacy.

Location
Rue de Rivoli (4th arr.)

Métro
Châtelet

Buses
38, 47, 58, 69, 70, 75, 76, 96

**Tour Eiffel (Eiffel Tower) C2

Despite oft-repeated doubts as to its stability, the Eiffel Tower is approaching its centenary (1989). Over 50 years ago it lost its title as the world's highest building to New York's Empire State Building but still has 5000 visitors a day (average over the year). The Eiffel Tower continues to be the symbol of Paris.

Location
Quai Branly (7th arr.)

Métro
Ecole Militaire, Bir Hakeim, Trocadéro

Tour Eiffel (view of the Palais de Chaillot)

Buses
42, 69, 80, 82, 87

Times of opening
1st and 2nd platforms: 10.30 a.m.–5.30 p.m. and 6.30–11 p.m.; 3rd platform: 10.30 a.m.–5.30 p.m. only

The designs and calculations for the tower were the work of Gustave Eiffel (1832–1923), an engineer from Dijon, and it was built for the World Fair in 1889. The tower is 307 m (1000 ft) high (320·75 m (1050 ft) to the top of the mast) and consists of 12000 steel components held together by 2·5 million rivets. Its method of construction distributes the total weight of 7500 tonnes in such a way that the pressure it exerts on the ground is only 4 kg per sq. cm (60 lb per sq. in), the equivalent of an average-sized adult on the seat of a chair.
People protested vigorously when it was being built and the construction company was obliged to give an undertaking to meet any claims for damages in the event of the tower collapsing on to surrounding buildings. However, the Eiffel Tower's greatest enemy, rust, is constantly kept under control by a team of experts equipped with special inspection cameras and if necessary every single part can still be replaced.
On foot one can only reach the 1st and 2nd platforms (57 m (185 ft), 350 stairs, and 115 m (375 ft), 700 stairs, respectively). It is preferable to use the lifts which travel from the base of the pillars to the 2nd platform. The 3rd platform (247 m (810 ft) high, length of sides 16 m – 50 ft), which is completely enclosed, is reached by a single lift. From here in fine weather one can see for 70 km (45 miles) in any direction but the 1st platform has the advantage of affording good views from close at hand of the nearby buildings and parts of the city. (There are restaurants on the first two floors.)

Tour Eiffel 

PEPSI-COLA
BAR
RAPPEL
CAFE
RESTAURANT

*Tuileries (Gardens of the Tuileries: Jardins des Tuileries) B3

Location
Between the Louvre and Place de la Concorde (1st arr.)

Métro
Tuileries, Concorde

Buses
24, 42, 52, 68, 69, 72, 73, 84, 94

Times of opening
9 a.m. until dusk

One of the largest and best-known parks in Paris is the Tuileries Gardens. When Catherine de Médicis had a palace built in 1563 on what is today the whole length of the Avenue du Général Lemonnier, close to the Palace of the Louvre, she named it the "Tuileries" after the tile-kilns that had stood on that site. In 1664 Colbert, Louis XIV's Minister of Finance, commissioned André Le Nôtre, later to be responsible for the park at Versailles, to design the Tuileries Gardens. The palace burnt down during the Paris Commune in 1871 and was never rebuilt.

Coysevox's Baroque statues of winged horses guard the entrance on the Place de la Concorde (see entry) through which, by way of terraces and ramps, one reaches the large octagonal fountain surrounded by 18th c. busts and statues by the sculptors Coustou and Coysevox (copy of a bust of Le Nôtre on the terrace of the Jeu du Paume). From the central avenue one has a unique view of the obelisk in the Place de la Concorde, the Champs-Elysées and the Arc de Triomphe (see entries) in one direction and the "Parterres" (formal lawns) of the Louvre Museum and the small triumphal arch "du Carrousel" in the other. To the left and right of the rather dusty "Grande Allée" you can rest on benches in the shade or watch the games of "boules" on the terraces by the Rue de Rivoli.

In this northern section there is also a Punch and Judy show as well as donkey rides for the children. Many children sail their model boats on the yacht pond at the other end of the central avenue (boats can be hired in the summer months).

*UNESCO (Unesco Building: officially Maison de l'UNESCO) C3

Location
Place de Fontenoy (7th arr.)

Métro
Segur

Bus
49

Times of opening
Visits by prior arrangement: tel. 5 66 57 57

This building is the headquarters of UNESCO, the United Nations Educational, Scientific and Cultural Organisation.

Jointly created in 1955–8 by its architects Marcel Breuer (USA), Pier Luigi Nervi (Italy) and Bernard Zehrfuss (France), it embodies a piece of modern architectural history.

Picasso's mural "Victory of Light and Peace over Darkness and Death" adorns the walls of the trapezoidal hall of the conference building. Outside it has a recumbent figure by Henry Moore (GB) and a black steel mobile by Alexander Calder (USA) and the two walls of the Moon and the Sun are decorated with ceramics by Joan Miró. Inside there are bronze reliefs by Hans Arp and tapestries by Le Corbusier.

Val-de-Grâce (church) C4

Location
277 Rue Saint-Jacques (5th arr.)

Métro
Port-Royal (RER)

The imposing Baroque church of Val-de-Grâce is part of a well-preserved 17th c. convent (nowadays a military hospital). Anne of Austria, wife of Louis XIII, bought the convent for the Benedictine nuns and vowed to endow it with a church if she gave birth to an heir to the throne (her marriage had been childless for 23 years). She kept her promise in 1645 after the birth of her son, the future Louis XIV, in 1643 and commissioned Jacques Lemercier to build the church, which was completed by Gabriel le Duc in 1667.

Buses
21, 38, 81, 83

Val-de-Grâce is the only Baroque church in Paris the architecture of which bears the stamp of Rome, the capital of 17th c. Baroque. Its architect Lemercier modelled the main façade, with its double row of columns, on that of St Susanna in Rome. The dome recalls the dome of St Peter's but is more ornate, with sculptured vases, windows and a frieze of fleurs-de-lys, and the initials "A" and "L", while its tambour is markedly three-dimensional with prominent pilasters and cornices and deep-set windows.

The interior of the church is also marked by the three-dimensional approach that governs the church's architecture and décor as a whole. The barrel-vaulted nave is divided into three sections, each with side-chapels. On the round arches there are reliefs representing the virtues (medallions: Christ's forefathers). At the intersection of the nave and chapels there is a stepped dais and a canopy supported by columns (reminiscnet of Bernini's baldachin over the High Altar of St Peter's – another echo of Rome).

In the cupola (40 m (130 ft) high, 17 m (55 ft) in diameter) the great fresco of God the Father surrounded by the Saints and Martyrs is the work of Pierre Mignard (1665). Anne of Austria's portrait can be seen in the fresco in the cupola of the chapel on the left of the choir. The chapel on the right is dedicated to St Louis and is the former Benedictine choir.

Château de Versailles (palace gates)

*Vaux-le-Vicomte (château, officially Château de Vaux-le-Vicomte)

Location
50 km (30 miles) SE

Times of opening
1 Nov.–15 March: Sat., Sun. 10 a.m.– noon and 2–6 p.m.:
15 March–31 Oct.: daily 2–6 p.m.

The Château of Vaux-le-Vicomte, 6 km (4 miles) NE of Melun (on the D215) is one of the finest of the 17th c. nobles' châteaux and served as the model for the palace and park at Versailles.

Nicholas Fouquet, Finance Minister of Louis XIV, called in the three greatest architects of that time to work on his project: Louis Le Vau (château), Charles Lebrun (interior) and André Le Nôtre (park). The magnificent château and park were completed in a relatively short time (1656–61) and cost Fouquet the enormous sum of 10 million "livres" (French pounds).

Fouquet's enjoyment of his property was short-lived. Accused of profiteering while in office, he was arrested at the instigation of his successor Colbert soon afterwards (he died in prison) and Vaux-le-Vicomte was confiscated. This château prompted Louis XIV to resolve to build for himself the finest palace in France, and with this in mind he seized part of the confiscated treasure (vases, statues, even trees and plants) and engaged Le Vau, Lebrun and Le Nôtre to create for him the palace to end all palaces, the focal point of power and splendour for all France – Versailles.

**Château et Parc de Versailles (palace and park of Versailles)

Location
Versailles, Département of Yvelines (78), 20 km (12 miles) SW, A13/12 or N10

Rail
from Montparnasse, Saint-Lazare and Invalides

Bus
171 (from Pont de Sèvres métro)

Times of opening
9.45 a.m.–5.30 p.m.; closed Mon.

Information
Office du Tourisme,
7 Rue des Réservoirs,
78-Versailles,
tel. 9 50 36 22

The Palace of Versailles with its parks and gardens is among the most beautiful, famous and historical sights in Europe. The architecture, interior, park and, in fact, the entire court of the French kings at Versailles in the 17th and 18th c. served as the model for many European royal and princely courts of that time. What was originally a small hunting lodge, built in 1631–4 by Philibert Le Roy for Louis XIII, was extended and rebuilt from 1661 to 1710 to become the royal seat of Louis XIV, the "Roi Soleil" (sun king). The architecture of Versailles is the work of Louis Le Vau, Jules Hardouin-Mansart and Robert de Cotte. Charles Le Brun was responsible for the interior and the gardens were landscaped by André Le Nôtre. Louis XIV's successors made little or no alterations apart from minor additions (Rococo apartments and the classicist Petit Trianon: Louis XV; garden extensions: Louis XV and Louis XVI).

Versailles was the residence of the French kings for over a century (1682–1789). The principles of absolute monarchy required the nobles of high rank to be in constant attendance at the court of the king. Thus Versailles was made the centre of power of absolutist France where the king, aloof from strong princes and growing unrest in Paris, was able to rule as an autocrat. Consequently Louis XIV's extravagant claim "l'Etat, c'est moi!" (I personify the State) can also be regarded as confirming the true state of affairs. The palace and park of Versailles provided the fitting setting for this abundance of power.

Exterior

Seen from the outside the palace is already impressive. Three broad avenues converge in the square in front of the palace (Place d'Armes). The former royal stables (Mansart, 1679–85)

Château de Versailles (park façade)

can be seen on both sides of the central avenue. Entering the forecourt through the palace gates the visitor is faced by the equestrian statue of Louis XIV (1835) where the forecourt becomes the Cour Royale – the courtyard formerly reserved for the royal family. This narrows to become the Cour de Marbre – the "marble courtyard" – which until 1830 was slightly higher and paved with coloured marble. The entrance to the palace and to the park is on the right side of the Cour Royale.
The oldest buildings are those fronting the Cour de Marbre. These were part of Louis XIII's hunting lodge, and contain the royal private apartments (1st floor). Le Vau enlarged the original building by adding on wings to house the State Apartments (Grands Appartements) on the 1st floor and the suites of the heirs to the throne on the ground floor. Mansart joined Le Vau's wings by building the Hall of Mirrors on the 1st floor overlooking the park and extended the palace by adding the N and S wings. The palace chapel (Mansart/Cotte) and opera house (Jacques-Ange Gabriel) completed the palace in its present form. The overall length of the park façade amounts to 680 m (2230 ft).

Interior

Today's visitor can still fully appreciate how the splendour revealed inside the palace must have impressed even royal contemporaries. Of the many rooms the following are particularly well worth seeing:
Galerie des Batailles (Gallery of Battles): in this gallery, which is 120 m (390 ft) long and 13 m (40 ft) wide and extends for almost the entire length of the S wing, the paintings of battles cover 14 centuries of French history. 82 busts of famous

military leaders line the walls and the Corinthian columns in the middle section of the gallery.

Salle du Sacre (Coronation room): the room gets its name from the painting by Jacques Louis David (1748–1825) of the coronation of Napoleon I and Empress Josephine.

Escalier de la Reine (Queen's staircase): the magnificent staircase with multi-coloured marble and gilded bronze reliefs on the ceiling fillet and over the doors leads to the state and private apartments of the queen. A recess in the centre of the 1st floor landing contains the king's coat of arms.

Salle des Gardes de la Reine (Hall of the Queen's Guards): the ceiling paintings and marble walls date from the time of Louis XIV. The paintings (1676–81) are by Noël Coypel (1628–1707). The central octagonal painting shows Jupiter in a silver chariot drawn by two eagles. The four pictures in the arches are classical representations of divine virtues.

Antichambre de la Reine (Queen's antechamber): visitors used to wait here before an audience with the queen in her drawing-room or bedchamber. The ceiling paintings (dating from Louis XIV) show famous women of antiquity (1673, Claude Vignon).

Salon de la Reine (Queen's audience chamber): the ceiling paintings (allegories of the arts and sciences, 1671, Michel Corneille) are all that remain from the time of Maria Theresa of Austria since in 1785 Marie-Antoinette transformed this room into its present form. The large Gobelin portrait of Louis XV (by P. F. Cozette from a design by Michel van Loos) dates from 1770.

Chambre de la Reine (Queen's bedchamber): 19 princes and princesses were born in this bedchamber which was created for

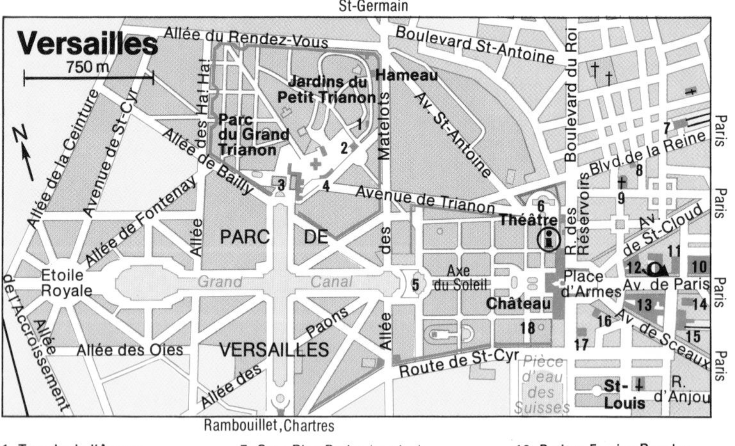

1 Temple de l'Amour
2 Petit Trianon
3 Grand Trianon
4 Musée des Voitures
5 Bassin d'Apollon
6 Bassin de Neptune
7 Gare Rive Droite (station)
8 Musée Lambinet
9 Notre-Dame
10 Préfecture
11 Palais de Justice
12 Grandes Ecuries Royales (stables)
13 Petites Ecuries Royales
14 Mairie (town hall)
15 Gare Rive Gauche (station)
16 Palais des Congrès
17 Bibliothèque (library)
18 Orangerie

Château de Versailles (Hall of Mirrors)

Maria Theresa of Austria, wife of Louis XIV. Queens also gave private audiences in this room. The Rococo ceiling showing the four virtues of a queen (charity, fertility, wisdom, fidelity) is of a later date (1729–35) and its "grisaille" paintings are the work of François Boucher (1703–70). Marie-Antoinette was responsible for the addition of the Gobelin medallions depicting Empress Maria Theresa of Austria, Emperor Joseph II and her husband Louis XVI. The little jewellery chest (1787, Schwerdtfeger) on the left of the queen's bed was a gift to Marie-Antoinette from the city of Paris.

Petits Appartements de la Reine (Queen's private apartments): these can be reached from the Queen's bedchamber and are funished as they would have been in Marie-Antoinette's time (1770–81)

Salon de la Paix (Salon of Peace): in the "classical" symmetry of Versailles this "Salon" (1680–6) was built to offset the Salon of War on the other side of the Hall of Mirrors. The ceiling is by Lebrun and the portrait of Louis above the fireplace is by Lemoyne.

Galerie des Glaces (Hall of Mirrors): after the annexation of Lorraine Louis XIV also acquired the dukedom of Burgundy in the Peace of Nijmegen (1678), thus consolidating France's supremacy in Europe. In that year the king decided to build a gallery which, with the Salons of War and Peace, completed the principal part of the palace and paid tribute in allegorical form to Louis XIV as the lord of war and peace. This celebrated Hall of Mirrors, which is 75 m (246 ft) long, 10 m (33 ft) wide and 12 m (40 ft) high, was based on plans by Jules Hardouin-Mansart (1646–1708) and the interior was designed by

Charles Lebrun (1619–90), director of the State Gobelins workshops. As with all galleries in hôtels, palaces and châteaux, the Hall of Mirrors served as a corridor (between the apartments of the king and queen) in which courtiers paid their respects. It was rarely used for solemn occasions. The Hall gets its name from the 17 arched panels of mirrors, each consisting of 18 mirror-panes (making 306 altogether), opposite the round-arched windows overlooking the park. It was in this historical hall that the new German Empire was proclaimed in 1871 and the Peace Treaty of Versailles was signed in 1919.
Since June 1980 the Hall has again been fitted out with (restored and reproduction) items of furniture, statuary and chandeliers (many in gilded plastic); the originals had been removed or destroyed before and during the Revolution. The paintings in the barrel-vaulted ceiling of the Hall of Mirrors are, taken as a whole, the most monumental ceiling paintings of their kind in France. They tell the story of Louis XIV's regency up till the Peace of Nijmegen.
Salon de l'Oeil de Bœuf (Ox-eye drawing-room): this drawing-room, named after its oval (ox-eye) window, dates from 1701 and originally contained paintings by the Italian painter Veronese. These were replaced by the portraits of the royal family. Worth noting is the frieze of children which, like the group of cherubs in the park, expresses the ageing king's wish for "more youth and less seriousness".
Chambre du Roi (King's bedchamber): Louis XIV's bedchamber was constructed in 1701 in what had been the main hall of Louis XIII's hunting lodge. It was here that the king died on 1 September 1715, and that the famous ceremonies of the "Lever du Roi" and the "Coucher du Roi" took place when the king granted morning and evening audiences. After many years of costly work the furnishings were restored to their original state in 1980.
Cabinet du Conseil (Council chamber): in the reigns of Louis XV and XVI all important decisions of state were taken in this room. The room's décor is a masterpiece of French Rococo (1755, based on designs by Jacques-Ange Gabriel).
Petits Appartements du Roi (king's private apartments): these can be reached from the council chamber. Dating from 1755, they were furnished in the Rococo style by Jacques-Ange Gabriel for Louis XV as somewhere to recover from the ceremonial etiquette of the court. Louis XV died in the first room (bedroom) on 10 May 1774.
Salon de la Guerre (Salon of War): this affords a unique view through the Hall of Mirrors to the Salon of Peace opposite on one side, and through the salons of the Grands Appartements on the other. The large oval stucco relief glorifying Louis XIV (between the corridors) is by Antoine Coysevox (1640–1720).
Salon d'Appollon (Salon of Apollo): "Apollo in the sun chariot accompanied by the seasons" (ceiling painting by Charles de la Fosse, a student of Lebrun) is the central allegorical theme from which Louis XIV derived his additional title of "le Roi Soleil" (the sun king). The walls are hung with priceless Gobelin tapestries and above the fireplace is the famous portrait of the king in the robe of ermine.
Salon de Mercure (Salon of Mercury): in the three salons of Apollo, Mercury and Mars the magnificent ceiling paintings are all that remain of the original décor (1670–80) – the marble was replaced by wood and the walls covered with fabric. The

Park of Versailles (Grand Trianon)

Park of Versailles (English Garden)

Grands Appartements were the staterooms where the king held court from 6 till 10 a.m.
Salon de Mars (Salon of Mars): this salon, with its ceiling painting by Audran, contains the famous picture of Marie-Antoinette with her children (1787, Madame Vigée-Lebrun).
Salon de Diane (Salon of Diana, 1675–80): the ceiling painting of Diana leading the hunt is by Gabriel Blanchard and the bust of Louis XIV is by Lorenzo Bernini.
Salon de Venus (Salon of Venus): here, too, as in the Salon de Diane, one finds, in the "cold and severe" marble décor, the style of the 1670s that originally characterised all seven of the Grands Appartements. This style echoed Louis XIV's determination to be remembered for his power and glory by constant reference to the heroes of classical antiquity. This theme is taken up in the marble walls and pillars, the classical-type statues (Louis XIV as a Roman emperor) and the paintings on the ceiling of Titus and Berenice, Antony and Cleopatra, Jason and Medea, Theseus and Ariadne, Europa and Jupiter, Amphitrite and Poseidon.
Salon d'Abondance (Salon of Plenty): the ceiling painting of the Goddess of Plenty, with her cornucopia, is by R. A. Houasse, a student of Lebrun. This room was used for the buffet at receptions.
Salon d'Hercule (Salon of Hercules): ceiling painting: Triumph of Hercules (1733–6; François Lemoine); two paintings by Veronese, gifts from the Republic of Venice (1664): "Elisha and Rebecca" (over the fireplace), "The Meal with Simon the Pharisee".

Palace Chapel (1699–1710, Jules Hardouin-Mansart, completed by his brother-in-law Robert de Cotte): the gallery with its Corinthian colonnade is on a level with the king's apartments (for the royal family only).

Musée de l'Histoire de France (Museum of the History of France): the history of France from the 17th to 19th c. in paintings and sculpture. (Visits by prior arrangement only. Information: Office du Tourisme, 7 Rue des Réservoirs, 78-Versailles, tel. 9 50 36 22.)

Opéra (opera-house – guided tours only): the plans for an opera-house at Versailles were drawn up by Jacques-Ange Gabriel (1698–1782) for Louis XV. It took only two years to build (1768–70) and was completed for the wedding of the future Louis XVI to Marie-Antoinette. Like the palace chapel and the east façade of the Louvre (see entry) it has a colonnade of Ionic columns. With its gilded, marble and mirror décor it is tastefully furnished to fit in with the rest of the palace.

The Park of Versailles

Palace and park together form one unit: without the palace the vast park would lack a focal point and lose its function as an imposing context for the Royal Court while without the park the palace would seem little more than an enormous building complex, a pent-up power source, lacking an appropriate setting. This is borne out by the history of the park since the plans for it were completed before the final plans (the Hall of Mirrors and the wings) for the palace took shape. On the other

▼ *Versailles (Bassin d'Apollon, Allée Royale/Tapis Vert, Palace)*

hand the way the park is laid out (with raised lawns, for example) conforms to the requirement to extend the imposing bulk of the palace out into the park.

The Park of Versailles is the perfect example of French landscape gardening in the 17th c. Its creator, André Le Nôtre (1613–1700), was the son of a gardener in the royal Jardins des Tuileries (see entry) in Paris and in this, his great masterpiece, he drew on his earlier landscape gardening for the Tuileries and for Vaux-le-Vicomte (see entry) in particular.

The main features of the "French gardens" (symmetry, geometrical topiary) which can rightly be described as unnatural, correspond to the ideals of French Classicism which saw these as expressing man's mastery over nature. The relationship between the palace and the park is of profound significance in so far as the palace symbolises the power of the monarch over his people in its domination of the park which, by its mastery over nature, reflects the Sun King's own mastery over nature. This is at its most apparent in the "Bassins" and the "Grand Canal" where artificial means are used to ensure that the water is always still.

The "English Gardens" near the Petit Trianon were added to Le Nôtre's French Gardens in the 18th c. and the contrast in the two styles is obvious. The English landscape garden copies nature by artificial means, with the possibility of acting out "genuine" rural life in its little "hamlet".

The Trianons (small châteaux) were the king's only private domain at Versailles. Elsewhere they were subject to the same rules of etiquette and ceremonial as all the other members of the royal court.

Château et Parc de Versailles

Tour

Bassin de Neptune (1679–84, designed by Le Nôtre): sculptuary (1740 by Adam, Bouchardon and Lemoyne): Neptune, with trident, and his wife Amphitrite, with sceptre, in the centre; Oceanus, on a unicorn, and Proteus, with sea creatures, at the sides.

Parterres: on the stone terrace, with steps leading down to the parterres (open terraces), there are four bronze statues (Bacchus, Apollo, Antony, a silenus) and two fine marble vases with reliefs by Antoine Coysevox (Turkish War and Peace Treaties of Aix-la-Chapelle and Nijmegen).

Parterre du Nord: the cosmic forces are represented by 24 statues in groups of four – the seasons and times of day, elements, continents, temperaments and literature.

Parterre d'Eau (centre): two pools with 24 bronzes, allegorical representations of the French rivers.

Parterre du Midi: the southern section of the terraces, with sumptuous flower ornamentation. View of the Orangery looking southwards.

Pièces d'Eau Suisses: behind the Orangery is the pool dug by the Royal Swiss Guard.

Bosquet de la Salle de Bal (Bosquet des Rocailles): an amphitheatre made out of natural stone for games and dancing (can only be visited during the fountains display).

Parterre de Latone: Latona is the Latin name for Leto, wife of Zeus, who is portrayed in this pool with her children Diana and Apollo fleeing from the wicked Lycians whom Zeus punishes by turning them into frogs.

Allée Royale (Tapis Vert): the royal avenue, also designated the "green carpet", runs between the pools of Latona and Apollo in the long axis of the park.

Colonnade (1685): Jules Hardouin-Mansart created this circular arcade (Ionic marble columns) as a particularly elegant setting for festivities (guided tours only).

Bassin d'Apollon: the figure of Apollo in the sun chariot (1670, Jean-Baptiste Tuby) is an allegory of the "Sun King", Louis XIV.

Canal: in Louis XIV's time golden gondolas, presented to him by the Republic of Venice, floated on the waters of the "Grand Canal" and the "Petit Canal".

Grand Trianon (1678–88): this little château, built for Louis XIV by Jules Hardouin-Mansart and Robert de Cotte, served as his own private domain, free from the etiquette of the court, where he and his favourite, Madame de Maintenon, each had their own wings. Napoleon was responsible for its subsequent restoration which is why its décor is partly Baroque and partly Empire (furniture).

Petit Trianon (1763–7, architect: Jacques-Ange Gabriel): Louis XV had this little château built for his mistresses. Louis XVI gave it to his queen, Marie-Antoinette.

English garden: this was laid out on the site of Louis XV's botanical gardens for Marie-Antoinette and contains a little hamlet with a farm, dairy, mill and dove-cot. Also worth seeing: Temple d'Amour (temple of love, 1778), Belvedere (octagonal pavilion, 1777), the Queen's Theatre (1780), French Pavilion (Gabriel, 1750).

Bosquet des Dômes: all that remains of the fine pavilion are its base, statues and reliefs. In the middle of the grove stands the group of Titans by Gaspard Marsy.

Bosquet des Bains d'Apollon: the Romantic-style trimmings were added to the famous Apollo group at a later date.
Ile des Enfants: on the NW edge of this grove there is a group of cherubs (*putti*) as playing children (1710) which dates from the time when the ageing Louis XIV wanted to see representations of "more youth".

*Bois de Vincennes C/D6

Location
SE outskirts (12th arr.)

Métro
Porte Dorée, Château de Vincennes

Buses
46, 86

The Bois de Vincennes on the SE edge of the city is the counterpart of the Bois de Boulogne (see entry) in the W and is roughly the same size. It lies on the Boulevard Périphérique and is bordered on the S and E by the Marne.
The forest here was enclosed for hunting by Philippe II Auguste in the 13th c. and in the 17th c. it was already becoming popular for outings. Louis XV restocked it with trees. Napoleon III gave it to the city of Paris for a park and nowadays its paths, tracks and man-made lakes make the Bois de Vincennes an attraction in its own right, apart from all else that it has to offer.
Lac Daumesnil: it is possible to walk around the lake and on the two islands (café-restaurant) reached by a small bridge. Boats can be hired for rowing on the lake.
See Zoo de Paris.
Lac de Saint-Mande.
See Château de Vincennes.
Parc Floral (gardens): the Parc Floral was established here following on from the Flower Show in 1969 and is a venue for art exhibitions as well as annual flower displays. It has an aquarium with exotic fish and reptiles as well as a sculpture garden, lake, children's playground and restaurant (open daily 9.30 a.m.–6 p.m.).
Cartoucherie (Théâtre du Soleil): See Practical Information, Theatres.
Lac des Minimes: rowing boats for hire, café-restaurant (on the small peninsula).
Hippodrome de Vincennes: see Practical Information, Sport.

*Château de Vincennes (castle)

Location
Vincennes, Avenue de Paris, E outskirts

Métro
Chateau de Vincennes

Bus
56

Times of opening
1 Oct.–31 March: 10–11.30 a.m. and 1.30–4 p.m.; 1 April–30 Sept.: 9.30 a.m.–12 noon and 1.30–5 p.m.; closed Tues.

Looking at the Château of Vincennes as it is today, a combination of medieval fortifications and Baroque castle, it is relatively easy to trace its history in architectural terms. The walls and nine towers of the fortification with the finest donjon (keep) in France enclose a spacious inner courtyard with four pavilions (living quarters) dating from the 17th c.
From the 11th c. the Forest of Vincennes (see Bois de Vincennes) belonged to kings of France who built a hunting lodge here (12th–13th c.) which became a castle (14th c.) and was finally one of their favourite residences (15th c.). With the defeat of the Fronde the castle became the prison for those opposed to absolutist monarchy in particular (the Prince de Condé, Cardinal Retz) and a century later for those opposed to the monarchy in general (Diderot, Mirabeau; the Marquis de Sade was also a prisoner here for several years). Cardinal

Mazarin ordered the building of the Pavillon du Roi and the Pavillon de la Reine in the 17th c. and the young King Louis XIV spent his honeymoon here in 1661.
Used as an arsenal by Napoleon, the castle was restored in the reign of Napoleon III by Viollet-le-Duc. Further restoration was required after 1944 because of the serious damage inflicted by German troops during their retreat.
Worth seeing:
Donjon (keep, *c.* 1330): this impressive keep served both as watch-tower and living quarters. It is five storeys high (52 m – 170 ft) with walls 3 m (10 ft) thick. The keep has four round towers at the corners and is surrounded by walls and a moat. (The tower-rooms were prison cells; museum since 1934.)
Ground floor: kitchen and stores; 1st floor: hall for receptions, study; 2nd floor: royal bedchamber (where Henry V of England died of dysentery in 1422) and chapel; 3rd floor: royal suite of rooms and treasury; 4th floor: servants' quarters; 5th floor: armoury. (Fine view from the roof terrace.)
Sainte-Chapelle (1379–1552): modelled on the Sainte-Chapelle (see entry) of the royal palace on the Ile de la Cité, the architecture of this palace chapel is still Gothic (Flamboyant façade, etc.) despite its not being complete until the Renaissance (beautiful Renaissance windows in the choir).
In the N oratory is the tomb of the Duc d'Enghien, the last Prince de Condé, shot on Napoleon's orders in 1814. (A column outside the walls at the foot of the Tour de la Reine marks the spot where he died.)
Pavillon de la Reine, Pavillon du Roi (1654–61): these are the last of the castle buildings and the work of Louis Le Vau. The Pavillon de la Reine was the home of Anne of Austria, the mother of Louis XIV. Cardinal Mazarin died in the Pavillon du Roi in 1661.

*Zoo de Paris (zoological gardens; also: Zoo de Vincennes) C/D6

Location
W section of the Bois de Vincennes (12th arr.)

Métro
Porte Dorée

Buses
46, 84

Times of opening
9 a.m.–6 p.m. daily

The zoo has a great many large open-air enclosures and fits well into the recreation area of the Bois de Vincennes (see entry).
The large number of native and foreign species (*c.* 600 mammals and 1700 birds) take up 17 ha (40 acres) of land and there is heated accommodation for the animals in the winter months.
From the 72 m (235 ft) high concrete "Rocks" one has a view over the Bois de Vincennes and its castle and, with good visibility, the eastern part of Paris.

Practical Information A–Z

Advance Booking (Location)

Advance booking (location) of tickets for theatre, opera, ballet, etc. is usually done over the phone (if one speaks French).

Tickets can also be bought in advance at several theatres and concert halls. The exact details are given in "L'Officiel" and "Pariscope" (see Programmes of Events).

There are also ticket agencies, especially around the Opéra and Champs-Elysées.

Airports (Aéroports)

Le Bourget

The smallest of Paris's airports, 40 km (25 miles) N of Paris. Information: tel. 8 34 93 90.
Connections with Paris:
Car: Autoroute A1, 40–70 min. (City centre).
Bus: RATP 350 (Gare du Nord, Gare de l'Est; 10th arr.) 30 min., RATP 152 (Porte de la Villette; 19th arr.) 25 min.

Charles-de-Gaulle/Roissy

50 km (30 miles) N. Information: tel. 8 62 22 80.
Connections with Paris:
Car: Autoroute A1, 50–90 min. (City centre).
Bus: RATP 350 (Gare du Nord, Gare de l'Est; 10th arr.) 50 min., RATP 351 (Place de la Nation; 12th arr.) 40 min. Cars Air France (Aérogare Centre Internationale, Porte Maillot, 16th arr.) 30 mins.
Rail: SNCF "Roissy Rail" (Gare du Nord; 10th arr.) 30 min.

Orly (Sud/Ouest)

14 km (9 miles) S. Information: tel. 6 87 12 34.
Connections with Paris:
Car: Autoroute A6, 40–60 min. (City centre).
Bus: RATP 215 (Place Denfert-Rochereau; 14th arr.) 25 min., RATP 183A (Porte de Choisy; 13th arr.) 50 min. Cars Air France (Aérogare des Invalides; 7th arr.) 40 min.
Rail: RER line C, also called "Orly-Rail".

Antique Shops (Antiquités)

Shops

Le Village Suisse
78 Avenue de Suffren (15th arr.); tel. 3 06 26 39
Métro: La Motte-Picquet
Open: 10.30 a.m.–12 noon and 2–7 p.m., closed Tues. and Wed.

La Cour aux Antiquaires
54 Faubourg Saint-Honoré (8th arr.); tel 0 73 43 99
Métro: Saint-Philippe-du-Roulé
Open: 10.30 a.m.–7 p.m.; closed Mon. and weekends.

Village Saint-Paul
Lots of shops in the Rues Saint-Paul, des Jardins, Saint-Paul, de l'Ave-Maria and the Quai des Célestins
Métro: Sully-Morland
Open: 11 a.m.–7 p.m., closed Tues. and Wed.

Also in Faubourg Saint-Germain (see entry) (Rue Jacob, Rue Bonaparte, Rue des Saints-Pères, 6th arr.).

Flea Markets

See Markets

Banks/Exchange Bureaus (Banques/Change)

Banks

Times of opening: 9 a.m.–12 noon and 2–4 p.m. (closed at weekends).

Exchange Bureaus

At all Airports (see entry) the exchange bureaus are open from 6 a.m. till midnight.
There are exchange bureaus at all Railway stations (see entry) except for Montparnasse. The times of opening are the same as for the banks.

Counters open late

The following stations and airport terminals have counters that stay open late and at weekends:

Gare du Nord: 7.30 a.m.–10 p.m.
Métro: Gare du Nord.

Gare d'Austerlitz: 7.30 a.m.–11.30 p.m.
Métro: Gare d'Austerlitz.

Aérogare des Invalides: 7.30 a.m.–11 p.m.
Métro: Invalides.

Aérogare Porte Maillot: 6 a.m.–11 p.m.
Métro: Porte Maillot.

Boat Trips (Excursions en bateau)

Bateaux-Mouches

Pont de l'Alma (8th arr.); tel. 2 25 96 10 and 3 59 30 30.
Métro: Alma-Marceau.
Daily: 10 a.m.–noon and 2–5 or 7 p.m. (every 30 min.); lunch: daily (except Mon.) 1 p.m.; dinner daily 8.30 p.m.

Vedettes Paris-Tour Eiffel

Pont d'Iéna (8th arr.); tel. 5 51 33 08 and 7 05 50 00.
Métro: Iéna.
Daily: 9.30 a.m.–noon and 1.30–5.30 p.m.; Sat., Sun. 9 p.m.

Vedettes Pont-Neuf

Pont-Neuf (Square du Vert-Galant; 1st arr.); tel. 6 33 98 38.
Métro: Pont-Neuf.
Daily: 10.30, 11 a.m., noon and 1.30–5 p.m., every 30 min.

La Patache-Autobus

Cruises on the Seine and the Paris canals between Pont de la Concorde and Bassin de la Villette (19th arr.).

Embarkation points:
15 Quai Anatole-France.
Métro: Solférino.
9 a.m.–12.30 p.m. (until 2 Nov.); closed Mon., public holidays.

Corner of Quai de la Loire and Avenue Jean-Jaurés.
Métro: Jaurés.
2–5 p.m. (until 2 Nov.); closed Mon., public holidays.

Appointments one day in advance: 19 Rue d'Athènes (9th arr.); tel. 8 74 75 30.

Guided Tours

See Guided Tours

Breakdown Service (Dépannage)

Automobile Clubs

The most important addresses for motorists are the French automobile clubs.

Automobile Club de France (ACF)
6–8 Place de la Concorde (8th arr.), tel. 2 65 34 70
Métro: Concorde

Breakdown Service

A 24-hour breakdown service is obtainable on the following telephone numbers:
Tel. 5 02 14 50
Tel. 2 36 10 00
Tel. 7 97 03 69
Tel. 2 31 34 00
Tel. 5 89 89 00
Lost car keys: tel. 7 07 99 99

Emergency Service

Emergency Service Telephone Number: 17 (Police Secours)

Petrol Stations

The following petrol stations are open round-the-clock:
Garage Saint-Honoré
58 Place du Marché Saint-Honoré (1st arr.)
Antar
42 Rue Beauborg (3rd arr.)
Shell
109 Rue de Rennes (6th arr.)
Esso
1 Avenue Matignon (8th arr.)
Total
53 Rue Marcadet (18th arr.)

Traffic Information

"Inter Service Route" gives information (in French) on traffic and road conditions, tel. (day and night) 8 58 33 33.

Main Dealer Garages

BL
196 Rue St Jacques: tel. 3 25 88 10
11 bis Boulevard Raspail; tel. 5 48 40 51
10, 12 Rue de Bellefond; tel. 2 80 69 52
82–84 Boulevard Voltaire; tel. 3 55 39 17
32 Avenue de la République; tel. 7 00 26 24
23 Rue Beccaria and 12 Place d'Aligre; tel. 3 43 55 00, 3 45 02 26
25 bis Rue Boulard; tel. 3 22 35 50
56 Rue Fondary; tel. 5 79 81 51
3 Rue Mademoiselle; tel. 8 28 42 57
62 Rue St Didier; tel. 7 23 88 00
35 Rue Paul Valéry; tel. 5 01 68 10, 5 01 67 05
30 Rue de Tilsitt; tel. 7 54 55 11, 7 54 55 12
53–55 Avenue de St Ouen; tel. 228 30 70
11–13 Rue Boursault; tel. 2 93 65 65
237 Boulevard Péreire; tel. 5 74 82 80, 5 74 61 14

Workshop 38 Rue Brunel; tel. 574 50 45
114 Rue Cardinet; tel. 755 97 60
3–5 Rue des Ardennes; tel. 2 03 30 75, 206 01 80

BMW
119 Boulevard Romain-Rolland (14th arr.); tel. 7 35 27 96

Citroën
42 Cours de Vincennes (12th arr.); tel. 3 43 57 80
75 Boulevard Lefebvre (15th arr.); tel. 8 28 95 79

Fiat
5 Boulevard Saint-Germain (5th arr.); tel. 0 33 67 78

Ford
89 Boulevard Raspail (6th arr.); tel. 2 22 73 80
58 Avenue Parmentier (11th arr.); tel. 8 05 29 02
76 Rue de Longchamp (16th arr.); tel. 5 53 18 40

General Motors (Opel, Vauxhall)
65 Boulevard Vincent Auriol (13th arr.); tel. 5 85 16 20
41 Rue de Vouillé (15th arr.); tel. 2 50 43 80

Mercedes
23 Boulevard de Courcelles (8th arr.); tel. 9 24 33 33
82–84 Boulevard Voltaire (11th arr.); tel. 3 55 39 17

Peugeot (Talbot)
75–77 Rue de Réaumur (2nd arr.); tel. 2 36 87 59

Renault
6–8 Rue de Valois (1st arr.); tel. 2 61 52 35

Rolls Royce
Franco Britannic Automobile SA
21 Avenue Kléber (16th arr.); tel. 5 00 85 19

Volkswagen
48 Rue de l'Arbre Sec (1st arr.); tel. 2 60 13 21
60 Boulevard Saint Marcel (5th arr.); tel. 7 07 59 59

Calendar of Events

January

Last Sunday: the Prix d'Amérique (horse-race), Hippodrome de Vincennes (see Sport).

March

Palm Sunday: the Prix du Président de la République (horse-race), Hippodrome d'Auteuil (see Sport).

Other events in March:

Festival International du Son.

Salon des Indépendants (Spring exhibition of visual arts) in the Grand Palais.

April

Foire Internationale (Paris International Fair): Parc des Expositions, Porte de Versailles (lasts until May).

May

International tennis championships, Stade Roland-Garros (see Sport).

Festival de l'Ile-de-France: concerts, guided visits. Information: 15 Avenue Montaigne (8th arr.); tel. 7 23 40 84 (lasts until July).

"Nuits de Sceaux" (music festival at Sceaux), see Excursions. Information: Royal Festival, 10 Rue Royale (1st arr.); tel. 2 60 31 84 (lasts until June).

Quatorze Juillet (Military parade on the Champs-Elysées)

June

Festival du Marais (music and drama in the Marais quarter). Information: 68 Rue François-Miron (4th arr.); tel. 8 87 74 31 (lasts until July).

July

14th July (Quatorze Juillet): Fête Nationale (national holiday) with military parade, dancing and fireworks.

Other events in July:
Festival Estival de Paris (Paris summer festival); classical and contemporary music.
Information: 5 Place des Ternes (17th arr.); tel. 2 27 12 68 (lasts until September).

Final stage of the Tour de France with the finish in the Champs-Elysées.

September

Salon d'Automne (autumn exhibition of visual arts) in the Grand Palais.

Internationale des Antiquaires (biennial antique dealers' fair, last held in 1980 in the Grand Palais; on until October).

Biennale de Paris
Exhibitions and happenings by young international avant-garde artists, all sections of the visual arts (biennial, last held in 1980; on until November).

Festival de la Danse (Ballet festival): important international ballet gathering (on until November).
Information: Main Tourist Office; tel. 7 23 61 72 (see Information).

Festival d'Automne (autumn festival): contemporary music, jazz, theatre, folklore (on until December).
Information: Main Tourist Office; tel. 7 23 61 72 (see Information).

October

Salon de l'Automobile (International car show): Parc des Expositions, Porte de Versailles.

International Film Festival.

Vendanges de Montmartre (Montmartre's wine harvest and wine festival held in the last vineyard in Paris, located on the corner of the Rue des Saules and the Rue de l'Abreuvoir as a reminder of the past).

The Prix de l'Arc de Triomphe (horse-race), Hippodrome de Longchamp (see Sport).

November

11th November: Armistice Day ceremony at the Arc de Triomphe (Anniversary of the armistice of 1918).

Camping

There are more than 100 camping sites in the Région Ile-de-France. The following bodies supply information in Paris:

Camping Club de France
218 Boulevard Saint-Germain (7th arr.); tel. 5 48 30 03
Métro: Bac.

Fédération Française de Camping et Caravaning
78 Rue de Rivoli (4th arr.); tel. 2 72 84 08
Métro: Châtelet.

Car Hire (Location de voitures)

Bail Auto
22 Place Vendôme (1st arr.); tel. 2 61 53 52.

Alfa
145 Rue de l'Université (7th arr.); tel. 5 51 49 69.

Europcar
42 Avenue de Saxe (7th arr.); tel. 2 73 35 20.

Hertz
Invalides Air-Terminal (7th arr.); tel. 5 51 20 49.

Autorent
11 Rue Casimir-Périer (7th arr.); tel. 5 55 53 49.

Avis
60 Rue de Ponthieu (8th arr.); tel. 2 25 82 50.

Central Auto Lafayette
4 Rue Buffault (9th arr.); tel. 7 70 54 81.

Hertz
12 Rue de Rocroi (10th arr.); tel. 2 85 32 03.

Eurocar
48 Avenue du Maine (15th arr.); tel. 7 34 89 83.

Cemeteries (Cimetières)

Cimetière de Montmartre

Main entrance: Rue Caulaincourt, under the bridge (18th arr.).
Métro: Place Clichy.
Open daily: 1 April–30 Sept.: 7.30 a.m.–6 p.m.; 1 Oct.–31 March: 9 a.m.–5 p.m.
Paris's third largest cemetery (1795) with the graves of Heinrich Heine (Avenue Hector Berlioz), Théophile Gautier (Avenue Cordier), Edgar Degas (Avenue Montebello), Jacques Offenbach (Avenue des Anglais), Stendhal (Avenue de la Croix) and many other famous people.

Cimetière de Montparnasse

Main entrance: Boulevard Edgar Quinet (14th arr.).
Métro: Edgar Quinet, Raspail.
Open: 10 a.m.–noon and 1.30–5 p.m.; closed Tues.

Second largest cemetery (1824) with the graves of Charles Baudelaire (Avenue de l'Ouest), Guy de Maupassant (in the SE), Ossip Zadkine (Avenue de l'Ouest) and André Citroën (Avenue Thierry).

Cimetière du Père-Lachaise

Main entrance: Boulevard de Ménilmontant (20th arr.).
Métro: Père-Lachaise, Philippe Auguste.
Open: daily 8.30 a.m.–5 p.m. (1 April–30 Sept.: 8.30 a.m.–6 p.m.).
Paris's largest and finest cemetery, named after the father confessor of Louis XIV, Père La Chaise. Monument of the Communards who were shot here at the "Mur des Fédérés" in 1871 and memorial for the victims of the German concentration camps. Also park and "City of the Dead" where many famous people are buried: Molière, La Fontaine, Balzac, Marcel Proust, Oscar Wilde, and Guillaume Apollinaire, David, Delacroix, Chopin, Bizet, Dr Guillotin (inventor of the guillotine), Edith Piaf.
(A plan of the graves is obtainable at the "Gardien" entrance.)

Dog Cemetery
(Cimetière des Chiens)

Pont de Clichy, 92-Asnières; tel. 7 93 87 04.
Métro: Porte de Clichy, Bus: 139, 140.
Open daily: 9–11.45 a.m., 2–5.45 p.m.; Sun. 2–5.45 p.m.

Chemists (Pharmacies)

Open at Night

Pharmacie des Arts
106 Boulevard Montparnasse (14th arr.); tel. 3 26 56 20
Métro: Vavin
Open: until 1 a.m.

Pharmacie Dhery
84 Avenue des Champs-Elysées (8th arr.); tel. 2 56 02 41
Métro: Franklin-D.-Roosevelt
Open: 24 hours.

Pharmacie Machelou
5 Place Pigalle (9th arr.); tel. 8 78 38 12
Métro: Pigalle
Open: until 1.30 a.m.

Pharmacie Mozart
14 Avenue Mozart (16th arr.); tel. 5 27 38 17
Métro: Muette
Open: until midnight.

Church Services (Services, Cultes)

Information

Information regarding all the churches, church services and religious communities in Paris is available from the following address:
Centre Religieux International: Palais des Congrès, Porte Maillot (17th arr.); tel. 7 58 21 47.

Catholic
37 Rue Spontini (16th arr.); tel. 7 04 31 49.
Métro: Porte Dauphine.

Protestant (Lutheran)
25 Rue Blanche (9th arr.); tel. 5 26 79 43.
Métro: Trinité.

Reformed
4 Rue de l'Oratoire (1st att.).
Métro: Louvre.

Jewish
44 Rue de la Victoire (9th arr.).
Métro: Trinité.

Services in English

British Embassy Church
5 Rue d'Aguesseau,
Métro: Madeleine/Concorde.

Christ Church
Boulevard Victor-Hugo.
Métro:
Neuilly-sur-Seine.

Saint-Georges
7 Rue Auguste-Vacquerie.
Métro: Kleber.

Eglise Ecossaise
17 Rue Bayard.
Métro: F. de Rooseveldt.

Cathédrale Américaine Sainte-Trinité
23 Avenue George-V.
Métro: Georges V.

Eglise Américaine de Paris
Quai d'Orsay.
Métro: Invalides/Chambre des Députés.

Paris A–Z, see Notre-Dame (10, 11.30 a.m.); see Saint-Eustache (11 a.m.); see Saint-Sulpice (noon); see Madeleine (11 a.m.).
Russian Cathedral (10 a.m.); 12 Rue Daru (8th arr.).
Métro: Ternes.

Cinémathèques

Cinémathèque Chaillot
Palais de Chaillot, corner of Avenue Albert-de-Mun and Avenue du Président-Wilson (16th arr.); tel. 7 04 24 24

Cinémathèque du Centre National d'Art et de Culture Georges Pompidou
Rue Rambuteau (corner of Rue Saint-Merri, 4th arr.); tel. 2 78 35 57.

Currency/Currency Regulations

Currency

The unit of currency is the French franc (F) which is made up of 100 centimes. There are banknotes for 10, 50 and 500 francs, and coins in denominations of 5, 10 and 20 centimes and ½, 1, 2, 5 and 10 francs.

Currency Regulations

There are no restrictions on the import of French or foreign currency. The export of foreign currency in cash is permitted up to a value of 5000 francs or to any higher amount which has been declared on entry into France. Up to 5000 French francs may be exported. It is advisable to take travellers' cheques and/or Eurocheque cards. Credit cards may also be used.

Customs Regulations

Visitors to France are allowed the usual duty-free allowances of alcohol and tobacco, etc. For goods bought in ordinary shops in Britain or another EEC country (i.e. duty and tax paid) the allowances are 300 cigarettes or 150 cigarillos or 75 cigars or 400 g of tobacco; 1½ litres of alcoholic drinks over 38·8° proof or 3 litres of alcoholic drinks not over 38·8° proof or 3 litres of fortified or sparkling wine, plus 4 litres of still table

Galeries Lafayette

wine; 75 g of perfume; and 375 cc of toilet-water. For goods bought in a duty-free shop, on a ship or on an aircraft, the allowances are two-thirds of these amounts (250 g of tobacco); the allowances of tobacco goods are doubled for visitors from outside Europe.

The duty-free allowances on return to Britain are the same as those for British visitors to France.

Department Stores (Grands Magasins)

La Samaritaine
75 Rue de Rivoli (1st arr.)
Métro: Châtelet, Hôtel-de-Ville.

Aux Trois Quartiers
17 Boulevard de la Madeleine (8th arr.)
Métro: Madeleine.

Galeries Lafayette
40 Boulevard Haussmann (9th arr.)
Métro: Chaussée d'Antin.

Au Printemps
64 Boulevard Haussmann (9th arr.)
Métro: Havre-Caumartin.

Diplomatic and Consular Offices in France (Ambassades)

United Kingdom

Embassy
35 Rue du Faubourg St-Honoré
F-75008 Paris; tel. (1) 2 66 91 42
Consular section: tel. 2 60 33 06

Consulates-General
105–9 Rue du Faubourg St-Honoré
F-75008 Paris
Tel. (1) 2 66 91 42

United States of America

Embassy
2 Avenue Gabriel
F-75008 Paris
Tel. (1) 2 96 12 02 and 2 61 80 75

Consulates-General
(Consular Section of Embassy)
2 Avenue Gabriel
F-75008 Paris
Tel. (1) 2 96 12 02 and 2 61 80 75
(Visas Section of Embassy)
2 Rue St-Florentin
F-75001 Paris
Tel. (1) 2 96 12 02 and 2 61 80 75

Canada

Embassy
35 Avenue Montaigne
F-75008 Paris
Tel. (1) 2 25 99 55

Consular Section
4 Rue Ventadour
F-75001 Paris
Tel. (1) 0 73 15 83

Electricity (Courant electrique)

Most electrical connections in Paris have been changed to 220 V but some hotels still have 110 V sockets. When sockets are unmarked it is better to ask.

Excursions (Excursions)

Visitors to Paris usually have little time for excursions except to Versailles and Fontainebleau.

The following places near Paris are of interest:

Breteuil (Park, Château)

35 km (22 miles) SW; take N306 to Saint-Remy-lès-Chevreuse, N838 left to Les Molières, D40 right towards Cernay, turn off to the right after approx. 5 km (3 miles).
RER-line B: Saint-Remy-lès-Chevreuse then by bus to the château.
Open daily: Park: 10 a.m.–6 p.m., Château: 2–6 p.m. (Sun. 11 a.m.–6 p.m.).
Restored 17th c. château. Historical attraction and appropriate setting for concerts and events of the Festival Estival de Paris (see Calendar of events).
The park of the château was laid out by Le Nôtre.

Champs (Park, Château)

20 km (13 miles) E; take N34 to Neuilly-sur-Marne, D33 right to Noisy-le-Grand, D75 left to Champs-sur-Marne.
Open: 10 a.m.–5 p.m., closed Tues.
The Château of the Marquise de Pompadour, mistress of Louis XV, at Champs-sur-Marne (formerly a village) dates from the early 18th c. Its sumptuously decorated and panelled interior is a magnificent example of original "Louis Quinze".

Fontainebleau (Forest)

The Forest of Fontainebleau (Forêt de Fontainebleau) is a popular recreation area (*c.* 23,000 ha – 57,000 acres). Walks are signposted. The wild and romantic scenery of the famous "Gorges de Franchard" is used as a training ground for mountaineering.
(Information: Club Alpin Français, 7 Rue La Boëtie, 8th arr.; tel. 2 65 54 45.)

Meudon (Terrace, Museum, Woods)

10 km (6 miles) SW; N10 to Pont de Sèvres, right: N187 to Meudon.
Open daily: 8 a.m.–5.30 p.m. (1 April–30 Sept.: 8 a.m.–8 p.m.).

The "Terrasse de Meudon" (terrace of the former château) affords beautiful views of the Seine valley and Paris. Other attractions: "Bois de Meudon" (wooded resort), aviation museum and Meudon Museum (see Museums).

Sceaux (Museum, Park, Château)

10 km (6 miles) SW.
Tel. 6 61 19 03; RER-line B: Parc de Sceaux.
Times of opening: see museum.
The former château built for Colbert, Minister of Finance, was destroyed during the French Revolution. The present château dates from the 19th c. and houses a museum (see Museums). During the summer a noted series of concerts ("Nuits de Sceaux") takes place in the Orangery of the château (built by François Mansart in the 17th c.). The park, designed by Le Nôtre, is one of the finest in the Ile de France.

Hotels (Selection)

In Paris reservations can only be made at the hotel in person. The official hotel reservation bureaus (see Information, Municipal Tourist Office) book rooms for the same day only.

Price Categories

The prices of the cheapest single room and the most expensive double room are established in accordance with the official state classification.

Luxury Hotels (Grand Luxe)

****Ritz, 15 Place Vendôme (1st arr.), 560–760F.

****Nova Park Elysées, Rue Pierre Charron (8th arr.), 1000–4000F.; suites to 35,000F.

****Meurice, 228 Rue de Rivoli (1st arr.), 443–748F.

****George-V, 31 Avenue George-V (8th arr.), 500–720F.

****Plaza-Athénée, 23–25 Avenue Montaigne (8th arr.), 540–650F.

****Crillon (de), 10 Place de la Concorde (8th arr.), 560–680F.

****L Scribe, 2 Rue Scribe (9th arr.), 550–750F.; apartment from 1000F.

****L Warwick, 5 Rue de Berri (8th arr.), from 550F.

Top Class Hotels

****Louvre Concorde, Place André Malraux (1st arr.), 320–370F.

****Edouard-VII, 39 Avenue de l'Opéra (2nd arr.), 315–400F.

****Littré, 9 Rue Littré (6th arr.), 265–390F.

****Relais Christine, 3 Rue Christine (6th arr.), 320–540F.

****Montalembert, 3 Rue Montalembert (7th arr.), 160–290F.

****San-Regis, 12 Rue Jean-Goujon (8th arr.), 265–420F.

****Commodore, 12 Boulevard Haussmann (9th arr.), 300–385F.

****Baltimore, 88 bis Avenue Kléber (16th arr.), 290–490F.

****Regent's Garden Hotel, 6 Rue Pierre-Demours (17th arr.), 220–300F.

****Map-Terrass, 12–14 Rue J.-de-Maistre (18th arr.), 210–290F.

****Abbaye Saint-Germain, 10 Rue Cassette (6th arr.), 195–300F.

***Deux-Iles (des), 59 Rue Saint Louis en l'Ile (4th arr.), 160–200F.

***Observatoire, 107 Boulevard St-Michel (5th arr.), 103–178F.

***La Bourdonnais, 3 Avenue de la Bourdonnais (7th arr.), from 145F.

***Bradford, 10 Rue Saint-Philippe-du-Roule (8th arr.), 180–200F.

***Blanche Fontaine, 34 Rue Fontaine (9th arr.), 155–185F.

***Terminus-Nord, 12 Boulevard Denain (10th arr.), 160–275F.

***Aiglon, 232 Boulevard Raspail (14th arr.), 135–185F.

***Frémiet, 6 Avenue Frémiet (16th arr.), 160–290F.

***Balmoral, 6 Rue du Général-Lanrezac (17th arr.), 170–255F.

Very Comfortable Hotels

**Ducs d'Anjou, 1 Rue Sainte-Opportune (1st arr.), 140–160F.

**Bretonnerie, 22 Rue Sainte-Croix-Bretonnerie (4th arr.), 70–200F.

**Nice, 155 Boulevard du Montparnasse (6th arr.), 122–145F.

**Saint-Germain, 88 Rue du Bac (7th arr.), 134–210F.

**L'Ouest-Hotel, 3 Rue du Rocher (8th arr.), 86–190F.

**Résidence Sémard, 15 Rue P.-Sémard (9th arr.), 95–140F.

**Nord (du), 17 Rue A.-Thomas (10th arr.), 90–140F.

**Carlton Palace, 207 Boulevard Raspail (14th arr.), 140–150F.

**Hotel Prima-Lepic, 29 Rue Lepic (18th arr.), 88–138F.

**Luxia, 8 Rue Seveste (18th arr.), 50–155F.

Good Average Hotels

*Sansonnet, 48 Rue de la Verrerie (4th arr.), 49–120F.

*Elysée (de), 12 Rue des Saussaies (8th arr.), 61–160F.

*Lux, 8 Avenue Corbera (12th arr.), 45–108F.

*Marceau, 13 Rue Jules-César (12th arr.), 46–130F.

*Trois Gares (des), 1 Rue Jules César (12th arr.), 45–95F.

See Inexpensive Accommodation

Inexpensive Accommodation

Inexpensive Accommodation

For Young People

There are several places offering inexpensive accommodation specially for young people, some of which are listed below:

Centre International de Séjour de Paris (CISP)
6 Avenue Maurice Ravel (12th arr.); tel. 3 43 19 01.
Métro: Picpus, Bel-Air, Porte de Vincennes.
200 beds; breakfast.

Le Fauconnier
11 Rue du Fauconnier (4th arr.); tel. 2 77 85 85.
Métro: Porte-Marie, Saint-Paul.
Breakfast.

Foyer International d'Accueil de la Mission Universitaire Française
18 Rue Mabillon (6th arr.); tel. 6 33 55 09.
Open: 1 June–1 Nov.
50 beds; no meals.

Foyer International d'Accueil de la Ville de Paris
30 Rue Cabanis (14th arr.); tel. 5 89 89 15.
Métro: Glacière.
430 beds; very suitable for groups; restaurant.

Maison Internationale des Jeunes
4 Rue Titou (11th arr.); tel. 3 71 99 21.
Métro: Faidherbe-Chaligny, Boulets-Montreuil.
150 beds; no meals.

B.V.J.-Centre International de Paris
20 Rue Jean-Jacques Rousseau (1st arr.); tel. 2 36 88 18.
Métro: Louvre, Halles, Palais-Royal.
170 beds; restaurant.

Maison des Clubs U.N.E.S.C.O.
13 Rue Vaugirard (6th arr.); tel. 3 26 50 78.
Métro: Odéon.
70 beds; no meals.

43 Rue de la Glacière (13th arr.); tel. 3 36 00 63.
100 beds; no meals.

Résidence International du Comité d'Accueil
14 Passage de la Bonne-Graine (11th arr.); tel. 3 55 62 66.
Métro: Ledru-Rollin.
160 beds; no meals.

Foyer International d'Accueil de Paris-Défense
19 Rue Salvador-Allende, 92006-Nanterre; tel. 7 25 91 34.
RER: Nanterre-Préfecture.
395 beds; cafeteria, restaurant.

Information (Renseignements)

Comité Régional de Tourisme

43 Avenue de Friedland, 75008-Paris.
Non-verbal information only and brochures for the Région Ile-de-France (surroundings of Paris).

Information Bureau in the City Hall

Hôtel de Ville, 29 Rue de Rivoli (4th arr.); tel. 2 78 13 00
Métro: Hôtel de Ville
Open: 8.45 a.m.–6.30 p.m., closed Sun., public holidays.
Provides general information about Paris.

Office de Tourisme de Paris
127 Avenue des Champs-Elysées (8th arr.); tel. 7 23 61 72
Open: 9 a.m.–10 p.m.
Information, brochures, hotel reservations (not by telephone) for Paris and surroundings. This head office is often extremely busy and it is advisable to apply to the branch offices for information and hotel reservations, but most brochures are obtainable at the head office only.

The branch offices dealing with hotel reservations and brochures are located in the four railway stations and the Congress Centre at Porte Maillot.
Gare du Nord (Métro: Gare du Nord); tel. 5 26 94 82
Open: Mon.–Sat. 8.30 a.m.–10 p.m.
Gare de l'Est (Métro: Gare de l'Est); tel. 6 07 17 73
Open: Mon.–Sat. 7 a.m.–1 p.m. and 5–11 p.m.
Gare des Invalides (Métro: Invalides); tel. 5 50 32 30
Open: Mon.–Sat. 9 a.m.–10 p.m.
Gare de Lyon (Métro: Gare de Lyon); tel. 3 43 33 24
Open: Mon.–Sat. 6.30 a.m.–noon and 5–11 p.m.
Palais des Congrès: Porte Maillot (17th arr.); tel. 7 58 22 45.
Métro: Porte Maillot.
(These times of opening only apply to the main season from 1 April–30 Sept.)

RATP tourist information centres
RATP, Paris's public transport undertaking (see Public transport), has two tourist information centres (Services touristiques) supplying general information and tourist tickets for bus, Métro, RER. They also book short weekend trips.
53 bis Quai des Grands-Augustins (6th arr.)
Métro: Pont-Neuf, Saint-Michel
Place de la Madeleine, next to the flower market (8th arr.)
Métro: Madeleine.
(Times of opening: see Travel bureaus)

Specially for Young People

The following organisations specialise in helping young travellers:
Centre d'Information et de Documentation de la Jeunesse (CIDJ)

101 Quai Branly (15th arr.); tel. 5 66 40 20
Métro: Bir-Hakeim
Open: 9 a.m.–7 p.m., closed Sun.
Information of every kind regarding accommodation, events, jobs.

Service Parisien d'Accueil aux Etudiants Etrangers
6 Rue Jeyn Calvin (5th arr.); tel. 7 07 26 22
Métro: RER Luxembourg
Open: Mon.–Fri. 9 a.m.–6 p.m.
Bureau for receiving foreign students: general information regarding accommodation, events, studying in France.

Lost Property (Bureau des Objets Trouvés)

Lost Property

Bureau des Objets Trouvés:
36 Rue des Morillons (15th arr.); tel. 5 31 14 80 and 5 31 82 10.
Métro: Convention.

Markets (Marchés)

Flea Markets
(Marchés aux Puces)

Porte de Clignancourt
Paris A–Z see Puces.

Porte de Montreuil (20th arr.)
Métro: Porte de Montreuil
Open: Sat.–Mon. 6 a.m.–5 p.m.

Porte de Vanves (14th arr.)
Métro: Portes de Vanves
Open: Sat., Sun. 2–5 p.m.

Flowers
(Marchés aux Fleurs)

Place Louis-Lépine (4th arr.)
Métro: Cité
Open: 8 a.m.–7.30 p.m.; closed Sun.

Place de la Madeleine (8th arr.)
Métro: Madeleine
Open: 8 a.m.–7 p.m.; closed Mon.

Place des Ternes (17th arr.)
Métro: Ternes
Open: 8 a.m.–7 p.m.; closed Mon.

Stamps
(Marchés aux Timbres)

Avenue Gabriel, Avenue Marigny (8th arr.)
Métro: Champs-Elysées-Clemenceau
Open: Sat., Sun., public holidays 8 a.m.–7 p.m., Thurs. afternoon.

Clothing
(Marché de la Friperie)

Carreau du Temple, 1 Rue Dupetit-Thouars (3rd arr.)
Métro: République
Open daily: 9 a.m.–noon, Mon. 9 a.m.–7 p.m.

Street Market

Birds (Marché aux Oiseaux)	Place Louis-Lépine (4th arr.) Métro: Cité Open: Sun. 9 a.m.–7 p.m. Quai de la Mégisserie (1st arr.) Métro: Châtelet, Pont-Neuf Open: 9 a.m.–7 p.m.; closed Sun. Lots of bird and animal stalls along the Seine.
Material (Marché aux Tissus)	Marché Saint-Pierre, Place Saint-Pierre (18th arr.) Métro: Anvers Open daily; closed Sun.

Museums (Musées)

Musée de l'Affiche	18 Rue de Paradis (10th arr.) Métro: Gare de l'Est Open: noon–6 p.m.; closed Mon., Tues.
Musée de l'Air	8 Rue des Vertugadins, 92-Meudon Rail: Montparnasse Open: 10 a.m.–5 p.m. Mon., Wed., Thur., Fri.; 10 a.m.–noon and 2–5 p.m. Sat., Sun., public holidays; closed Tues.
Musée des Antiquités Nationales de France	Paris A–Z, see Saint-Germain-en-Laye
Musée de l'Armée	Paris A–Z, see Musée de l'Armée

Musée d'Art et d'Essai
Paris A–Z, see Palais de Tokyo

Musée d'Art Juif
42 Rue des Saules (18th arr.)
Métro: Lamarck-Caulaincourt
Open: 3–6 p.m. Tues., Thurs., Sun.
Jewish art, Polish religious objects.

Musée d'Art Moderne de la Ville de Paris
Paris A–Z, see Musée d'Art Moderne de la Ville de Paris

Musée des Arts Décoratifs
(Pavillon de Marsan) 107 Rue de Rivoli (1st arr.)
Métro: Palais-Royal
Open daily: 10 a.m.–noon and 2–5 p.m.; closed Mon., Tues.
History of decorative arts (furniture and everyday objects from the Middle Ages to the early 20th c.).

Musée des Arts et Traditions Populaires
6 Route du Mahatma-Gandhi, Bois de Boulogne (16th arr.)
Métro: Sablone, Porte Maillot; Bus: 73
Open daily: 10 a.m.–5.15 p.m.; closed Tues.
French folk-art.

Maison de Balzac
47 Rue Raynouard (16th arr.)
Métro: Passy, Muette
Open daily: 10 a.m.–5.40 p.m.; closed Mon., Tues.
Home of Honoré de Balzac containing numerous documents and a library of works by and about Balzac.

Musée des Bas-Reliefs
Paris A–Z, see Musée de l'Armée

Musée des Beaux-Arts de la Ville de Paris
Paris A–Z, see Petit Palais

Bibliothèque Nationale
58 Rue de Richelieu (2nd arr.)
Métro: Bourse, Palais-Royal
Open daily: noon–6 p.m.
Important exhibitions relating to books and the history of art.

Musée Bossuet
Meaux (77), 50 km (30 miles) E of Paris
Rail: from Gare de l'Est
Open: 2–6 p.m.; closed Tues., public holidays
Archaeology, art and history of the region in the former palace of Bossuet, court preacher to Louis XIV.

Musée Bourdelle
16 Rue Antoine-Bourdelle (14th arr.)
Métro: Montparnasse
Open: 10 a.m.–5.45 p.m.; closed Mon.
Works by the sculptor Bourdelle (student of Rodin) and temporary exhibitions of modern sculpture.

Musée Carnavalet
Paris A–Z, see Musée Carnavalet

Centre de la Mer et des Eaux
195 Rue Saint-Jacques (5th arr.)
Métro: Luxembourg
Open: 10 a.m.–5.30 p.m.; closed Mon.
Film shows including the research work of Jacques Cousteau.

Musée des Céramiques de Sèvres
4 Grande-Rue, 92 Sèvres
Métro: Pont de Sèvres
Open: 9.45 a.m.–noon and 1.30–5.45 p.m.; closed Tues.
Extensive collection of porcelain throughout history and from many countries.

Musée Cernuschi	7 Avenue Vélasquez (8th arr.) Métro: Villiers, Monceau Open: 10 a.m.–5.40 p.m.; closed Mon., Tues., public holidays Municipal museum of Chinese art.
Musée de la Chasse et de la Nature	(Hôtel Guénégaud) 60 Rue des Archives (3rd arr.) Métro: Rambuteau Open: 10 a.m.–6 p.m.; closed Tues., public holidays Museum of the hunt and weapons, 16th and 17th c. Flemish and German paintings.
Musée du Cinéma	(Palais de Chaillot), Place du Trocadéro (16th arr.) Métro: Trocadéro Open 9.30, 11.30 a.m., 2.30, 4.30 p.m.; closed Mon. Guided tours only. History of the cinema in documents, costumes and movie-making equipment.
Musée de Cluny	Paris A–Z, see Musée de Cluny
Musée Cognacq-Jay	25 Boulevard des Capucines (2nd arr.) Métro: Opéra, Madeleine Open: 10 a.m.–5.40 p.m.; closed Mon. A sumptuously furnished museum with Rococo interiors established by the Cognac-Jay family (founders of La Samaritaine Department Store).
Musée des Collections Historiques de la Police	Ibis, Rue des Carmes (5th arr.) Métro: Maubert-Mutualité Open: Wed., Thur. 2–5 p.m. Police historical crime museum.
Musée Condé	Paris A–Z, see Musée Condé
Musée Eugène Delacroix	6 Rue de Furstenberg (6th arr.) Métro: Saint-Germain-des-Prés Open: 9.45 a.m.–5.15 p.m.; closed Tues. Sketches and paintings by the master of the French Romantic movement.
Musée du Dix-Neuvième Siècle	(Formerly: Gare d'Orsay), Quai Anatole-France (7th arr.) Métro: Solférino "A museum of the 19th c." is due to be housed in the former station by 1983, covering every aspect of popular culture in terms of architecture, painting, sculpture, photography, etc. It will have an exhibition area of 1500 m² (1790 sq. yd).
Musée de l'Ecole Supérieure des Mines	60 Boulevard Saint-Michel (6th arr.) Métro: Luxembourg Open: 2.30–5.30 p.m.; closed Mon. Geological collection of more than 100,000 different types of rock.
Musée des Enfants	12 Avenue de New-York (8th arr.) Métro: Alma-Marceau Open: 10 a.m.–5.45 p.m.; closed Mon. Children's museum with different events and exhibitions.

Musée des Equipages

Château Vaux-le-Vicomte (itinerary and visiting hours see Paris A–Z, Château Vaux-le-Vicomte)
Coaches and carriages from recent centuries.

Manufacture des Gobelins

42 Avenue des Gobelins (13th arr.)
Métro: Gobelins; Museum and guided tours of the studios
Open: Wed., Thur., Fri. 2–4 p.m.
State factory where tapestries (gobelins) are still being made by the same methods as in past centuries.

Musée Grévin

10 Boulevard Montmartre (9th arr.)
Métro: Montmartre (9th arr.)
Métro: Montmartre
Open daily: 2–7 p.m.; Sun., public holidays 1–8 p.m.
Very popular waxworks presenting historical tableaux and celebrities.

Musée Guimet

Paris A–Z, see Musée Guimet

Musée de l'Histoire de France

(Hôtel de Soubise), 60 Rue des Francs-Bourgeois (3rd arr.)
Métro: Rambuteau
Open: 2–5 p.m.; closed Tues.
History of France from the Merovingian period (7th and 8th c.) until the Second World War.

L'Historial

Rue Poulbot (near the Place du Tertre; 18th arr.)
Métro: Anvers, Pigalle
Open daily: 10 a.m.–noon and 2–6 p.m.
Historical waxworks of the Butte de Montmartre (Paris A–Z, Butte, see Montmartre)

Musée Historique de la Ville de Paris

Paris A–Z, see Musée Carnavalet

Musée de l'Homme

Paris A–Z, see Musée de l'Homme

Musée Français de l'Holographie

4 Rue Beaubourg, opposite the Centre Pompidou (see entry) (4th arr.)
Métro: Rambuteau
Open daily: noon–7 p.m.
This new museum of the laser age houses the precursors of the hologram (three-dimensional photographic images).

Maison Victor Hugo

6 Place des Vosges (4th arr.)
Métro: Saint-Paul
Open: 10 a.m.–5.40 p.m.; closed Mon., Tues., public holidays
Victor Hugo lived in this house on the Place des Vosges (see entry) between 1832 and 1848. Since 1903 it has been a museum exhibiting mementoes, furniture, illustrations of his works and 400 of his drawings.

Musée de l'Ile de France

Sceaux (92)
RER line B: Parc de Sceaux
Open daily: 2–7 p.m.; closed Tues.; Wed., Thurs., Sat., Sun., 10 a.m.–noon
The history of the Ile de France in documents, paintings, coins, ceramics and other craft objects.

Musée Instrumental du Conservatoire Supérieur de Musique de Paris

14 Rue de Madrid (17th arr.)
Métro: Europe
Open: Wed.–Sat. 2–6 p.m.
Temporary exhibitions of musical instruments.

Musée Jacquemart-André

158 Boulevard Haussmann (8th arr.)
Métro: Saint-Philippe-du-Roule
Open: 1.30–5.30 p.m.; closed Mon., Tues.
18th c. European paintings and Italian Renaissance paintings; temporary exhibitions.

Musée de Jeu de Paume

Paris A–Z, see Musée du Jeu de Paume

Musée de la Légion d'Honneur

2 Rue de Bellechasse (7th arr.)
Métro: Solférino
Open: 2–5 p.m.; closed Mon.
Orders of chivalry from the Middle Ages until the present (insignia and documents).

Musée du Louvre

Paris A–Z, see Louvre

Musée du Luxembourg

Paris A–Z, see Palais du Luxembourg

Musée de la Marine

Paris A–Z, see Musée de la Marine

Musée Marmottan

2 Rue Louis Boilly (16th arr.)
Métro: Muette
Open: 10 a.m.–6 p.m.; closed Mon.
Charming museum in a private mansion with a collection of Flemish paintings (16th c.), Empire furniture and Impressionist paintings.

Musée de Meudon

11 Rue des Pierres, below the terrace (see Excursions), Meudon (92)
Open: Wed., Thur., Sat., Sun. 2–6 p.m.
The pretty house which the poet François Rabelais lived in when he was a priest was bought by Molière's widow, Armande Béjart, after his death. Richard Wagner, Auguste Rodin and the author Louis-Ferdinand Céline later stayed here. The present museum houses mementoes of those who lived here as well as Meudon glassware, documents relating to the former Château of Meudon and Redouté roses.

Musée de la Mode et du Costume

(Palais Galliéra) 10 Avenue Pierre 1er de Serbie (16th arr.)
Open: 10 a.m.–5.40 p.m.; closed Mon., Tues., public holidays
Museum of fashion (civilian uniforms and fashionable dress from 1735 until the present).

Musée Gustave Moreau

14 Rue de la Rochefoucault (9th arr.)
Métro: Trinité
Open: 10 a.m.–1 p.m. and 2–5 p.m.; closed Mon., Tues.
The former home and studio of the symbolist painter houses a unique museum containing about 1000 paintings and 7000 drawings.

Musée des Monuments Français

Paris A–Z, see Musée des Monuments Français

Monnaie de Paris

Paris A–Z, see Monnaie de Paris

Musée de Montmartre

17 Rue Saint-Vincent and 12 Rue Cortot (18th arr.)
Métro: Anvers, Pigalle
Open: Mon.–Sat. 2.30–5.30 p.m., Sun. 11 a.m.–5.30 p.m.
History of the "Free Commune" of Montmartre.

Musée National D'Art Moderne

Paris A–Z, see Musée National d'Art Moderne

Musée National des Arts Africains et Océaniens

293 Avenue Daumesnil (12th arr.)
Métro: Porte Dorée
Open: 9.45 a.m.–noon and 1.30–5.15 p.m.; closed Tues.
Collections of African and Oceanic art.

Muséum National d'Histoire Naturelle

Paris A–Z, see Muséum National d'Histoire Naturelle

Musée National de la Renaissance

Château d'Ecouen, 95 Ecouen
Rail: Gard du Nord
Open: 9.45 a.m.–12.30 p.m. and 2–5.15 p.m.; closed Tues.
One of the most beautiful Renaissance châteaux in the Région Ile-de-France. Because of restoration work in progress only parts of it are open to the public.

Musée National des Techniques (Consérvatoire National des Arts et Métiers)

292 Rue Saint-Martin (3rd arr.)
Métro: Réaumur-Sébastopol
Open: Mon.–Sat. noon–5.45 p.m., Sun. 10 a.m.–5.30 p.m.
Technological museum: astronomy, automata, early cars and trains (models), agricultural and industrial technology, printing techniques, photography, weaving and spinning.

Musée de Neuilly

12 Rue de Centre; 92 Neuilly
Métro: Pont-de-Neuilly
Open: 2.30–5 p.m.; closed Tues., public holidays
Collection of old automata that are set in motion once a day at 3 p.m. – Museum of Woman.

Musée Nissim de Camondo

63 Rue de Monceau (17th arr.)
Métro: Villiers
Open: 10 a.m.–noon and 2–5 p.m.; closed Mon., Tues., public holidays
18th c. Rococo furniture and tapestries, costume exhibition.

Musée Notre-Dame de Paris

10 Rue du Cloître (4th arr.)
Métro: Cité
Open: during exhibitions 2–6 p.m.; closed Tues., otherwise Sat. 3–6 p.m. only.
History of the Ile-de-la-Cité.

Musée de l'Opéra

Paris A–Z, see Opéra

Musée de l'Orangerie

Jardins des Tuileries, Place de la Concorde (1st arr.)
Métro: Concorde
Open: varies according to exhibition. Usually 10 a.m.–5 p.m.; closed Tues.
"Nymphéas" by Claude Monet, Guillaume-Walter collection (Post-Impressionists).

Musée de l'Ordre de la Libération

51 bis Boulevard de Latour-Maubourg (7th arr.)
Métro: Latour Maubourg
Open: 2–5 p.m.; closed Sun.
An exhibition by the French "Order of Liberation" of

documents concerning the Resistance and the deportations during the German occupation (1940–4) as well as some of General de Gaulle's manuscripts.

Palais de la Découverte

Paris A–Z, see Palais de la Découverte.

Palais de Tokyo

Paris A–Z, see Palais de Tokyo

Musée de la Photographie

78 Rue de Paris, 91-Bièvres
Open: 10 a.m.–noon and 2–6 p.m.; closed Tues.
Rail: Gare de Lyon
Museum of the history of photography.

Musée Picasso

(Hôtel Salé), 5 Rue de Thorigny (3rd arr.)
Métro: Sébastien-Froissart
Paintings from Picasso's private collection (by Cézanne, Douanier Rousseau, Degas, Corot, Gauguin, Matisse) and works from Picasso's estate, housed since 1980 in the mansion of Aubert de Fontenay who collected the salt tax (hence "Hôtel Salé")

Musée de la Poste

34 Boulevard de Vaugirard (15th arr.)
Métro: Montparnasse
Open: 10 a.m.–5 p.m.; closed Thurs.
History of the postal service and philately.

Musée de la Préhistoire

Paris A–Z, see Saint-Germain-en-Laye

Musée de Radio-France

(Maison de Radio-France), 116 Avenue du Président Kennedy (16th arr.)
Métro: Ranelagh, Passy
Open: 10 a.m.–noon and 2–5 p.m.; closed Mon.
Radio and TV news and history of the studios of Radio-France. Tour of the studios.

Musée Rodin

Paris A–Z, see Musée Rodin

Rotonde de la Villette

1 Square Léon-Paris, Place de Stalingrad (19th arr.)
Métro: Stalingrad
Open: by prior appointment only, Mon.–Fri.
City of Paris centre for archaeological research with exhibitions concerning excavations in Paris.

Musée Roybet-Fould
Poupées anciennes

178 Boulevard Saint-Denis, 92-Courbevoie
Métro: Pont-de-Levallois
Open: 2–6 p.m.
Fine museum of dolls and toys. Sculpture by Antoine Carpeaux (19th c.).

Musée du S.E.I.T.A.

2 Avenue Robert Schuman (7th arr.)
Métro: Invalides
Open: 11 a.m.–6 p.m.; closed Sat., Sun.
Museum of the state tobacco industry.

Musée de la Serrure Bricard

1 Rue de la Perle (3rd arr.)
Métro: Chemin-Vert
Open: 10 a.m.–noon and 2–5 p.m.; closed Mon., Tues., public holidays
Old locks and wrought-iron work

Musée des Transports Urbains

60 Avenue Sainte-Marie, 94160-Saint-Mandé
Métro: Porte Dorée
Open: 15 April–31 Oct. Sat., Sun. 2.30–6 p.m.
Original Parisian urban transport vehicles.

Music

Concert Halls (Salles de Concert)

Paris is a metropolis that is famous for its music. Concerts are given almost daily in one or other of its concert halls. Details of these can be found in "L'Officiel des Spectacles" and "Pariscope".

Salle Pleyel
252 Faubourg Saint-Honoré (8th arr.); tel. 2 27 06 30.

Salle Gaveau
45 Rue La Boëtie (8th arr.); tel. 2 25 29 14.

Centre International de Paris, Palais de Congrès
Porte Maillot, 24 Boulevard Pershing (17th arr.); tel. 7 58 22 22.

Salle Cortot
78 Rue Cardinet (17th arr.); tel. 9 24 80 16.

Théâtre des Champs-Elysées
15 Avenue Montaigne (8th arr.); tel. 3 59 37 03.

Palais de Chaillot
Place du Trocadéro (16th arr.); tel. 7 27 81 15.

Radio-France
116 Avenue du Président Kennedy (16th arr.); tel. 5 24 15 16.

Opera and Light Opera

The three main venues for opera and light opera are:

Opéra
Place de l'Opéra (9th arr.); tel. 7 42 57 50.
Métro: Opéra.

Salle Favart (Opéra Comique)
5 Rue Favart (2nd arr.); tel. 7 42 72 00.
Métro: 4-Septembre.

Théâtre Musical de Paris
Place du Châtelet (4th arr.); tel. 2 33 40 00.
Métro: Châtelet.

Night-life

Cabarets and Revues

Its "Cabarets and Revues" have made Parisian night-life famous throughout the world.

A typical "Revue"

Among the best-known are:

Alcazar
62 Rue Mazarine (6th arr.); tel. 3 29 02 20.

Crazy Horse Saloon
12 Avenue Geroge-V (8th arr.); tel. 7 23 32 32.

Folies Bergère
32 Rue Richer (9th arr.); tel. 2 46 77 11.

Lido
116 Avenue des Champs-Elysées (8th arr.); tel. 5 63 11 61.

Moulin Rouge
Place Blanche (18th arr.); tel. 6 06 00 19.

Paradis Latin
28 Rue du Cardinal-Lemoine (5th arr.); tel. 3 25 28 28.

Tour Eiffel
Champ-de-Mars (15th arr.); tel. 5 50 32 70.

Discothèques

Discothèques currently in fashion include:

La Baie des Anges
23 Faubourg-du-Temple (10th arr.); tel. 2 08 54 06.
Métro: République.

Galaxy Club
40 Rue des Blancs-Manteaux (4th arr.); tel. 2 71 43 22.
Métro: Rambuteau.

La Panthère Rose
38 Rue de Ponthieu (8th arr.); tel. 3 59 76 38.
Métro: Franklin-D.-Roosevelt.

La Palace
8 Rue du Faubourg-Montmartre (9th arr.); tel. 2 46 10 87.
Métro: Rue Montmartre.

Le Tabou
33 Rue Dauphine (6th arr.); tel. 3 25 66 33.
Métro: Odéon.

Whisky à Gogo
57 Rue de Seine (6th arr.); tel. 6 33 74 99.
Métro: Odéon.

Wonder Club
38 Rue du Dragon (6th arr.); tel. 5 48 90 32.
Métro: Saint-Germain-des-Prés.

Jazz Clubs

Some suggestions for jazz fans:

Au River-Bop
67 Rue Saint-André-des-Arts; tel. 3 25 93 71.
Métro: Saint-Michel.

Slow-Club
130 Rue de Rivoli; tel. 2 38 84 30.
Métro: Louvre.

Caveau de la Montagne
18 Rue Descartes; tel. 5 34 82 39.
Métro: Monge.

Le Petit Journal
71 Boulevard Saint-Michel; tel. 3 26 28 59.
Métro: Luxembourg.

Music Halls

International and French singing stars and pop-groups appear on the bill at the following music halls:

Bobino
21 Rue de la Gaîte (14th arr.); tel. 3 22 74 84.
Métro: Edgar-Quinet.

Olympia
28 Boulevard des Capucines (2nd arr.); tel. 7 42 25 49.
Métro: Madeleine.

Night Clubs, Dance Halls

Popular night clubs and dance halls in Paris include:

La Coupole
102 Boulevard Montparnasse (14th arr.); tel. 3 20 14 20.
Métro: Vavin.

New Jimmy's
124 Boulevard Montparnasse (14th arr.).
Métro: Vavin.

Stereo-Club (Chez Simone)
6 Rue Arsène-Houssaye (8th arr.); tel 5 61 07 32.
Métro: George-V.

Striptease

A host of striptease joints, bars, sex shops and porno cinemas are located on the southern fringe of the Butte de Montmartre (see Paris A–Z, Butte, see Montmartre) between Place Pigalle and Place Clichy, and in the Rue Saint-Denis (1st arr.).

Parking (Parkings)

1st and 2nd Arrondissement

Parking Saint-Honoré
58 Place du Marché-Saint-Honoré.

Parking Vendôme
Place Vendôme.

Parking Samaritaine-Louvre
Place du Louvre (near the church of Saint-Germain-l'Auxerrois).

3rd and 4th Arrondissement

Parking Centre Beaubourg
Rue Rambuteau (underground garage of the Centre Pompidou).

Parking Sully
5 Rue Agrippa-D'Aubigné.

Parking Notre-Dame
Place du Parvis Notre-Dame.

Parking Cogedim
33 Rue Beaubourg.

5th and 6th Arrondissement

Parking Soufflot
22 Rue Soufflot.

Parking Saint-Sulpice
Place Saint-Sulpice.

Parking Mazarine
27 Rue Mazarine.

Parking Montparnasse-Raspail
138 bis Boulevard du Montparnasse.

Parking Saint-Germain
169 Boulevard Saint-Germain.

7th Arrondissement

Parking Invalides
Esplanade des Invalides (opposite 23 Rue de Constantine).

8th Arrondissement

Parking Concorde
Place de la Concorde (opposite Rue Boissy-d'Anglas).

Garages de Paris
25 Place de la Madeleine.

Ponthieu
60 Rue de Ponthieu.

Parking Champs-Elysées-George-V
Rue de Galilée (opposite 130 Avenue des Champs-Elysées).

9th Arrondissement

Parking Galéries Lafayette
54 Boulevard Haussmann.

Parking Paramount Opéra
4 Rue de la Chaussée-d'Antin.

Parking Olympia
7 Rue Caumartin.

Parking Anvers
41 Boulevard de Rochechouart.

10th Arrondissement

Parking Gare du Nord
18 Rue de Dunkerque.

14th Arrondissement

Grand Garage Raspail
14 Rue Campagne-Première.

Parking Edgar Quinet
Boulevard Edgar Quinet.

18th Arrondissement

Grand Garage de la Place Blanche
4 Rue Coustou.

Parks and Gardens (Jardins, Parcs)

Jardins Albert-Kahn

92 Boulogne-Billancourt, 6 Quai du 4 Septembre
Métro: Porte de Saint-Cloud then bus 72.
Open daily: 2–6 p.m. from 1 May to 15 Nov. closed the rest of the year.
Different types of gardens in one park.

Jardin Fleuriste de la Ville de Paris

3 Avenue de la Porte d'Auteuil (16th arr.)
Métro: Porte d'Auteuil.
Open: 1 April–30 Sept.: 10 a.m.–6 p.m.; 1 Oct.–31 March: 10 a.m.–5 p.m.
Civic nurseries with plants on display in the open and in greenhouses.

Parc des Buttes-Chaumont

19th Arrondissement
Métro: Buttes-Chaumont.
City park on one of the highest points in Paris.

Parc Monceau

Boulevard de Courcelles (8th arr.)
Métro: Monceau.
The "aristocrat" of Paris's public parks.

Parc Montsouris

Boulevard Jourdan (14th arr.)
RER: Cité Universitaire.
Very pretty little park opposite the Cité Universitaire Internationale.

Parc de Saint-Cloud

Rue de Saint-Cloud, 92-Saint-Cloud
Métro: Pont de Sévres (cross Seine bridge then right).
Open: 7 a.m.–9 p.m. (accessible by car).
Classical gardens laid out by Le Nôtre (Paris A–Z, see Versailles).

Pets

Certificate of Vaccination

Dogs and cats can be taken into France if they have a certificate of vaccination against rabies not less than a month or more than a year old. (In view of the quarantine regulations on re-entry into Britain most British visitors will, of course, leave their pets at home.)

Police (Police)

Police Stations

Place du Marché Saint-Honoré (1st arr.); tel. 2 61 09 19.
5 Place des Petits-Pères (2nd arr.); tel. 2 60 96 06.
5 Rue Perrée (3rd arr.); tel. 2 78 40 00.
Place Baudoyer (4th arr.); tel. 2 77 67 21.
Rue Basse des Carmes (5th arr.); tel. 3 29 21 57.
78 Rue Bonaparte (6th arr.); tel. 3 29 76 10.
116 Rue de Grenelle (7th arr.); tel. 5 55 40 81.
1 Avenue Selves (8th arr.); tel. 2 25 88 80.
6 Rue Drouot (9th arr.); tel. 2 46 30 26.
1 Rue Hittorf (10th arr.); tel. 6 07 57 77.
Place Léon Blum (11th arr.); tel. 3 79 75 56.
5 Rue Bignon (12 arr.); tel. 6 28 26 85.
144 Boulevard de l'Hôpital (13th arr.); tel. 5 70 11 99.
112 Avenue du Maine (14th arr.); tel. 3 20 14 80.
154 Rue Lecourbe (15th arr.); tel. 5 31 14 40.
73 Rue de la Pompe (16th arr.); tel. 5 03 13 20.
19 Rue Truffaut (17th arr.); tel. 2 92 05 50.
77 Rue du Mont-Cenis (18th arr.); tel. 6 06 43 84.
2 Rue André Dubois (19th arr.); tel. 6 07 57 79.
6 Place Gambetta (20th arr.); tel. 6 36 86 04.

Emergency Telephones (Police-Secours)

There are police emergency telephones (tel. 17) all over Paris.

Police Prefecture

The police prefecture (Préfecture de Police) is located on the Ile de la Cité, Place Louis Lépine (4th arr.).

Post (PTT)

Information

Weekdays 8 a.m.–10 p.m.; tel. 2 80 67 89.

Stamps

Stamps (timbres) can be bought in post offices and tobacconists (bureaux de tabac).

Head Post Office (Poste principale)

52 Rue du Louvre (1st arr.)
Métro: Sentier, Les Halles, Louvre.
The only post office which is open day and night.

Times of Opening

Weekdays 8 a.m.–7 p.m., Sat. 8 a.m.–noon.

Postal Rates

Letters within France: 1.40F. Postcards inside France: 1.20F. The postage on letters (up to 20 g) to the United Kingdom is 1.60F; to the United States and Canada it is 2.30F. The postage on postcards to the United Kingdom is 1.60F; to the United States and Canada it is also 1.60F.

Telephoning

See Telephone

Programmes of Events

Weekly Programmes

"L'Officiel des Spectacles" and "Pariscope": two weekly publications listing events for the forthcoming week, starting with Wednesday, and available at all kiosks.

The "Office de Tourisme de Paris" in the Champs Elysées (see Information) has plenty of leaflets giving details of current events.

Programme of Events in English

By dialling tel. 7 20 88 98 you can hear a recorded message giving information about all kinds of events such as concerts, exhibitions, ballet, etc.

Public Holidays (Jours fériés)

1 January (Jour de l'An); 1 May (Fête de Travail); 14 July (Fête Nationale); 15 August (Assomption); 1 November (Toussaint); 11 November (Fête de l'Armistice 1918); 25 December (Noël); plus Ascension day, Easter Monday, Whit Monday.

Public Transport (Transport publics)

Information

RATP provides a 24-hour service concerning public transport in Paris (Métro, bus, RER). Tel. 3 46 14 14.

Buses

Since there are only 56 bus routes in Paris (143 in the suburbs) it is slightly more difficult to use the bus, but the journeys are also more enjoyable because the individual tourist can get better aquainted with the Paris that lies above ground.

The tickets are the same as for the Métro and can be purchased from the bus driver.

However, a ticket is only valid for a specific section without changing.

Ten-trip "carnet": the same as for the Métro:

Métro

The Métro system is the most effective means of transport for the visitor because it covers the whole City, is relatively low-priced and it is easy to find one's way.

When using the Métro remember that although the lines are numbered they are generally referred to by the name of the station at the end of the line, so that if, for example, you want to travel from Cité in the direction of Montparnasse you follow the signs for "Porte d'Orléans" which is at the end of the line. Blue signs indicate the direction ("Direction") and stations where you can change trains ("Correspondances") are indicated on the platform by a yellow illuminated sign.

The maps inside the coaches show the stations on the line you are travelling on and indicate where you have to change (Correspondances) to connect with other lines.

Single ticket (ticket/billet): valid for one journey of any length including changes and obtainable from ticket offices at Métro stations. It is necessary to feed this into the automatic barriers at the entrance where it is magnetically checked and cancelled.

They are comparatively expensive (3F. in 1980) and frequent users of the Métro would do better to get a tourist season ticket (see below) or a ten-trip "carnet". A single ticket works out about 40% cheaper if bought in a "carnet" of 10 tickets (17F.50 in 1980).

RATP

RATP (Régie Autonome des Transport Parisiens), which is part State-owned, is Paris's most important transport undertaking with 36,000 employees and three forms of transport – Métro, buses, RER.

RER

There are three RER (Réseau Express Régional) express lines: RATP (see entry) operates the A and B lines and SNCF (see entry) operates the C line.

The fare depends on the length of the journey. By paying extra it is possible to change from RER to Métro but a fresh ticket is required to change from one RER line to another. Tickets are obtainable from automatic machines in RER stations.

Ten-trip "carnet": not available.

Tourist season ticket: see below.

SNCF

The French national railways, SNCF (Société Nationale des Chemins de Fer Français), operate the international and inter-city lines (Grandes Lignes), the commuter trains (Banlieue) and the C RER line.

Fares depend on the length of the journey. Single tickets only and season tickets for the week or the month are available. Single tickets can be obtained from ticket offices and automatic machines in the stations.

Tourist Season Ticket (Billet de Tourisme)

It is possible to buy a tourist season ticket for 2, 4 or 7 days (35, 53 and 88F. in 1980) permitting unlimited use of the RATP (see entry) network (bus, Métro, RER) in Paris and the suburbs. It can be used for 1st and 2nd class travel on the Métro and RER.

The tourist ticket cannot be used on the C RER line which is operated by SNCF (see entry).

Tourist tickets can be bought at:
60 main Métro stations;
6 Railway stations (see entry): Gare de l'Est, du Nord, de Lyon, Saint-Lazare, des Invalides, Montparnasse; RATP tourist offices (see Information).

To use the ticket, feed the individual coupons into the automatic barriers at Métro and RER stations.

On buses just show the ticket to the bus driver (do not insert it into the bus ticket machine because it cannot then be used again!).

Running Times

The Métro runs every day from 5.30 in the morning until 1.15 at night. Trains run at 1½ minute intervals in the rush hour and at 5 to 10 minute intervals the rest of the day and at weekends.

Buses generally run between 6.30 a.m. and 9.30 p.m. at 5 to 10 minute intervals in the rush hour and at up to 30 minute intervals the rest of the time. Very few lines operate on Sundays and public holidays.

On the RER lines, which run daily from 5.30 in the morning to 12.30 at night, waiting times are also longer – up to 30 minutes – but they run at 5 to 10 minute intervals during rush hour.

Railway Stations (Gares)

The six main stations are linked to the Métro-system (the names of the station and the Métro are the same).
All the stations apart from Montparnasse and Saint Lazare have a tourist office operated by the City of Paris (see Information) and apart from Montparnasse they all have exchange bureaus (see Information).
The Gare du Nord has a special reception bureau for young people.

Gare d'Austerlitz (also Gare d'Orléans)
55 Quai d'Austerlitz (13th arr.)
Information: tel. 5 84 16 16; Reservations: tel. 5 84 15 20
Trains for S and SW France, Spain, Portugal.

Gare de l'Est
Place du 11 Novembre 1918 (10th arr.)
Information: tel. 2 08 49 90; Reservations: tel. 2 06 49 38
Trains for E France, S Germany, Luxembourg, N Switzerland, Austria.

Gare de Lyon
20 Boulevard Diderot (12th arr.)

Information: tel. 3 45 92 22; Reservations: tel. 3 45 93 33
Trains for S, SE and Central France, Italy, Switzerland and the Alps.

Gare Montparnasse
17 Boulevard Vaugirard (15th arr.)
Information: tel. 5 38 52 29; Reservations: tel. 5 38 52 39
Trains for W France (particularly Brittany).

Gare du Nord
18 Rue de Dunkerque (10th arr.)
Information: tel. 2 80 03 03; Reservations: tel. 8 78 87 54
Trains for N France, N Germany, Belgium, Great Britain and the Netherlands.

Gare Saint-Lazare
13 Rue d'Amsterdam (8th arr.)
Information: tel. 5 38 52 29; Reservations: tel. 3 87 91 70
Trains for Normandy and Great Britain.

Gare (Aérogare) des Invalides
Quai d'Orsay (7th arr.)
No longer has international rail connections but serves the RER line C (see Public Transport) to Orly airport (see Airports).

Seat Reservations

At all stations: Mon.–Sat. 8 a.m.–10 p.m. and Sun. 8 a.m.–7 p.m.

Information

Mon.–Sat. 7 a.m.–9 p.m., Sun. 9 a.m.–1 p.m. and 2–7 p.m.
Telephone information for all stations: daily 8 a.m.–10 p.m.; tel. 2 61 50 50.

Restaurants (Selection)

French restaurants normally offer a choice between a "menu" or "á la carte". The most inexpensive menu can offer a choice between several dishes for each course but other dishes are not available outside the menu and courses cannot be served out of order. Anyone eating á la carte is of course free to choose which dishes they have and what order they have them in.

The restaurants are listed according to the five main categories of the current Paris restaurant guide. It is well worth also venturing to outlying parts of the City.

Although international cuisine plays an important role in cosmopolitan Paris only restaurants offering French cuisine could be included in this context (prices as of late 1980).

Luxury Restaurants

Le Gand Vefour
17 Rue du Beaujolais (1st arr.); carte 155–200F.

La Tour d'Argent
15 Quai de la Tournelle (5th arr.); carte 180–270F.

L'Archestrate
84 Rue de Varenne (7th arr.); carte 185–250F.

Maxim's (Rue Royale)

Maxim's
3 Rue Royale (8th arr.); carte 250–400F.

Taillevent
15 Rue Lamenais (8th arr.); carte 145–185F.

Lasserre
17 Avenue Franklin-D.-Roosevelt (8th arr.); carte 165–200F.

Le Vivarois
192 Avenue Victor-Hugo (16th arr.); carte 140–190F.

Nouvelle Cuisine (New Cuisine)

La Chamaille
81 Rue Saint-Louis-en-l'Ile (4th arr.); carte 120F., menu 60F.

Jacques Cagna
14 Rue des Grands-Augustins (6th arr.); carte 140–190F.

Au Trou Gascon
40 Rue Taine (12th arr.); carte 110–140F.

Le Duc
243 Boulevard Raspail (14th arr.); carte 120–170F.

Le Planteur
2 Rue de Cadix (15th arr.); carte 100F, menu 50F.

Rostang
10 Rue Gustave-Flaubert (17th arr.); carte 120–160F..

Les Semailles
3 Rue Steinlen (18th arr.); carte 160–180F.

Le Petit Pré
1 Rue de Bellevue (19th arr.); carte 90–130F.

Cuisine Traditionelle (Traditional Cuisine)

Taverne Nicolas Flamel
51 Rue de Montmorency (3rd arr.); menu 90F.

Chez Julien
1 Rue du Pont-Louis-Philippe (4th arr.); carte 100F. menu 75F.

Chez Toutoune
5 Rue de Pontoise (6th arr.); menu 75F.

Café de la Paix, Opéra
Place de l'Opéra (9th arr.); carte 130F.

Brasserie Flo
7 Cour des Petites Ecuries (10th arr.); carte 80F.

Julien
16 Rue du Faubourg-Saint-Denis (10th arr.); carte 100F.

Les Marronniers
53 bis Boulevard Arago (13th arr.); carte 120F., menu 50F.

La Coupole
10 Boulevard du Montparnasse (14th arr.); carte 80F.

L'Artisan
5 Rue de Vesigny (18th arr.); carte 90F.

Cuisine Régionale/ Spécialités (Regional Cuisine and Specialties)

La Main à la Pate
35 Rue Saint-Honoré (1st arr.); carte 90F., menu 70F.

La Clef des Champs
38 Rue Croix-des-Petits-Champs (1st arr.); menu 60F.

L'Ambassade d'Auvergne
22 Rue du Grenier-Saint-Lazare (3rd arr.); carte 120F.

L'Auberge "In"
34 Rue du Cardinal-Lemoine (5th arr.); vegetarian cuisine; carte 40F.

Androuet
41 Rue d'Amsterdam (8th arr.); cheese; carte 100F., menu 80F.

Auberge de Riquewihr
12 Faubourg Montmartre (9th arr.); carte 120F.

Ty-Coz
35 Rue Saint-Georges (9th arr.); carte 130F.

Pyrénees-Cevennes
106 Rue de la Folie-Méricourt (11th arr.); carte 100F.

A Sousceyrac
35 Rue Faidherbe (11th arr.); carte 120F.

Le Train Bleu
Gare de Lyon, 20 Boulevard Diderot (12th arr.); specialties from Lyons; carte 120F.

Chex Laurent
11 Rue des Acacias (17th arr.); carte 75F., menu 54F.

Charlot
128 bis Boulevard de Clichy (18th arr.); carte 130F.

Au Cochon d'Or
192 Avenue Jean-Jaurès (19th arr.); meat specialties (formerly La Villette meat market); carte 100F.

Relais des Pyrénées
1 Rue du Jourdain (20th arr.); carte 120F.

Cuisine Bistro (Bistro Cuisine)

Aux Crus de Bourgogne
3 Rue de Bachaumont (2nd arr.); carte 80F.

L'Assiette au Bœuf
9 Boulevard des Italiens (2nd arr.); menu 40F.

La Crèmerie Polydor
41 Rue Monseigneur-Le-Prince (6th arr.); carte 40F.

Bistro de la Gare
59 Boulevard du Montparnasse (6th arr.); menu 40F.

Thoumieux
79 Rue Saint-Dominique (7th arr.); menu 26F.80, carte 60F.

La Galatée
3 Rue Victor-Massé (9th arr.); menu 30F.

Le Petit Pot
180 Rue du Faubourg-Saint-Antoine (12th arr.); menu 40F.

Chez Grand-Mère
92 Rue Broca (13th arr.); menu 38F., carte 55F.

La Route du Beaujolais
17 Rue de Lourmel (15th arr.); menu 34F., carte 75F.

Maison Quere Henri Martin
125 Rue de la Tour (16th arr.); carte 20F.

Sightseeing (Conférences, Visites, Excursions)

Guided Visits (Conférences)

Several organisations arrange guided visits daily to points in the city of particular cultural or historical interest. These visits last 1–1½ hours and the commentary is in French. Subjects, times and starting points are published in "Officiel" (see Programmes of Events) under "Conférences".

Excursions Outside Paris

Some travel agencies specialise in city tours but also arrange excursions to places outside Paris.

Excursions to places outside Paris.

Excursions of this kind (usually at the weekend) can also be booked at the RATP and SNCF travel bureaus:

Services Touristiques de la RATP
53 bis Quai des Grands-Augustins (6th arr.); tel. 3 46 42 03.
Métro: Pont-Neuf, Saint-Michel.
Open: Mon.–Fri. 8.30 a.m.–noon, 1–4.45 p.m.; Sat., Sun., public holidays 8.30 a.m.–noon, 2–4.45 p.m.
Place de la Madeleine, near the flower market (8th arr.); tel. 2 65 31 18.
Métro: Madeleine.
Open: Mon.–Fri. 7.30 a.m.–6.45 p.m.; Sat., Sun., public holidays 6.30 a.m.–6 p.m.

Bureaux de Tourisme de la SNCF
in the Railway stations (see entry) Gare du Nord, de l'Est, de Lyon, d'Austerlitz, Montparnasse and Saint-Lazare.
General Information: tel. 2 61 50 50.

Guided Tours by Coach

Paris-Vision
214 Rue de Rivoli (1st arr.); tel. 2 60 30 01 and 2 60 31 25.
Métro: Tuileries.

Cityrama/Rapid-Pullmann
4 Place des Pyramides (1st arr.); tel. 2 60 30 14.
Métro: Palais-Royal.

American Express
11 Rue Scribe (9th arr.); tel. 0 73 42 90.
Métro: Bourse.

Cityrama/Théâtres-Voyages-Excursions
21 Rue de la Paix (2nd arr.); tel. 7 42 06 47.
Métro: Opéra.

Sightseeing Flights

Viewing Paris from the air is expensive but well worth it.

Air 2000
6 Avenue Maurice Ravel (12th arr.); tel. 3 43 19 01.
Booking: a fortnight in advance Mon.–Thurs., 10 a.m.–5 p.m.

Sightseeing flights from several airports in the suburbs: Aéroports du Bourget, de Saint-Cyr, de Toussus-le-Noble.

Heliport de Paris
Métro: Balard.
Booking in advance: tel. 5 54 12 55 and 5 57 75 51.
Flights over the Défense quarter and Versailles.

Boat Trips

See Boat trips

Son et Lumière

"Son et Lumière" literally means "Sound and Light" and there are many "Son et Lumière" performances in places of particular interest to tourists throughout France. These usually present a kind of historical pageant, with words and music and highly theatrical lighting effects, of events connected with the particular building.
In Paris there is a "Son et Lumière" in French and English in the courtyard of the Hôtel des Invalides (see Paris A–Z, Hôtel des Invalides).

Sport

Boxing and Wrestling

Cirque d'Hiver, 110 Rue Amelot (11th arr.).
Métro: Filles-du-Calvaire.
Pavillon de Paris, 211 Avenue Jean-Jaurès (19th arr.).
Métro: Porte de Pantin.

Football and Rugby

Parc des Princes, 24 Avenue du Commandant-Guilbaud (16th arr.).
Métro: Porte de Saint-Cloud.
Paris's largest football stadium (capacity 50,000) is also used for other events.

A day at the races

Tennis

Stade Roland-Garros, 2 Avenue Gordon-Bennett (16th arr.)
Métro: Porte d'Auteuil.
Site of the French International championships.

Racecourses (Hippodromes)

Hippodrome d'Auteuil, Bois de Boulogne.
Métro: Porte d'Auteuil.

Hippodrome de Longchamp, Bois de Boulogne.
Métro: Porte d'Auteuil.

Hippodrome de Vincennes, Bois de Vincennes.

Taxis

Since 1937 the number of taxis in Paris has been restricted by law to 14,300. Consequently a taxi licence is hard to come by – and the same is often true of a taxi when you need one!

Fares

The fare is made up of a basic charge plus a time supplement. A higher basic charge is applied at the railway stations.

The daytime rate (A) applies from 6.30 a.m. to 10 p.m. when the more expensive night rate (B) comes into force. Journeys outside the city boundaries are charged at the C rate.

Taxi-drivers expect a tip of 10 to 15%.

Minicabs

A selection of phone numbers: 2 52 94 00; 7 35 22 22; 2 05 77 77; 6 57 11 12; 2 00 67 89; 2 03 99 99, 7 39 33 33.

Telephone

International Calls

At post offices (see Post) you can ask for an international line (communication internationale) or use a pay-phone for international calls. These pay-phones can also be found on the street and in the Métro stations and have more than one coin slot.
To make an international call:
1. Hold coins ready, lift the receiver and wait for the first dialling tone.
2. When you hear the tone dial the international prefix 19 and wait for the second dialling tone.
3. When you hear the second tone dial the country code (UK – 44) followed straight away by the area code (omitting prefix "0") and then the local number.
4. Wait until the subscriber answers then insert coins. A rapid broken tone indicates that the money has been used up but the line will remain open if more coins are inserted immediately.
International calls can be made in many cafés.
A call to Great Britain costs about 0F. 50 for 11 seconds.

Calls in France

The same procedure as for international calls but using the prefix 16 instead of 19 (wait for dialling tone) followed by the area code and local number.

Local Calls (City and Greater Paris)

At post offices and most cafés it is necessary, for local calls, to ask for a phone token (*jeton*) which has to be inserted in the single slot before dialling the number (wait for the dialling tone). With the older type of phone you press a button when the subscriber answers and the coins then drop and make the connection.

For a local call the street pay-phones require 2×20 centimes if they are the older model and a 50-centime coin if they are the new type.

Day and Night

There are two places where phone calls can be made to anywhere and at any time, day or night. These are:

the Head Post Office (see Post) and
the Post Office at: 8 Place de la Bourse (2nd arr.); Métro: Bourse; tel. 2 33 16 62.

Theatres (Selection)

Boulevard Theatres (Théâtres Boulevard)

Antoine
14 Boulevard de Strasbourg; tel. 2 08 77 71.
Métro: Strasbourg-Saint-Denis.

Atelier
Place Charles-Dullin; tel. 6 06 49 24.
Métro: Anvers.

Carré Silvia Monfort
106 Rue Brancion; tel. 5 31 28 34.
Métro: Porte-de-Vances.

Comédie des Champs-Elysées
15 Avenue Montaigne; tel. 7 23 37 21.
Métro: Alma.

Daunou
7 Rue Daunou; tel. 2 61 69 14.
Métro: Opéra.

Edouard VII
Place Edouard-VII; tel. 7 42 57 49.
Métro: Opéra.

Fontaine
10 Rue Fontaine; tel. 8 74 82 34.
Métro: Blanche.

Gymnase-Marie-Bell
38 Boulevard de Bonne-Nouvelle; tel. 2 46 79 79.
Métro: Bonne-Nouvelle.

Mathurins
36 Rue des Mathurins; tel. 2 65 90 00.
Métro: Havre-Caumartin.

Michodière
4 bis Rue de la Michodière; tel. 7 42 95 22.
Métro: 4-Septembre.

Montparnasse
31 Rue de la Gaîté; tel. 3 20 89 90.
Métro: Montparnasse, Edgar-Quinet.

Nouveautés
24 Boulevard Poissonière; tel. 7 70 52 76.
Métro: Montmartre.

Palais-Royal
38 Rue Montpensier; tel. 2 97 59 81.
Métro: Bourse, Palais-Royal.

Rond-Point (Compagnie Renaud-Barrault)
Corner of Champs-Elysées and Avenue Franklin-D. Roosevelt.

Variétés
7 Boulevard Montmartre; tel. 2 33 09 92.

Cafés-Théâtres

Café d'Edgar
58 Boulevard Edgar-Quinet; tel. 3 20 85 11.
Métro: Edgar-Quinet.

Café de la Gare
41 Rue du Temple; tel. 2 78 52 51.
Métro: Hôtel de Ville.

Bec Fin
6 Rue Thérèse; tel. 2 96 29 35.
Métro: Palais-Royal.

Coupe-Chou
94 Rue Saint-Martin; tel. 2 72 01 73.
Métro: Rambuteau.

Cour des Miracles
23 Avenue du Maine; tel. 5 48 85 60.
Métro: Montparnasse.

La Vielle Grille
1 Rue du Puits-de-l'Ermite; tel. 7 07 60 93.

Experimental Theatre

Théâtre de la Cité Internationale Universitaire
21 Boulevard Jourdan (14th arr.); tel. 5 89 38 69.

Théâtre de la Commune
2 Rue Edouard-Poisson, 93 Aubervilliers; tel. 8 33 16 16.

Maison des Arts André Malraux
Place Salvador-Allende, 94 Créteil; tel. 8 99 94 50.

Théâtre des Amandiers
7 Avenue Pablo-Picasso, 92 Nanterre; tel. 7 21 18 81.

Théâtre Gérard Philippe
59 Boulevard Jules-Guesde, 93 Saint-Denis; tel. 2 43 00 59.

Théâtre Jean Vilar
Place Stalingrad, 93 Suresnes; tel. 7 72 38 80.

Cartoucherie de Vincennes
Avenue de la Pyramide, Bois de Vincennes; tel. 3 74 24 08.
Métro: Château de Vincennes (then bus 306 to "Route du Champs-de Manœuvre").
Three groups, including "Théâtre du Soleil" (A. Mnouchkine).

Children's Theatre

The only theatre in Paris that puts on plays exclusively for children:

Théâtre Roland-Pillain
(Théâtre du Petit Monde), 262 Faubourg Saint-Honoré (8th arr.); tel. 7 00 23 77.
Métro: Ternes.
Open: Wed., Sun.

Puppet Theatres

Jardin d'Acclimatation
(see Paris A–Z, Jardin d'Acclimatation)
Sat., Sun., Wed. 3.15 and 4.30 p.m.

Marionnettes du Champs-de-Mars
Champ-de-Mars (7th arr.).
Métro: Ecole Militaire.
Daily: 3.30 and 4.15 p.m.

Marionnettes du Luxembourg
Jardin du Luxembourg (see Paris A–Z, Jardin du Luxembourg).
Daily: 4 p.m.

Marionnettes des Champs-Elysées
Jardin du Carré-Marigny.
Métro: Franklin-D.-Roosevelt.
Wed., Sat., Sun. from 3 p.m.

Guignol du Parc Montsouris
Parc Montsouris (see Parks).
Wed., Sat., Sun. from 3 p.m.

Théâtre de la Petite Ourse
Jardins des Tuileries (see Paris A–Z, Jardins des Tuileries).
Métro: Tuileries.
April–July.
(For exact details see programme of events in "L'Officiel du Spectacle").

Opera and Light Opera

See Music

National Theatres (Théâtres Nationaux)

The national theatres include:

Comédie Française
2 Rue de Richelieu (1st arr.); tel. 2 96 10 20.
Métro: Palais-Royal.

Odéon
1 Place Paul-Claudel (6th arr.); tel. 3 25 70 32.
Métro: Odéon.

Chaillot
Palais de Chaillot, Place du Trocadéro (16th arr.); tel. 7 27 81 13.
Métro: Trocadéro.

Théâtre de l'Est Parisien (TEP)
17 Rue Malte-Brun (20th arr.); tel. 6 36 79 09.
Métro: Gambetta.

Théâtre de la Ville
Place du Châtelet (4th arr.); tel. 2 74 10 19.
Métro: Châtelet.

Civic Theatres
(Théâtres Municipaux)

Civic theatres are:

Théâtre Marigny
Carré Marigny, Jardin des Champs-Elysées (8th arr.); tel. 2 25 20 74.
Métro: Champs-Elysées-Clemenceau.

Théâtre des Ambassadeurs
1 Avenue Gabriel (8th arr.); tel. 2 65 97 60.
Métro: Champs-Elysées-Clemenceau.

Time

French Summertime – i.e. Central European Time (CET) plus 1 hour – operates from early April to late September.

Times of Opening (Heures d'ouverture)

Shops

Retail shops usually open from 9 a.m. to 7 p.m. Grocers generally open earlier. Each quarter has at least one shop which stays open until 10 p.m. Shops normally only shut on Sunday but if they open on Sunday they shut on Monday or Wednesday.

Butchers and grocers are open until noon on Sun. The bakers in a quarter arrange for at least one of them to stay open all day Sun. Most shops are closed for lunch from 1 to 3 p.m.

Department Stores

Open 9.30 a.m.–6.30 p.m. Mon. to Sat.
Open on Wed. until 10 p.m.: Bazar de l'Hôtel de Ville (BHV) and Samaritaine. Many department stores close at lunchtime.

Churches

Churches are normally open from 8 a.m. to 7 p.m. but close at lunchtime from noon to 2 p.m.
Visitors should avoid sightseeing during Mass.

Museums

The opening times of museums are given in their entry in the Paris A–Z section and under "Museums" in the "Practical Information" section.
NB: All "national" museums (Musée National de . . .) are closed on Tues.

Post Offices

Mon.–Fri. 8 a.m.–7 p.m.; Sat. 8 a.m.–noon.

Parks and Gardens

Public parks and gardens are open until sunset from 10 a.m. in the winter (1 Oct.–31 March) and from 8 a.m. in the summer (1 April–30 September).

Places of Interest

See Paris A–Z.

Tips (Pourboire)

Cafés, Restaurants

The menu card on the counter should state: "Service compris" (service included) or "Service non compris" or "Service en sus" (service not included). The rate for waiters is 12–15% but an extra tip is always welcome.

Hotels

Waiters, chambermaids, etc., but not the owner get a small tip.

Cinemas, Theatres

Usherettes insist on a tip (about 1 F per person). Their earnings often consist solely of tips.

Taxis

10–15%.

Tourist Information

See Information.

Traffic

Driving in Paris traffic calls for special skills besides experience. The driver needs to be agile and alert, to fit in with the traffic flow and to cope with the failure of other drivers to use their indicators.
Nervous drivers should stay off the roads between 11 in the morning and 8 at night.

Taxi and Bus Lanes

Lanes marked with broad white lines at the side of medium and arterial roads are for buses and taxis and may not be used by other cars before 8.30 at night. Besides risking a heavy fine, the offending driver will be furiously hooted at by bus and taxi drivers who will if necessary eject him from their territory!

Parking on the Road

When parking on the flat leave the car in neutral with the handbrake off to avoid damage from other drivers attempting to park.

Entering Main Roads

Although traffic from the right should have priority this cannot be relied upon when entering main roads or roundabouts.

Travel Bureaus (Agences de voyages)

In Paris

French Government Tourist Office
Head Office: 8 Avenue de l'Opéra (1st arr.); tel. 7 66 51 35.
Métro: Palais-Royal.

In Great Britain

French Government Tourist Office
178 Piccadilly, London W1V 0AL; tel. (01) 493 3171.

A French institute (Institut français), consulate or general consulate can be found in most of Great Britain's larger cities.

In the United States of America

610 Fifth Avenue, New York, NYC 10021.

9401 Wilshire Boulevard, Beverly Hills, CA 90112.

645 N. Michigan Avenue, Suite 430, Chicago, IL 60601.

323 Geary Street, San Francisco, CA 94012.

In Canada

372 Bay Street, Suite 610, Toronto, Ont. M5H 2W9.

1940 Sherbrooke Street West, Montreal, Que. H3H 2W9.

City Office of Some Airlines

Airline addresses and telephone numbers are obtainable from the Paris office of the airlines –
Aeroport de Paris, 291 Boulevard Raspail (14th arr.); tel. 3 20 15 00.

Air France
119 Avenue des Champs-Elysées (8th arr.); tel. 7 20 70 50.
Reservation by telephone possible.

British Airways
91 Avenue des Champs: Elysées (8th arr.); tel. 7 78 14 14.

British Caledonian
3 Rue de la Paix (2nd arr.); tel. 2 61 50 21.

Pan Am
1 Rue Scribe (9th arr.); tel. 2 66 45 45.

TWA
101 Avenue des Champs-Elysées (8th arr.); tel. 7 20 54 33.

Air Canada
39 Boulevard de Vaugirard (15th arr.); tel. 2 73 84 00.

Air France Abroad

158 New Bond Street, London W1Y 0AY: tel. (01) 499 9511 and 499 8611.

666 Fifth Avenue, New York, N.Y. 10019.

1 Place Ville-Marie, Suite 3321, Montreal H3B 3N4, P.Q.

National Railways (Offices, Information)

British Rail
12 Boulevard de la Madeleine (8th/9th arr.); tel. 2 66 90 53.

French Railways

Société Nationale des Chemins de Fer Français (SNCF)
16 Boulevard des Capucines (9th arr.).

179 Piccadilly, London W1V 0BA; tel. (01) 493 4451–2.

610 Fifth Avenue, New York, NY 10020; tel. (212) 582 2110.

2121 Ponce de Leon Boulevard, Coral Gables, Florida 33134; tel. (305) 445 8648.

11 East Adams Street, Chicago, Illinois 60603; tel. (312) 427 8691.

9465 Wilshire Boulevard, Beverly Hills, California 90212; tel. (213) 272 7967.

323 Geary Street, San Francisco, California 94102; tel. (415) 982 1993.

1500 Stanley Street, Montreal H3A 1R3, P.Q.; tel. (514) 288 8255–6.

Travel Documents

Passports

Visitors from Britain and most Western countries require only a valid passport (or a British Visitor's Passport) to enter France.

Driving Licence/ Car Documents

British and other Western driving licences and car documents are accepted in France and should accompany the driver.

Green Card

Although nationals of EEC countries do not need an international insurance certificate (green card) it is desirable to have one since otherwise only third-party cover is provided.

Country of Origin

All foreign cars visiting France must display an international distinguishing sign of the approved pattern and design showing the country of origin.

Travelling to Paris

By Car

A number of companies operate car ferries between Great Britain and France and it is advisable to find out from your travel agent which is the most suitable crossing. The following are examples of the fastest crossings:
Dover–Calais/Boulogne (90 min. by car ferry, 30 min. by Hovercraft) via Lille to the Autoroute du Nord.
Folkestone–Boulogne (105 min.) via Lille to the Autoroute du Nord.
Newhaven–Dieppe (4 hr) via Rouen to the Autoroute de Normandie.
Portsmouth–Le Havre (6 hr) via Rouen to the Autoroute de Normandie.
Southampton–Le Havre (overnight) via Rouen to the Autoroute de Normandie.

Distances are shorter by the national roads (routes nationales) but the journey takes longer.

The present speed limits are 130 km per hour (80 m.p.h.) on motorways, 110 km per hour (70 m.p.h.) on expressways, 90 km per hour (55 m.p.h.) on national and departmental roads and 60 km per hour (35 m.p.h.) in built-up areas unless otherwise signposted.

Tolls are payable on the motorways.

French petrol prices are higher than the European average but they are standardised throughout France (including on motorways) by the Government.

By Coach

Travel by coach is becoming increasingly popular and Paris is a favourite destination for city tours. Many companies offer a variety of inexpensive tours and there are regular coach services to Paris from London and certain other towns in Britain. Check with your local travel agent.

By Air

Buses and trains run between Paris and the three Airports (see entry).

NB: Taxis may only charge the single fare to or from the airport.

Several companies offer car hire with or without driver.

Exchange bureaus at the airports are open from 6 a.m. till midnight.

By Rail

Apart from the normal train services linking up with the Channel ferries, through-carriages run overnight between London and Paris:
London Victoria–Paris Gare St Lazare (10 hr);
London Charing Cross–Paris Gare du Nord (7 hr);
London Waterloo (East)–Paris Gare du Nord (7 hr); and
London–Paris Overnight "The Parisienne".

Both stations in Paris have Information, Banks/Exchange bureaus, Taxis and connections with Public transport (see entries).

Further details and reservations from the British Rail Travel Centres at Waterloo Station, London SE1 or Birmingham New Street (tel. 021–643 4444 ext. 2593).

Useful Telephone Numbers at a Glance

Emergency Services:	Telephone No.
– AA London	19–44–1–954–7373
– Ambulance	8 87 27 50
– Breakdown (English-speaking service)	5 32 22 15
– Doctor (SOS Médecins)	3 37 77 77 and 7 07 77 77
– Fire brigade (Sapeurs-Pompiers)	18
– Police (Police Secours)	17
– RAC London	19–44–1–686–2525
– Vet (8 p.m.–8 a.m., SOS Vétérinaires)	8 71 20 61
Information (Renseignements):	
Airports (Aéroports):	
– Le Bourget	8 34 93 90
– Charles-de-Gaulle/Roissy	8 62 22 80
– Orly	6 87 12 34
Automobile Club de France	5 53 39 59
Dialling Codes (indicatifs):	
– to Paris (from all countries)	0 03 31
– to Great Britain	19–44
Embassies (Ambassades):	
– Great Britain	2 66 91 42
– United States of America	2 96 12 02 and 2 61 80 75
– Canada	2 25 99 55
Events (English)	7 20 88 98
Lost Property (Bureau des Objets Trouvés)	5 31 14 80
Postal Services (Postes-PTT)	2 80 67 89
Railways (SNCF)	2 61 50 50
Road Conditions (Inter Service Routes)	8 58 33 33
Stations (Gares):	
– Main Office	2 61 50 50
– Gare de l'Est	2 08 49 90
– Gare du Nord	2 80 03 03
– Gare de Lyon	3 45 92 22
– Gare d'Austerlitz	5 84 16 16
Students	7 07 26 22
Touring Club de France (English speaking service)	5 32 22 15
Tourist Information/Tourist Office	7 23 61 72
Young Persons (accommodation, jobs)	5 66 40 20

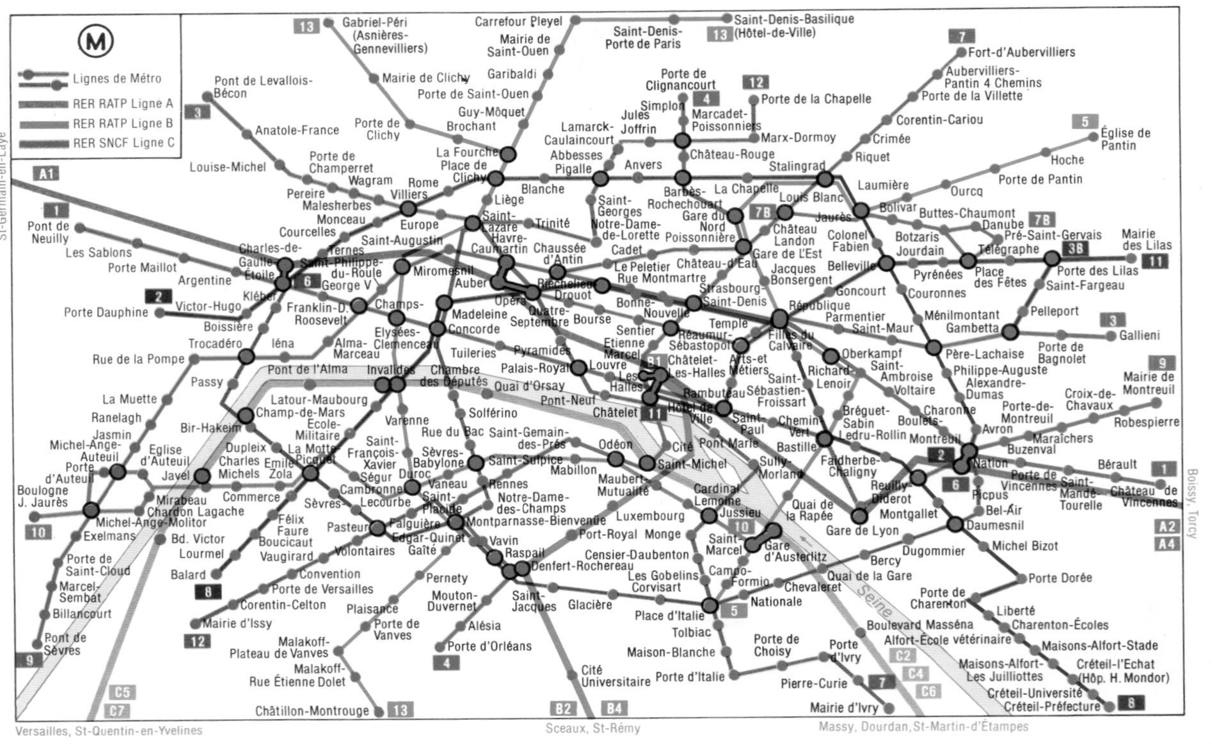

Lignes de Métro
RER RATP Ligne A
RER RATP Ligne B
RER SNCF Ligne C
St-Germain-en-Laye
Boissy, Torcy
Versailles, St-Quentin-en-Yvelines
Sceaux, St-Rémy
Massy, Dourdan, St-Martin-d'Étampes
A1
A2
A4
B2
B4
C2
C4
C5
C6
C7
Seine
Gabriel-Péri (Asnières-Gennevilliers)
Carrefour Pleyel
Mairie de Saint-Ouen
Saint-Denis-Porte de Paris
Saint-Denis-Basilique (Hôtel-de-Ville)
Fort-d'Aubervilliers
Aubervilliers-Pantin 4 Chemins
Porte de la Villette
Corentin-Cariou
Crimée
Riquet
Église de Pantin
Hoche
Porte de Pantin
Ourcq
Laumière
Mairie de Clichy
Garibaldi
Porte de Saint-Ouen
Guy-Môquet
Brochant
Porte de Clichy
Pont de Levallois-Bécon
Anatole-France
Louise-Michel
Porte de Champerret
Pereire
Wagram
Malesherbes
Villiers
Rome
La Fourche
Place de Clichy
Porte de Clignancourt
Simplon
Jules Joffrin
Marcadet-Poissonniers
Porte de la Chapelle
Marx-Dormoy
Lamarck-Caulaincourt
Abbesses
Pigalle
Anvers
Château-Rouge
Barbès-Rochechouart
La Chapelle
Stalingrad
Louis Blanc
Jaurès
Bolivar
Buttes-Chaumont
Danube
Pré-Saint-Gervais
Mairie des Lilas
Porte des Lilas
Saint-Fargeau
Télégraphe
Place des Fêtes
Botzaris
Jourdain
Pyrénées
Belleville
Colonel Fabien
Château Landon
Gare de l'Est
Gare du Nord
Poissonnière
Blanche
Liège
Saint-Lazare
Trinité
Saint-Georges
Notre-Dame-de-Lorette
Cadet
Le Peletier
Rue Montmartre
Château-d'Eau
Jacques Bonsergent
Goncourt
Couronnes
Ménilmontant
Pelleport
Gambetta
Gallieni
Porte de Bagnolet
Pont de Neuilly
Les Sablons
Porte Maillot
Argentine
Charles-de-Gaulle-Étoile
Ternes
Courcelles
Monceau
Europe
Saint-Augustin
Havre-Caumartin
Chaussée d'Antin
Saint-Philippe-du-Roule
Miromesnil
Auber
Opéra
Richelieu-Drouot
Quatre-Septembre
Bourse
Bonne-Nouvelle
Strasbourg-Saint-Denis
République
Parmentier
Saint-Maur
Père-Lachaise
Philippe-Auguste
Alexandre-Dumas
Mairie de Montreuil
Croix-de-Chavaux
Robespierre
Porte-de-Montreuil
Maraîchers
Buzenval
Avron
Porte Dauphine
Victor-Hugo
Kléber
George V
Franklin-D. Roosevelt
Champs-Élysées-Clemenceau
Madeleine
Concorde
Boissière
Trocadéro
Iéna
Alma-Marceau
Rue de la Pompe
Passy
Pont de l'Alma
Invalides
Chambre des Députés
Tuileries
Pyramides
Palais-Royal
Louvre
Sentier
Étienne Marcel
Réaumur-Sébastopol
Temple
Arts-et Métiers
Filles du Calvaire
Oberkampf
Saint-Ambroise
Voltaire
Richard-Lenoir
Châtelet-Les-Halles
Les Halles
Saint-Sébastien-Froissart
Quai d'Orsay
Pont-Neuf
Châtelet
Hôtel de Ville
Rambuteau
Saint-Paul
Chemin Vert
Bréguet-Sabin
Ledru-Rollin
Charonne
Boulets-Montreuil
Bastille
Pont Marie
Cité
Saint-Michel
Odéon
Sully-Morland
Faidherbe-Chaligny
Reuilly-Diderot
Nation
Porte de Vincennes
Saint-Mandé-Tourelle
Bérault
Château de Vincennes
Picpus
Bel-Air
Daumesnil
Montgallet
Gare de Lyon
Quai de la Rapée
La Muette
Ranelagh
Jasmin
Michel-Ange-Auteuil
Porte d'Auteuil
Église d'Auteuil
Boulogne J. Jaurès
Michel-Ange-Molitor
Exelmans
Porte de Saint-Cloud
Marcel-Sembat
Billancourt
Pont de Sèvres
Mirabeau
Chardon Lagache
Javel
Charles Michels
Émile Zola
Dupleix
Bir-Hakeim
Champ-de-Mars
Latour-Maubourg
École-Militaire
La Motte Picquet
Commerce
Bd. Victor
Lourmel
Balard
Félix Faure
Boucicaut
Vaugirard
Sèvres-Lecourbe
Cambronne
Varenne
Saint-François-Xavier
Ségur
Duroc
Vaneau
Sèvres-Babylone
Rue du Bac
Solférino
Saint-Germain-des-Prés
Saint-Sulpice
Mabillon
Rennes
Notre-Dame-des-Champs
Saint-Placide
Montparnasse-Bienvenüe
Falguière
Pasteur
Volontaires
Edgar-Quinet
Gaîté
Vavin
Raspail
Denfert-Rochereau
Convention
Porte de Versailles
Corentin-Celton
Mairie d'Issy
Pernety
Plaisance
Porte de Vanves
Mouton-Duvernet
Alésia
Porte d'Orléans
Malakoff-Plateau de Vanves
Malakoff-Rue Étienne Dolet
Châtillon-Montrouge
Saint-Jacques
Glacière
Cité Universitaire
Maubert-Mutualité
Cardinal Lemoine
Jussieu
Luxembourg
Port-Royal
Monge
Censier-Daubenton
Les Gobelins
Corvisart
Saint-Marcel
Gare d'Austerlitz
Campo-Formio
Place d'Italie
Nationale
Chevaleret
Tolbiac
Maison-Blanche
Porte d'Italie
Porte de Choisy
Porte d'Ivry
Pierre-Curie
Mairie d'Ivry
Quai de la Gare
Bercy
Dugommier
Michel Bizot
Porte Dorée
Porte de Charenton
Liberté
Charenton-Écoles
Boulevard Masséna
Alfort-École vétérinaire
Maisons-Alfort-Stade
Maisons-Alfort-Les Juilliottes
Créteil-l'Echat (Hôp. H. Mondor)
Créteil-Université
Créteil-Préfecture